F. L. Steinmeyer, L. A. Wheatley

The miracles of our Lord in relation to modern criticism

F. L. Steinmeyer, L. A. Wheatley

The miracles of our Lord in relation to modern criticism

ISBN/EAN: 9783743336391

Manufactured in Europe, USA, Canada, Australia, Japa

Cover: Foto ©Thomas Meinert / pixelio.de

Manufactured and distributed by brebook publishing software (www.brebook.com)

F. L. Steinmeyer, L. A. Wheatley

The miracles of our Lord in relation to modern criticism

THE
MIRACLES OF OUR LORD
IN RELATION TO MODERN CRITICISM.

PRINTED BY MURRAY AND GIBB,

FOR

T. & T. CLARK, EDINBURGH.

LONDON, ... HAMILTON, ADAMS, AND CO.
DUBLIN, ... JOHN ROBERTSON AND CO.
NEW YORK, . . . SCRIBNER, WELFORD, AND ARMSTRONG.

THE MIRACLES OF OUR LORD

IN RELATION TO MODERN CRITICISM.

BY

F. L. STEINMEYER, D.D.,

ORDINARY PROFESSOR OF THEOLOGY IN THE UNIVERSITY OF BERLIN.

TRANSLATED, WITH THE PERMISSION OF THE AUTHOR, FROM THE GERMAN BY

L. A. WHEATLEY.

EDINBURGH:
T. & T. CLARK, 38 GEORGE STREET.
1875.

TRANSLATOR'S PREFACE.

THERE is no need of apology for introducing to the English reader one of the works of so accomplished a divine as Professor Steinmeyer, whose learning and subtlety of mind have placed him in a high position among the theologians of Germany.

Dr. Steinmeyer is principally known by his *Beiträge zum Schriftverständniss*, a work which shows him to be an able expounder of Scripture, and worthy of being a preacher to the University of Berlin, a position he held for many years in addition to his professorship, but which he has lately resigned on account of the claims of his chair. He ranks highly as an exegete, as may be inferred from the present work, which will be found a contribution to exegesis as much as to apologetics; and in order that it may be more available for the former purpose, a list of the passages of Scripture elucidated is appended.

With regard to the style, it might be presumed, from the author being a fervid orator, that the sentences would flow 'in well-rounded periods.' This is, however, not the case, as Dr. Steinmeyer's strength lies principally in the power he possesses of evoking thought in his hearers or readers.

Dr. Steinmeyer has brought to his task an unbiassed judgment, and is careful to give fair play to his opponents; and in order to do justice to this characteristic, I have, in quoting from Strauss' work, given the words of his English translator instead of my own, so that there might be no danger, through my own prepossessions, of my misinterpreting him.

The quotations of Scripture are taken from the authorized version.

The method of treatment employed by the author is a new one in this country. He does not attempt to explain the miracles, still less does he exclude from them the supernatural element; but, as will be seen in his introduction, he takes the broad ground of the omnipotence of God, which no theist can deny, and then shows the *probability* of Jesus having performed miracles, by suggesting and explaining the motives which might have induced Him to put forth His almighty power.

CONTENTS.

	PAGE
INTRODUCTION:	
1. The Problem,	1
2. Method of solving it,	7
3. Value of the Solution,	22
JESUS AS A WORKER OF MIRACLES,	32

THE MIRACLES OF JESUS.

FIRST GROUP.—MIRACLES CONSIDERED AS SIGNS OF THE KINGDOM OF HEAVEN,	50
The Healing of Peter's Mother-in-law,	51
The Healing of the Woman with an Issue of Blood,	54
The Healing of the Woman who had an Infirmity Eighteen Years,	65
The Healing of the Man with the Dropsy,	70
The Healing of the Man with the Withered Hand,	73
SECOND GROUP.—MIRACLES CONSIDERED AS SYMBOLS,	78
The Healing of the Sick of the Palsy,	78
The Cleansing of the Lepers,	88
The Captain at Capernaum,	102
The Healing of the Blind,	108
The Healing of the Deaf and Dumb,	120
THIRD GROUP. — MIRACLES AS WITNESSES OF THE POWER OF THE KINGDOM OF HEAVEN,	128
1. The Liberation of those possessed,	129
The Canaanitish Woman,	140
The Possessed at Gadara,	150

	PAGE
The Possessed who was Blind and Dumb,	165
The Healing of the Possessed at Capernaum,	171
The Lunatic,	173
2. The Raising from the Dead,	187
The Daughter of Jairus,	191
The Young Man at Nain,	202
The Raising of Lazarus,	209
FOURTH GROUP.—MIRACLES AS PROPHECIES,	222
Peter's Draught of Fishes,	223
The Money in the Mouth of the Fish,	230
The Stilling of the Tempest,	239
The Miraculous Feedings,	249
The Turning of the Water into Wine,	259
The Cursing of the Fig-tree,	263
PASSAGES OF SCRIPTURE REFERRED TO,	271

THE MIRACLES OF OUR LORD.

INTRODUCTION.

I. THE PROBLEM.

DAVID FREDERICK STRAUSS, in his work on the *Life of Jesus*, seeks in two ways to free the German people from the oppressive yoke of faith, in order to furnish a contribution towards the solution of that problem which, according to his view, is offered to Protestantism.

He endeavours, on the one hand, to prove the incredibility of the sources, that is, the unauthenticity of the four Gospels, partly on account of the want of a sufficient testimony from without; partly on account of the relation in which they stand one to another; and partly from the tendency each has to follow the other, and thus betray a much later time of authorship. On the other hand, his exertions are directed towards the extirpation of what he calls the 'miracle delusion.' He wishes to show that Christianity is no supernatural revelation; that its Founder is no God-man; and that His life was no chain of miracles, but that, in reality, everything happened quite naturally;—and his assurance is, that by this means he will break up that authority which demands a blind obedience; that he will remove from the spiritual office—from the priesthood, standing in a position above the congregation—the historical basis indispensable to it; and lastly, that he will prepare a ground for the planting of the essentials of Christianity which would then remain, the real saving truths, in the place of its transitory elements, of its already half-destroyed covering.

Whoever feels himself compelled, either for the sake of the duties belonging to his office, or from a pure impulse from within, to endeavour to assist in paralyzing the effects of a work whose author may be considered to have spoken the last word in the cause of unbelief, must necessarily accompany the author of the *Life of Jesus* on one of two paths. However, the reflection occurs, whether it be possible to treat it in the nature of an alternative, as these paths by no means run parallel, and whether it be possible to restrict oneself to one or the other. Whoever declines to believe in miracles, can hardly fail to be prejudiced against the credibility and authenticity of those records in which such deeds of God are related and testified to; at least he would reserve to himself a position within which the arbitrary will of criticism could, without hindrance, dispose of them. And, on the other hand, to him who considers the Gospels as later inventions of the Christian Church, not only the necessity, but even the motive is present, yea, every interest, to prevent his acknowledging miracles. No one has drawn the knot of this connection so close as Strauss himself. 'If a miracle,' as he expresses it, 'is incompatible with history, the Gospels can be no historical sources; and if the Gospels are really historical records, miracles are not to be separated from the history of the life of Jesus.' The question is equally the same, if, while the two-edged sword with which he conducts the combat delivers its blows not preponderatingly on one of its sides, its other is used only as a weapon for subsidiary services. We leave on one side the question as to which of the two was first in his own case: whether he arrived at the unauthenticity of the sources from the impossibility of miracles, or attained his standpoint from the opposite course, neither the scope of the work before us nor the frank explanation of its author can leave us in uncertainty as to the just decision. However high a value he concedes to historical investigation, he himself expressly declines to have any purely historico-critical interest in it. He adds that there is no need of our entering into purely critical questions, in order to refuse the acceptation of miracles. And he could not express himself plainer than he has done (*Leben Jesu*, p. 150, Eng. trans. vol. i. p. 200): 'It is absolutely impossible to conceive a case in which the investigator of history will not find it more probable, beyond all comparison, that he has to deal with an untrue account rather than with a miraculous fact.' This is no chance remark, but an assertion which can indeed be considered as the programme for all his subsequent investigations. We therefore follow Strauss' own leading, when we seek to oppose the *denial of miracles in the evangelical narratives*, which has found in him its representative.

It may appear as if, in keeping *this* point in view, we are restricted to a region in which a method quite different from the purely historico-exegetical one would be required. Strauss, indeed, lays great stress on this, that the mere historian, from his standpoint, must refuse even to acknowledge the miracles in the evangelical narrative. For, as the historical investigator has not merely to arrange *what* has happened, but also to state *how* one event must have proceeded from the other, so he can by no means allow an occurrence to pass which breaks through the chain of what is natural, and permits that which is unnatural to enter in. But he adds, that the historian, especially in so far as he is a scientific man, must have his philosophy, and thus he would also be supported by it in refusing to believe in miracles on philosophic grounds; or, in other words, that the philosophical historian may attack the truth of the miracles in the Gospel narrative, for the very reason that he is not in a position to admit the conception of a miracle.

It has often been asserted, that the rejoinders which were called forth by the critical edition of Strauss' *Life of Jesus*, published in the year 1835, have, notwithstanding their merits, missed the desired effect, because, various as are the points of view taken, they left unheeded the deepest ground, out of which have sprung the assertions of the critic. Should the combat with Strauss be fought out in the battle of Theism against Pantheism and Atheism? If this were really the case, theology would have no cause to appear on the battle-field. It would be impossible to require it, as such, to fight the opponent of Christianity with the weapons of *philosophy*. Franz Buddeus, in his excellent work, *Theses Theologicæ de Atheismo*, puts himself in strong opposition to Spinoza on the miracles in Holy Scripture (ch. iii. § 5); but he contents himself with the point, that all the errors of the philosopher have proceeded from the false supposition, that '*Deum et naturam unum idemque esse.*' Against this fundamental error he simply protests, without in any way refuting it. In the same way, Rothe, in his treatise on the Miracles (*Zur Dogmatik*, Gotha 1863, p. 80, etc.), explains that it may be perfectly conceivable that miracles should be denied by the pantheist, who knows of no other causality than that of nature, whether as *natura naturans*[1] or as *natura naturata*, and for whom

---

[1] This is an expression which Nitzsch in his *System d. Christlehre*, § 85, as also Twesten in his *Dogmatik*, ii. p. 176, have made available in the interest of the simple rejection of Pantheism.

that causality which we call God does not exist; also it is easily to be understood how Schleiermacher, partly from his tendency towards Pantheism, partly from his deterministic representations of the preservation and government of the world, should have arrived at a similar result; but it is *not* conceivable how the conception of a miracle can furnish any difficulty to a theist.[1] Now, if a theology is conceivable only on the standpoint of Theism, we cannot reasonably desire it to enter into the latest fundamental views of philosophy, from which has resulted, in Strauss' case, the impossibility of miracles. But apart from this, a 'Life of Jesus' thus prepared would in no manner correspond with that of the author. We have here to do with a work of conciliatory tendency. As it was intended for the *people*—for the *German people* especially—Strauss knew very well that he would have a difficulty to reach them by a philosophical explanation. No popularizing of Spinoza, however well done, would be able to take away, from even a section of the people, their present faith in miracles. It would not even have earned the

[1] Rothe had formerly introduced Weisse as a striking example of this, but afterwards he recalled the expression of his amazement at this thinker. An author has lately appeared, who acknowledges himself as a modern example of this kind, viz. O. Bagge, who has published *Princip. d. Mythus*, etc., the Principle of the Myth in the Service of Christian Positivism,—an Essay for, and yet against Strauss,—Leipzig 1865. He asserts that he stands on the true, unclouded field of Theism, and yet that he looks upon miracles as only the popular childish conception of the unknown workings of nature. He can oppose nothing to what Strauss has explained in this sense, that there can be no grosser theological suicide than the bare assertion of the traditional belief in miracles. The author appears to have a different conception of Theism than the one here advanced (of which Zeller says: 'If God is thought of, in the sense of ordinary Theism, as a supernatural Will, there must necessarily be the working of this Will, that is, a miracle'). He has not defined to us what his Theism is; but it must be that undefined and undefinable 'something,' like the same *something*, that *remainder* which is still left to him out of the evangelical narratives. This *latter* 'something' is just as inconceivable a minimum as is the difference between this author and Strauss.

thanks and applause of those in whom that faith was already lost. Nowhere has he treated it from the standing ground of outspoken Pantheism; but, in its place, he accepts that of scepticism. He pronounces on Hume's Discussions the commendatory judgment, that they are of such a general convincing power, that the matter can really be considered as satisfactorily settled by them. From them he borrows his view of the *internal improbability* of miracles. The burden of this improbability is shown to be so heavy, that everything which could be brought towards the justification of miracles is as a feather in the scale against a hundredweight. And he is not satisfied with this general assertion; but against each several Gospel narrative of a miracle, he produces the grounds on account of which it is neither probable nor credible that it could have taken place in the manner related. A sharp eye can discover everywhere in the background Spinozism, which has nevertheless quite other arguments at its disposal. However, it is not these, but solely those of scepticism, as stated, which are made available. If this treatment can reckon on finding a good point of union in the abhorrence of miracles, inherent in the thinkers of moderate intellect as well as in the savant of little experience, it also promises to effect a more prompt reception of the myth theory. For if it had been proved that the biblical narratives could only be received as true histories by heaping improbability on improbability, a method of exposition by which each difficulty of that nature disappears brings its own recommendation. Here, then, is the problem which the apologist has to solve. He has to prove that these improbabilities really do *not* exist, but are adroitly produced and brought in, while they never occur of themselves to the unprejudiced and critical reader. On the other hand, the miraculous accounts in the Gospel history have in themselves the highest *internal probability*,—a probability which appears the brighter, the more the biblical narrative is considered.

II. METHOD OF SOLVING THE PROBLEM.

Before we describe the way and the manner in which we intend to solve the problem, it will be necessary to declare to *which* of the miracles we wish to attach the proposed proof. It may be objected to our making a selection, such as is in accordance with our judgment, that by such a selection the point of the proof, although here and there in single cases successful, is broken as a whole. We would meet this objection by stating that we consider the problem *in some sense* soluble, even in those miracles which we deliberately exclude from our investigation. We make a distinction between those miracles wrought by the word and power of Jesus Himself, and those which were wrought by the glory of the Father *on* the Son. With regard to the latter (the supernatural birth of Jesus, and His resurrection from the dead), they do seem undoubtedly to elude a manner of consideration such as we intend to use towards the others. The schoolmen had a very firm consciousness of this, especially Thomas Aquinas. He makes the distinction between ' miracula quæ sunt ad fidei confirmationem,' and those ' de quibus ipsa est fides.' As an example of this last, he expressly points out the birth of Jesus by the Virgin ; and he continues : ' Illa sunt facta in multorum conspectu, hæc vero voluit Deus esse occulta, ut fides probaretur, quando ea amplectitur *propter scripturarum assertionem.*' A similar feeling is betrayed in the distinction, by Augustine, between ' miracula visibilia et invisibilia.' As this Father says : ' Illa ad illuminationem vocant, ista vero vocatos illuminant.' Both have been decided by the circumstance that the apostle places these miracles, which happened *on* Christ, as the pith and centre of *His* gospel; and, on this ground, did not consider it admissible to give any secondary foundation to the faith in them, by the side of the 'assertio scripturarum.' At the same time, we do *not* say that they should absolutely not be considered with any regard to the point of view laid down. The question is certainly allowable, where there may be probability, and where improbability,—whether it is the accepted fact, that the diligence of the apostles and the rise of the Christian Church are the fruits of the resurrection of Jesus, as really accomplished, or of a supposition which the disciples had imagined, and then persuaded themselves of its truth; whether we take the view, that the teaching and acts of Jesus (the impression produced, and the consequent results being included) are the operation of One, not like us below, and of this world, but who has come from above; or if we take the opposite one, that Jesus also proceeded from a natural development, —an improver, certainly, of the human ideal, but neither the first of them nor the last. However, this is not the probability which we have in our mind; for we do not mean any proceeding from *reflection*, but exclusively that which comes by *intuition*. It is therefore on this account that we must naturally confine our consideration to those miracles which, by their nature, can be placed in the light of *such* a probability, to those whose details the eye can follow, that is, to the miracles of *Our Lord Himself*.[1]

---

[1] This is the place to announce a still further restriction of our material, to which we find ourselves necessitated. We will not leave the miracles related in the fourth Gospel unconsidered, but we cannot devote more than a cursory attention to them. It is impossible to obtain any light on the result of their probability, by going into details in a work, whose single parts cannot, with impunity, be taken away from their connection with the whole.

The supposition that a glance at the way in which they happened is really granted to us, hardly stands in opposition to the assertion, on which Rothe lays great stress, that in a miracle the *process* does not positively take place—that it is the effect alone which we can observe. Strictly speaking, this proposition will only apply specially to those miracles which we have determined to put aside as not to be considered.

The miracle of the supernatural birth of Jesus, or that of His resurrection from the dead, could have been seen as happening by no human eye; they were perceptible only to the God-man Himself, and to the Risen One Himself. Even with regard to the miracles of Jesus Himself, we must unhesitatingly exclude as many 'as, from their original connections and surroundings, no one could have seen;'—the peculiar process by which the bread was increased, and the wine was transformed, was certainly excluded from the view of witnesses. However, the manner in which our Lord acted, the circumstances among which He accomplished His miracles, and the words which He then spake (that is, all that which the older apologetics call the 'circumstantiæ'),—all belong to the process, and are the very data by which we must assure ourselves of their probability, and especially urge for the settlement of the question; and on them, in each individual case, pre-eminently depends the question as to the motive.

It will now be seen from this preface what is the way in which we expect to solve our problem. We have no intention of appealing simply to the feelings, or even to sober sense, though this could be easily done, without it being able to be said that we have made our observations unsuitably. It appears to some, that the evangelical narratives of the miracles cannot be brought better into the bright light of probability, than by drawing a comparison between them and those contained in the apocryphal Gospels. We do not undervalue the importance of such a point of view; but, in opposition to the latest criticism, it is far too inadequate. Strauss himself would allow an important, even if a gradually decreasing, difference between these twofold species of narratives; he would pronounce a judgment something to this effect: that in the former we have the formation of myths on the part of the Christian Church; while in the latter we have the vagaries of the unbridled fancy of individuals. But still less have we in view to raise the question, by means of any *explanation* of miracles, of the amount of their probability. From all such attempts, and from the manner in which they are always employed, we ourselves decidedly and expressly dissent. 'In the very conception of a miracle, it is understood that it is unexplainable, as it is the work of God performed without any intermediate agency; but to *explain* an event, is to point out the intermediate means between it and its causality' (Rothe, in the work before quoted, p. 100). 'It is the character of miracles, that they cannot be explained by the natures of created things' (Leibnitz, *Theodicée*, § 207). Notwithstanding the evident correctness of the above propositions, the most unfortunate and the most unprofitable attempts at explanation have been constantly renewed, from the earliest times of the Church unto the present. The endeavours employed have been manifold, diverging from one another in various minor degrees; but they have all been compelled to return to a double method of treatment.

It was only to be expected that Christian apologetics, from the beginning until now, should have entered into the objections which present themselves to thinkers of moderate intelligence, as to the antagonism between miracles and the laws of nature as empirically established. If they could not, and ought not, to have kept themselves free from these matters, they could at least have employed no more irrelevant means, than by seeking to show that this antagonism did *not* exist, but was only *apparent*, and at the same time exerting themselves to mitigate and weaken it.[1]

The definition which Augustine has given to a miracle, 'miraculum voco quidquid arduum aut insolitum supra spem vel facultatem mirantis apparet' (*de util. cred.* c. 16), convinces us that he would not have been averse to this method. We understand him to consider the miracle also as simply an acceleration of the work of nature. The key with which he seeks to open to the light of reason the event at Cana— 'ipse fecit vinum in nuptiis, qui omni anno hoc facit in vitibus; illud autem non miramur, quia omni anno fit; assiduitate amisit admirationem'—suits also other miracles of the Lord (similar expressions of this Father are to be found collected in the little work of Nitzsch, *Augustine's Doctrine of Miracles*, Berlin 1865, p. 81 and following), as, for instance, the cursing of the fig-tree, in so far that the tree would at last have withered of itself; or the many accounts of healing in the Gospels, for an illness which is not fatal is gradually mitigated by the healing power of nature. We are unable to discover any real difference between a method of considering them of that kind, and the end attained by

[1] It is hardly necessary to remark, that we cannot employ, according to our view, such a manner of explaining the miracles as Paul Venturini and others have used in treating them. We are silent regarding it, not because the reasons for not accepting a folly well-nigh forgotten would be superfluous, but on the ground that by this method it is attempted to explain away the miracles as such. We are concerned alone with that method of exposition which preserves the miracles themselves intact, and seeks merely to justify them from the suspicions raised against them from the point of view of the laws of nature.

those who pass them over, in consideration of our deficient insight into the laws of nature. In both cases, the miracle threatens either to evaporate in mist, or to be raised up as a pure delusion before our eyes. If there really exists such a peaceful harmony between miracles and the laws of nature, that the former are the products of the latter,—only that these latter are either not known to us, or, if known to us, have been placed in an unusually rapid flow,—then, in fact, the conclusion is as good as drawn, that everything is a miracle, and again, that nothing is a miracle.[1] There is, at the most, a necessity for the adoption of a generally held *providentia extraordinaria*, — a providence which, by means of the combination of single factors, will produce those effects of nature before which human reason is silent. We certainly know that all who move within these barriers, and especially Augustine himself, do not draw out these consequences, or can even be considered to acknowledge them; but then the whole labour they have expended has been purely in vain. For if, for the purpose of the miracle, the *causæ secundæ* experience an extraordinary influence, if the laws of nature have been set in motion in a

---

[1] O. Bagge has lately (in his work quoted before, p. 88 and following) represented this oft-repeated proposition in such a manner that he points it out as a reality on theistic grounds, and as the true solution of the problem in question. Consequently he arrives at the hackneyed phrase, that man himself is a miracle, without, indeed, knowing that Montaigne had already written: 'I know no greater miracle in the world than man himself, only we forget it, because we are accustomed to it;' it even, though far otherwise intended, is to be found in Augustine (*de Civitate Dei*, x. 12). It is one of the many services of Strauss, that he has contributed to set aside this perversion of the conception of a miracle, this misuse of the expression. Especially in one of his controversial works, *die Halben und die Ganzen*, Berlin 1865, he has proved by evidence that hollow declamations on the miracles, such as Schenkel has promulgated, could only be possible when the same expressions are used for two different things (in work quoted, p. 45). We ought also to discontinue reviving afresh the assertion, which has now become trite, that where no knowledge of the laws of nature existed, as in the Old Testament, there could have been no miracle. The

forcible manner, that is, in a manner which is *not* founded in their own organic processes, but rather in decided opposition to them, is there not then a real injury to it,—an injury from which one would have willingly preserved the miracle-worker? Where is then the harmony?

The Church dogmatics of the Evangelical Church, and even the scholasticism of the middle ages, have, on this account, always been averse to moderate in this manner between the two conceptions. It has done the opposite. Thomas Aquinas says (*de potentia Dei*, quæst. vi. art. 2) of miracles, that they take place ' præter naturam, supra naturam, contra naturam ; ' and the Lutheran theologians have resolutely adhered to these definitions. It is an axiom of the *systema novissimarum controversiarum* of Zacharias Grape (Rostock 1722), in the section on Providence, that ' miracula cum natura non esse concilianda.' Here and there we find the *contra* less insisted on. Hopfner (*Loc. theol.* 1673), in Loc. x. *de miraculis*, contents himself with the *præter* and *supra* ('miracula sunt opera Dei præter et supra naturæ ordinem facta'). Löscher, however, returns to the full strictness of the definition, in his

' discovery' that the Old Testament contains no expression of a conception of nature, supports this view just as little as do a few passages in the Psalms; which are quite irrelevant. We will allow no one to dissuade us from believing, that even an eye partially closed to a recognition of nature's laws is in a position to recognise a miracle, that is, an action performed as such, which has not proceeded from the series of final causes, but from the immediate divine causality. Buddeus has very suitably destroyed the tender, artistically spun web of this opinion by the simple remark : ' Ita comparata sunt miracula biblica, ut cœcum menteque destitutum esse opporteat, qui vim ad hæc requiri infinitam non agnoscat.' Similarly, J. Lulofs, Professor of Philosophy, Mathematics and Arts at Leyden, in his edition of the theses of Buddeus, which appeared in 1767 : ' Leges naturæ per innumera experimenta et per observationes repetitas *omnibus* innotuerunt.' It is evident, as founded on fact, that the Israelitish consciousness for the recognition of a miracle had been sufficiently organized, and has been very satisfactorily explained lately by M. Baumgarten, in his *Nachtgesicht Sacharias*, vol. ii. p. 405 and following.

controversies with the Deists. 'Solus Deus,' he declares in his *theologia pretiosa*, 'potest tum *supra* naturæ *vires*, tum *contra* naturæ *leges* agere, *quorum utrumque requiritur ad verum miraculum*.' Moreover, Buddeus speaks not only in his *Theses de atheismo*, but also in his *Institutiones theolog. dogmat.* (lib. ii. c. 1), quite particularly of a *suspensio legum naturæ* in a miracle; in fact, he even raises it to a constitutive element of the conception. Rothe declares that he does not quite agree with these definitions; he inclines rather to the formula, that miracles and the laws of nature cannot come into conflict, because they are not antagonistic. A miracle is performed just *immediately* by the absolute causality of God, who has *not* submitted Himself, His freedom, His will, to the laws of nature, and has not confined His efficacy within it. All biblical theologians have willingly given their assent to this exposition, as well as their thanks for this frank and open explanation. However, there is between him and the Church dogmatics no real difference on this point; for even the latter do not intend to assert anything further than that the immediate divine causality enters into the place of the *causæ secundæ*, which are completely excluded. In fact, there is a sense in which the contested *contra* is not only completely allowable, but is indispensable. For if an effect occurs, which certainly would not have happened *if* the laws of nature had been left to their own organic processes, we must then agree that it has resulted *contra* leges naturæ. Critically, a *contra* would only occur in the case that the non-natural effect was one against nature, or rather an unnatural one. It needs no evidence to prove that this was never the case with the miracles of Jesus. It will enter into no man's mind ever to consider restored health as an unnatural occurrence. The words of our Lord, when He healed the man who had the dropsy (Luke xiv. 5), or the woman with an infirmity (Luke xiii. 6), occur quite apropos to this point of view, that He was taking away the unnatural condition, and, on the other hand, restoring the natural one. And this is applicable not only to the effects themselves, but also to the relation in which they were placed towards nature. Everywhere they range themselves in it; they submit to its laws, and are subject to its operations. The life to which Lazarus was awakened was no supernatural one, but the very same, and with the same conditions as before. Those who were miraculously fed and cured were not on that account made free from the necessity of again buying their food, and of again preserving their health in the usual natural way.[1] We advance, lastly, for the *contra*, as comprehended in our views, the claim that, in a *teleological* sense, it is essentially requisite in a miracle; for only those effects which bear the impression on their face, force themselves on the senses as having happened miraculously. Werensfels' definition, that ' miraculum est opus potentiæ divinæ extraordinarium, *in sensu incurrens*, admirationemque videntium excitans,' finds its surer support in the significative declaration of our Lord, that He performs His works by the finger of God (Luke xi. 20). The words refer to Ex. viii. 15. There the Egyptian magicians say, when they cannot imitate the miracles of Moses: 'The finger of God is here;' it is obviously a work of God, a miracle; and on this is grounded the censure of the stiff-necked and invincible obduracy of Pharaoh which follows.

It is only another form of this manner of treatment

---

[1] Compare M. Baumgarten, *d. Nachtgesichte Sacharias*, ii. p. 405: 'A miracle always enters into the natural order of things, but only so far as that the effect is at once ended; nature being in the process like the surface of the ocean, which is at one moment broken by a stone, but at the next annihilates all traces of it.'

in *explaining* the miracles, to expect to find the key in a power of nature of a higher kind which Jesus had at His disposal. The analogies which have been drawn, before and after Olshausen, from the electrical currents of magnetism, are now very generally discredited. However, Rothe has lately again spoken of a real process of nature, even if an extraordinary one, on which many miracles appear to rest. This declaration would be hardly reconcilable with the earlier expressed explanations of this theologian, if he had not prefaced it with the remark, that he has here in view only a part (and that by no means a large one) of the miracles of Jesus, and especially not the extraordinary ones, but only the ordinary ones, such as the curing of the sick. In *these* it is indisputable that there may have been some really earthly powers of nature at work, but only such as at present we cannot see, or which are not yet familiar to our experience, but which deeper searching physiologico-anthropological investigation will bring more and more to the light of day. The distinction between extraordinary and ordinary miracles, which Rothe here makes, has in some sense been always made previously. By the side of miracles 'proprie et specifice, stricto et rigoroso sensu sic dicta' (called also 'miracula primi ordinis'), there have been shown 'miracula secundaria, comparative talia, miracula quoad nos, non simpliciter.' These definitions are to be found not only in Leibnitz (in his *Conformité de la foi avec la raison*, § 3, in his *Theodicée*, and in the collection of minor works), but also in Gerhard, Höpfner, Löscher, Buddeus, and even in the Schoolmen. The latter certainly do not allow to these 'miracula secundaria' the definition of 'miracula,' but characterize them as only 'mirabilia' or 'miranda;' while the former desire that expressions should be used such as 'ostenta' (Löscher), 'prodigia' (Höpfner), or 'portenta' (Buddeus). In this distinction, Church dogmatists take this course, partly in order to be able to keep false miracles—those of the devil, of Antichrist, and of false prophets—separate from those that are divine; and partly they wish, even in the circle of these latter works of God, to distinguish those which have proceeded chiefly from the action of providence, and those which show an immediate interference of God '*contra leges naturæ*,' for they could only impute to *these* latter a forced power of demonstration. But on no consideration would they have considered themselves pledged to divide the miracles of Jesus into extraordinary and ordinary, into objective and subjective; they were to them, jointly and severally, 'miracula proprie sic dicta.'

The only exegetical support on which the view, now on the decline, that Jesus often cured sicknesses by the bodily touch or by the use of media, is sustained, partly falls to the ground from the fact that, in numerous cases, this neither did happen nor could have happened, and partly vanishes under the earnestly considered question (first raised by Buddeus, and since thoroughly examined by S. J. Baumgarten in his *Untersuchung. Theol. Streitigkeiten*, Halle 1762, i. p. 658), whether the ground of the effect is really to be sought for in these touches and media themselves, or if the action is not rather to be explained by the motives which lead to it. Moreover, this fancy can only be asserted in subjective feelings. If the feelings are appealed to, as to whether the turning of the water into wine at Cana is not on a much higher platform than perhaps the healing of the mother-in-law of Peter, the decision desired would in *this* instance be obtained. But whoever would speak merely according to purely objective standards, would mercilessly level the ground. The 'mirabilia' may be subjected to this difference of rank, for one may appear to me more wonderful than another (although even in this region there is never a complete harmony between the feelings of individuals), but the 'miracula' *never*. The healing of the mother-in-law of Peter is, in the same 'sensus strictus et rigorosus,' a miracle, just as much as the increasing of the bread. It is impracticable in the one case to state it as the mere effect of the powers of nature, and in the other as the work of the immediate interposition of God. It is difficult to contradict the saying of Löscher: 'Diligenter distinguendum est inter naturæ vires, quæ nobis cognitæ nondum sunt, et inter ordinem naturæ, de quo nobis sufficientes constat.' The healing of the mother-in-law of Peter did *not* result 'secundum ordinem naturæ;' at least the witnesses present did not understand it in this way, nor did the evangelists relate it in this sense.

A *second* attempt has been made to *explain* the miracles of Jesus, by employing the intervention of psychology. The miracles of Jesus appeared a troublesome and difficult problem to Schleiermacher, in whose theology there was no place left for the conception of a miracle, but who, nevertheless, firmly held to the authenticity of the fourth Gospel. For the sake of the biblical narratives, but certainly also on deeper grounds, he was not averse to allow them in some sense ('We *have a presentiment,*' as he characteristically says in his *Glaubenslehre,* ii. § 103,—'we have a presentiment that, in relation to the Redeemer, there was a higher order than the natural one—that extraordinary powers must have been at His command'); and yet he did not feel himself able to acknowledge them in the sense of the narrator. How he escaped from this dilemma, is evident from the lately published *Vorlesungen über das Leben Jesu,* Berlin 1864.[1] In the

---

[1] The publication of these essays has pleased no one so much as Strauss. The real admirers of Schleiermacher were deeply grieved by it. It is cer-

first place, he, by the employment of various means, puts aside from consideration the most inconvenient narratives: some on account of the 'natural explanation' (quite unworthy and peculiar to him); others by the fact that the representation of the evangelists is destitute of completeness and of probability, in such a degree that an hypothesis is justifiable (*Vorlesungen*, p. 238 and following). Thus there remains to him only the healing of the sick and of the demoniacs. But he succeeded in showing these as the effects of a dominating over an oppressed will, as assertions of the power of the spiritual over the psychical and physical, so much the easier, the more he took into account the specific worthiness and peculiarity of Jesus. Thus, he justified his 'presentiment,' that the power of working miracles was at the command of the Redeemer, without destroying the foundations of his theology, in which there was no place for the conception of a miracle.[1] And thus here is, in fact, a point where he nearly approaches Strauss, notwithstanding the diversity of their premises and of their points of issue.

It would be a useless labour to prove what violence is done, by this attempt at explanation, to the evangeli-

tainly not to be justified in the interest of science, and any consideration of piety must be withheld from it. It must certainly have pleased Strauss to have another precursor in his way of understanding the life of Jesus—at least as regards miracles—besides Reimarus. The opinion has hitherto been held, that Schleiermacher, in his *History of the Development of Theology*, had effected a conversion of rationalism in the direction of faith, and that opinion is partly correct. However, Strauss asserts that Schleiermacher was in advance of his age, in so far that he, though perhaps he had no clear conception of it, has aimed at the standpoint advanced by himself, without being able to attain it. The lectures on the life of Jesus now published give an appearance of probability to this assertion; for, as regards the working of miracles of our Lord, *considering the actual results*, we can discover no difference between the two authors.

[1] Schleiermacher, in his practical exposition of Scripture, expresses himself more favourably with regard to miracles. In his explanation of Acts ii. 22 (*Sermons*, iii. p. 448), he is indignant against those who take objection to the miracles of our Lord, and complain of them as a hindrance to

cal narratives, and especially to the accounts in the fourth Gospel, which is so expressly acknowledged as authentic. On the other hand, the biblical argument, which is always brought forward in its favour, demands a short examination. The circumstance is noticed, that our Lord often demanded faith before He would help—that He was able to perform only a few cures in Nazareth, on account of the 'want of faith' of the inhabitants. The fact is also advanced, that the confidence of the sick in the physician forms an important factor in the cure. But, in the first place, it is not the fact that all who were wonderfully healed entertained such a confidence. Naaman mocked at the means of cure recommended to him by Elisha; he yielded to it only on the solicitation of his servants with the most decided mistrust, even in complete unbelief, and still he became clean. Thus also many, among others the 'impotent' man at Bethesda, who received help from Jesus without in the least surmising in Him a helper. The 'faith' which the Lord requires in the cases which are shown us, has very little to do with the so-called confidence in the benevolent physician. Remarking on the words of Jesus to the woman who had an issue of blood, 'Thy faith hath made thee whole' (Matt. ix. 22), Strauss says: 'He could not have expressed Himself more truly, modestly, correctly, and precisely.' We shall see in proper time that even this singular case will be judged quite otherwise. Besides, the biblical language, especially in places such as John iv. 48, 'Except ye see signs and wonders, ye will not

their faith; and he here asserts that they are rather a welcome witness of the satisfaction of the Father in the Son—sensible representations of the heavenly voice: 'This is my beloved Son.' We can, however, have no real confidence in this exposition, when the speaker at the same time continues, in an extremely energetic, almost overheated manner, to carry out his favourite proposition, that miracles are really of no importance for the planting and cherishing of our faith.

believe,' sanctions the idea that the 'faith' is in a region to which the miracle must first lead the way. In any case, it could not be requisite to the *power*, but only to the *will* of Jesus,—not the preliminary to the earthly, sensible result, but only to serve towards the attainment of a higher purpose.

If we decidedly renounce every attempt to make the miracles probable by means of *explanation*, what other way is there offered for our aim? No one can *explain* a miracle, but one can and must *conceive* it. However, we must not let ourselves be here content with the sense in which Rothe (p. 100 of *Dogmatik*), while expressly declining the one, requires the other. Certainly the miracle *is* conceived as soon as it has been acknowledged as an immediate work of *God*. But even to this end we must also glance into the suppositions on which this work of God every time rests. Löscher with justice remarks, in his *Theologia pretiosa:* 'Miracula semper supponunt actum interiorem voluntatis divinæ et fundamenta sufficientiæ extraordinariæ actionis Dei.' Twesten has also explained how essential this teleological point of view is for the conception of a miracle: 'The mere inexplicability of an event by any known effective causes is not of itself sufficient to make us see in it a special result of divine causality. It is necessary to a miracle that it should signify some end, and that significance is the divine object recognisable by us' (*Dogmatik*, ii. p. 117).[1] In its application to the miracles of Jesus, the demand herein founded, that the motive must be shown which moved our Lord to work miracles *in general*, and then each single miracle which He performed *in particular*, is left

[1] The one-sided accentuation of this view would, however, endanger a weakening, and even destruction, of the conception of a miracle. But if we are first convinced that the miracle rests principally on its relation to the *effecting* cause, we can then do full justice without hesitation to the question regarding the *end* in view.

undecided. If these motives are shown, and that *not* from general considerations, but from the existing text itself, from the 'event' which our eyes perceive, then *are* the miracles conceived, and therewith are they then brought into the light of a complete probability.

We are confirmed in the accuracy of this method, of which we will make use throughout, by nothing more than by the use made of it by Strauss himself. We see him, in fact, striving not only to show the general grounds on which the authors of the Gospels represented their Messiah as a worker of miracles; but in each special case he makes it his chief business to discover the cause for which they might have imputed to Him this wondrous work. We will also move in the same path, but we will certainly strive after an opposite end. *To us* the biblical narratives are truth; consequently *we* seek in *Jesus Himself* the motives of the miracles related. To the author of the *Life of Jesus* they are but fictions; he has consequently to search for the motives of the legendary poets who formed them.

III. THE VALUE OF THE SOLUTION.

It is very important that we should show at once the point of view from which we would throw light on the question before us. Our intention is not to measure the value which the justification of miracles can claim *for itself*. But the measure of the value attached concerns exclusively the proof of the *probability* of the miracles of Jesus, partly in general, and partly of each single one in particular. Thus, we have not to consider of what profit it is to have caused the acknowledgment of miracles in general; but the question is, What and how much is gained if the miracles of Jesus are made to stand in the light of probability?

The apologetic value of miracles has never been

settled by theologians. Some have esteemed it very high, others lower; but there have also not been wanting some who will not grant it any value. Buddeus has taken a very extreme view, for he declares: 'Non modo religionis christianæ veritatem, sed et numinis existentiam *valide* ex miraculis demonstrari posse.' On the other hand, Joh. Gerhard is by no means inclined to raise such a claim for them. This theologian (who has devoted only a very cursory discussion to the part 'de miraculis' in his *Locus de notis ecclesiæ*, xxiii. 11) gives the well-known propositions: 'Per miracula non possunt probari oracula,' and, 'Miracula, si non habent doctrinæ veritatem conjunctam, nihil probant.' And he calls attention apart from the *dictum probans* (Deut. xiii. 1) to the circumstance that miracles can be also performed by the devil,[1] by heathens, and by heretics. His intention was certainly not to deny *all* power of convincing to miracles; he expressly guards himself from saying that 'miracula *nihil* probare.' He only demands that there should be the most accurate valuation of it in the doctrine: 'Miracula sunt doctrinæ tesseræ et sigilla; quemadmodum igitur sigillum literis avulsum nihil probat, ita quoque miracula sine doctrina nihil valent;' 'miracula fuerunt buccinæ et præcones quibus evangelium primitiis commendabatur.' It was, however, evidently quite in this sense that Höpfner lays down the canon: 'Fides semper magis niti debet verbo et sacramento, quam miraculis.' To him the miracle is of secondary importance, perhaps

---

[1] Gerhard passes over this fact naturally in a totally different sense, and for quite other ends than was done by Spinoza, as well as modern theologians (Schleiermacher, *Glaubenslehre*, i. p. 101). Rothe (*Zur Dogm.* 110) and Twesten (*Dogmatik*, i. p. 366), by simply recalling the passage in Matt. xii. 24, have shown with what injustice *these* writers have raised the reproach expressed against the apologetical value of miracles. A sword which is despised as quite blunt and unsuitable, and which one is ashamed to wear, should not be sharpened for a momentary use.

even a subordinate affair; and he has so little evaded the circle in which, with this standpoint, he must move, that he rather cites with approval the assertion of Theophylact: 'Prædicatio per miracula confirmatur miracula autem per prædicationem.'

The importance of miracles has always been recognised in the Lutheran dogmatics. It was universally taught that 'finem miraculi esse, ut agnoscatur et confirmatur veritas cœlestis.' However, its immediate power was gradually remarkably weakened. The circumstance is noteworthy, that this doctrine was more and more removed from the *locus de revelatione*, and referred to that *de munere Christi triplici*. In the explanation of miracles, the conception of them was always to be found in the first place, the apologetical side in the last.[1] In modern times, the possibility of proving miracles has been resolutely opposed. Schleiermacher, while calling attention to some witnesses in Scripture, is the chief spokesman (as is known) in this direction (*Glaubenslehre*, i. p. 100 and following) : 'The delusion seems everywhere more and more to have prevailed, that the efficacy of these circumstances has somehow

---

[1] It is not that the power of our Lord's working miracles was immediately subordinated as a constitutive element to the 'munus propheticum,' as soon as it had received an assured place in the *locus de officio Christi* (which, by the way, did not happen early—even Gerhard evidently delayed it). Scattered traces of this are to be found even in older expositions (thus Brochmann, in his *Systema Theologia*, 1633, reckons as part of the prophetical office of Christ : ' Quod stupendis, omnemque finitam potentiam excedentibus operibus doctrinam confirmavit ') ; but Gerhard and his followers place this office only in the *functio docendi* under especial stress on the *efficacia doctrinæ*. In the first place, Buddeus teaches expressly : ' Miraculis insuper Jesus doctrinam suam confirmavit ; quæ quum propria virtute ederet, iis pondus doctrinæ suæ addidit, eamque ita comparatam esse ostendit, ut de divina ejus origine et veritate nemini dubitare fas sit.' The editor of the theses of Buddeus, *De Atheismo*, Lutofs, seeks to mediate between him and Gerhard, and proposes the formula : ' Miracula non probant veritatem doctrinæ, sed divinam missionem eorum, qui istius doctrinæ fuerunt præcones.'

always supposed faith as existing, and therefore they cannot have produced it.' The characteristic expressions, 'seems' and 'somehow,' should be noted.[1] But in this he is followed by others. M. Baumgarten (*Geschichte Jesu*, p. 168 and following), basing his argument on certain passages of the Bible detached from their context, guards himself against an unjust underestimation of miracles for apologetical ends; however, on the same doubtful supports, he also earnestly warns against an over-estimation of them. Rothe even (*Zur Dogm.* 111) candidly declares: 'I place the apologetical importance of miracles quite in the background; in *our* days it is of very little weight.'

Why should this be? Why must it be so? And why especially in our days? It is perhaps that, in favourable cases, miracles are only of importance for the 'fides humana,' while the 'fides divina' must be thoroughly grounded on the 'testimonium Spiritus sancti.' We can conceive that they may be kept separate the one from the other; but in reality, the one depends closely on the other. Where the grounds of reason do not go hand in hand with the faith of the heart, there is then wanting the peace of deep conviction — there are conflicts in view which may lead to a fatal breach. Or is it, that even the 'fides humana' in the miracles has only a rotten support, for which moreover a rich compensation is offered in means of proof in some other manner? A rotten support! In how far is it

---

[1] The principal ground on which the integrity of Schleiermacher's character as a theologian has appeared doubtful to many, is that he, although, as is known to every one, conscious of other grounds, did not scruple to support himself on specious arguments from Scripture. In the present case he calls attention to the fact that our Lord repeatedly forbade His miracles to be published abroad. Any one acquainted with Scripture would know that Christ as often expressed a prohibition 'that one should tell no one that He was the Christ.' Schleiermacher might find a difficulty in drawing from this last the inferences which he had from the first.

so weak? It is quite an erroneous assertion of Schleiermacher, that miracles can only be of service in the case of the immediate perception of them; and on the other hand, that they lose their power according to the ratio of distance in time and space. For there is absolutely no real difference between one which we saw with our own eyes, and one in a credible trustworthy report. Here and there the 'operatio Dei' is in like manner 'in sensus incurrens.' Just as one can mistrust the report, so can one also distrust one's own eyes. The right or the wrong is in both cases sufficiently similar.[1] And the rich compensation? In what does it consist? We are mistrustful even beforehand of a compensation for an 'adminiculum fidei' given of God, particularly when it is so opportunely offered to us and urged on us by the hands of Lessing.

It is only a new manner of expressing the well-known proposition of the latter, when Schleiermacher continues: 'What in our day takes the place of miracles, is the historical account of the condition, extent, and duration of the spiritual operations of Christ.' Without estimating the value of this boasted new proof, or wishing to suspect it in and on account of itself, we at any rate dispute its title to hold the dignity of a compensation for that which it has taken away from us. It would indeed be a strange thing to endeavour to restrict to contemporaries the measure of St. John's

[1] Our experience has lately given most striking confirmation to this. Whoever has read the work of Renan will be reminded of the author's acknowledgment, that he would by no means recognise a miracle, even if his own eyes had beheld it. On page 36 of the French edition can be seen what other sort of proofs he considers necessary. Weisse also declares, 'I should not trust my eyes if I saw a supernatural miracle pass before them.' Well, *stat pro ratione voluntas*. But then would be accomplished the saying of S. J. Baumgarten (*Untersuchung. Theol. Streit.* i. p. 661), that it would be that all history must completely give up every historical proof, and even the certainty of the senses and of experience.

words (John xii. 37), 'Though He had done so many miracles before them, yet they believed not on Him,' or that of the similar complaint of our Lord Himself (John xv. 24); and to consider the simple conclusion of the man who was born blind, who had been healed (John ix. 33), 'If this man were not of God, he could do nothing,' as binding only on those then present. But it is more than strange when these assertions are maintained in the face of the declaration of the evangelist: these (that is, the signs) are written that ye might believe that 'Jesus is the Christ' (John xx. 31). Γέγραπται is the word used. Now John must then have been of opinion that the miracles of Jesus written of by him have the same power of conviction for his readers, and indeed for *all* readers, even to the latest times, as, when seen, they had for the immediate witnesses. Even if, as we are assured, we had other means to attain faith, we should in no way be recompensed for the loss of this proof. This theory of compensation generally rests on a delusion which is easily proved. Let us look narrowly at the supposition, that though at one time miracles were of an irreparable importance, at the present they have none. If this means, that formerly it was necessary that miracles should *happen*, while now there is no necessity for them, there is no dispute on the subject. This has not only been granted, but expressly affirmed. Augustine (*de Civitate Dei*, c. 22): 'Quisquis adhuc prodigia, ut credat, requirit, magnum est ipse prodigium, qui mundo credente non credit.' Of a similar opinion is Chrysostom in his *Homiliæ* 13 *in Joann*. Höpfner says: 'Miracula sunt veritatis cœlestis signa, sed temporaria, non perpetua, et ad fundationem ecclesiæ necessaria; doctrinâ confirmatâ iis non amplius opus est.' Gerhard observes: 'Nequaquam Christus generalem promissionem dedit, quod miracula etiam post prædicationem evangelii in mundo receptam ordinarie et perpetuo in ecclesia vigere debeant.' If, however, it means that once the interposition of miracles was needed for *faith* in the revelation of God, while now the necessity has passed away, the assertion intended in this sense cannot harmonize with the acknowledgment, as strongly asserted, that a miracle is a constitutive element of revelation. How can I sincerely believe a revelation, if a 'constitutive element' of it, and that the very one 'by which God is revealed to the purblind eye,' is to be cast aside?[1]

We therefore consider the apologetical value of miracles considerably higher than is granted to them by the public opinion of modern theology. The interest which we maintain for them is higher than the mere historical one; they must be available for other services to us, than only to bridge over the 'yawning chasm of the history of the world.'[2] But we repeat it, this is not at present our purpose. The question is rather this: What and how much is gained when the miracles of Jesus have, in the sense indicated, been brought into the light of probability? We believe that something considerable is thereby gained. The fact has been proved in the cases of Rothe, of Schleiermacher, and even in others of earlier times, that there are numerous minds which may find a stumbling-block

[1] Notwithstanding our best endeavours, we have been unable to understand the distinction made by Rothe (*Zur Dogm.* p. 80): 'The question is not by what *we* now could recognise a miracle as such; but it is asked, by what could a revelation when it happened have been evident as a revelation to those to whom it was immediately addressed?' How am I to begin to accept miracles as mere historical occurrences, if when they happened they were expressly and exclusively intended to make the revelation evident as such? Then should I indeed separate what God has joined together.

[2] If they had not this higher significance, how is it to be explained that attempts are made with such untiring persistency to do away with them, from the most varied points of view, and by means of the most manifold manœuvres? They must certainly belong to those things which are most uncomfortable for polemics.

in the miracles of Jesus, without on that account being specially incredulous of a divine revelation. In consideration of this fact, Rothe (here completely agreeing with Weisse) warns us that we must not altogether alienate from the Christian faith the present generation, by exacting from them an acknowledgment of the biblical miracles. No one will deny the justice of the problem which this much respected man has proposed to the Church of the present, to win back those who are estranged from it, even though many may not agree to the manner and way in which he has lately formulated it at the 'Protestantentag' at Eisenach. But the great question is, whether it can in any way be furthered by the purely negative proceeding of dispensing the heretical self-will from accepting miracles. The saying, 'I will not force on you the belief in miracles,' is on that account a hazardous one, because the supposition in reality nowhere occurs, 'that the light of revelation appears in other things to minds offended at miracles, that Christian ideas have sprung up in them, that they in the light of this sun have entered into life.' If we must always put aside everything against which one has 'an instinctive perception,' how much of Christianity, and what sort of Christianity, would remain?

Even Strauss himself does not wish to take Christianity away from the present generation;[1] but he only wished to purify it from the transient representations of the time; and he assures us that, after the taking away of these elements, there really is 'still something, and that not a little,' of it left (*Die Halben und die Ganzen*, p. 128). Not a little?

For religious need there remains just so much, that

---

[1] When the above was written Strauss was an Hegelian; he has, however, since become a Materialist, and his antipathy to Christianity, as evinced in his *Old and New Faith*, has increased.—T.

is as extremely little as his criticism from the historical side has left of what really constitutes the life of Jesus. At any rate, not an atom remains of that which the Apostle Paul calls *his* gospel, besides which there can be no other, even though an angel from heaven should announce it, — not an atom of that gospel which has overcome the world.

It is an indubitably just saying, 'Beneficia non obtruduntur.' But in the question before us it cannot be used otherwise than in the comprehensive sense, that the most comprehensive benefit, the gospel, is to be obtruded on no one. The Church has neither the power nor the right, either tacitly or expressly, to dispense from the acceptation of any truth which it acknowledges. Apart from the disloyalty of it, we would deny its wisdom. Thus, even though we wish to take into consideration the fact that the miracles of Jesus in the evangelical history are at present a stumbling-block to many, our present path must be a different one.

We do *not* suffer, we do *not* counsel that they should be placed on one side; but we seek rather to construct a heartfelt upright reconciliation with them, and for this end we will strive to place them in the light of probability. We may assert that in some such sense the ancient Church itself pursued the same end and the same path.[1] There was not the slightest necessity for the early Christian apologists to prove the historical certainty of the miracles of Jesus, as they were not attacked even by a Celsus. They had, however, to illustrate the intrinsic character of these deeds of our Lord, and to defend them from false suspicions; they had to show their difference from the workings of magicians, and especially the harmony in which they stand with the faith of Christians.

---

[1] We recommend for comparison the detailed communications of Baur in his *Dogmengeschichte*, Leip. 1865, Pt. i. p. 352 and foll.

Our problem is, as we have now repeatedly shown, a double one. The one is of a general, the other of a special nature. We have first to show in particular the probability of Jesus working miracles; and then the probability of each single miracle which, according to the reports of the evangelists, was performed by our Lord.

I.

JESUS AS A WORKER OF MIRACLES.

It is evident that the question, whether it is conceivable and probable that our Lord should manifest a power of working miracles, stands in close connection with the presuppositions held regarding His person. Whoever considers Jesus nothing but a man, although a 'pattern of the human ideal,' must also consider the actual miracles which He is said to have wrought as improbable, incomprehensible, and impossible; and according to the view he takes of the original narratives, he will either go the way of rationalism, or—if he holds a perfectly free position with regard to their sources—will continue his path unimpeded to a complete denial of them. Strauss could only find it comprehensible, and at the same time really probable, that Jesus, by exciting the imagination, may have effected cures which bore in them the appearance of the miraculous: 'Sufferers regularly crowded upon him in order to touch his garments, because they expected to be cured by doing so. And it would have been strange indeed, if there had been no cases among all these in which the force of excited imagination, and impressions half spiritual, half sensuous, produced either actual removal or temporary mitigation of their complaints; and this effect was ascribed to the miraculous power of Jesus' (*Leben Jesu*, 266; Eng. trans. i. 365).

Miracles in this sense, 'according to the mode of thought of the period, and of his contemporaries, he *must* perform, whether he would or not.'¹ Strauss was necessitated by his standpoint to refer to the region of legend all which is not opened by this key. Our purely positive tendency precludes us from a thorough contest with the Myth theory which he has offered to the German people. We will here content ourselves with showing the reasons why he has until now neither succeeded, nor ever can succeed, in obtaining applause and acknowledgment, notwithstanding all the expenditure of acuteness and learning, as well as the energy of will, with which he has striven to carry out that theory. Welcker's declaration, that 'a myth sprouts out of the mind, as a germ breaks through the earth,' may be just in relation to a time which is *before* history; but it is quite inapplicable to *the* time here treated of: *there* it unavoidably leads to absurdities. Whoever reads the attempt which Strauss has made (*Leben Jesu*, p. 154; Eng. transl. i. p. 206) to illustrate the manner in which, according to this theory, the evangelical accounts of miracles have come into existence, will not be so much astonished that he has employed it, as that he can suppose that a man with sound sense could find it acceptable. But it appears, in fact, that he is more and more inclined to abandon the hypothesis of such a 'generatio æquivoca' as a position as good as lost, and to put in the place of this unconscious formation of legends the conscious fabrication of them. On the other hand, he indeed protests that he has completely given up the former; but when he acknowledges that,

¹ If Strauss had not assured us that he had not read Renan's work until after the completion of his own, we should have entertained the suspicion that he had borrowed this phrase from that writer, who, as is known, often assures us that Jesus was a worker of miracles 'contro cœur.' At any rate, it agrees better with the fantastic Frenchman than with the clear sober thinker. Singularly, however, it has also gained the assent of Zeller (compare his *Vorträge und Abhandlungen*, Leips. 1865, p. 489).

in consequence of Baur's proofs of the fact of *intentional* fabrication, he now grants far more justice and importance to it than formerly, his language betrays plainly enough the change of opinion which has come over him.

His position has thereby become untenable; and so long as he holds to it, so long as the fourth Gospel in particular is to him nothing more than a novel with an apologetic tendency,[1] so long will he attract others less and less to him. If he selects the eleventh chapter of St. John in order to justify his views, he can, on the ground of his discussions, certainly maintain the full amount of the assertion, that 'the history of Lazarus in St. John cannot be held without dizziness' (*die Halben und Ganzen*, p. 124); but, in truth, it would make the head of any impartial person grow giddy, if he is to believe the conception that a Gentile Christian in the second century has composed it. We put quite out of sight the moral side of the question; but Strauss must necessarily show (as the question is now no more one regarding unconscious productions of an uncertain subject, 'the Church,' but regarding the conscious literary activity of an individual) that, among the Gentile Christians of the second century, men were not wanting who may have been qualified for such a task. We take all connoisseurs of the literature of this century to witness, whether there is even the slightest trace of any qualification of that sort to be found. There have been certainly in all times poetical geniuses; but who would have been able to have created unaided, in form and substance,

---

[1] Strauss has been, however, urged to receive the idea of 'known fabrication' by no means only by the Gospel of St. John. He felt himself necessitated to it also in regard to the accounts of miracles in the synoptical Gospels. For even if the latter had arisen from being founded on prophetical texts,—as, for instance, the passage of Isa. xxxv. 5,—the supposition of an intentional fiction is here also indispensable.

the eleventh chapter of the fourth Gospel, when in possession merely of an 'idea,' and some names? In comparison to him, all the known poets would be extremely subordinate spirits. It would be difficult for any one to demand the acceptance of such a monstrosity.

The position of Schleiermacher is apparently formed differently, and yet *not* so in reality. As this theologian, in the interest of the defence of 'Ebionitism,' holds fast to the specific worthiness of the Redeemer, and thus 'surmises' that the power of working miracles may have been at His command, he would certainly find it conceivable and probable that Jesus should have also used this power. But as his interest was equally pressing, and perhaps preponderating, to exclude 'Doketism' in all, even its most subtle forms, he could acknowledge that probability only so far as he was able on one side to conceive a miraculous deed as an ordinary act of Christ;[1] and, on the other side, to set up an analogy between Christ's manner of working and that of another man's, that is, in so far as the key of the psychological method of explanation (as mentioned before) unlocked it for him. Hence, probably, only single miracles were selected by him, and these even merely for the sake of showing the authority of the narrator of them, but not at all on account of Jesus' power of working miracles in general. As regards the latter, we get the impression that Schleiermacher rather concealed it, as in his *Life of Jesus* he has placed it very characteristically under the heading, 'Zeit ausfüllung.'

But how is it now with those who more or less decidedly believe that Jesus is the Christ, the Son of

---

[1] See Schleiermacher's *Glaubenslehre*, ii. p. 136: 'Christ used His powers of working miracles as every one uses his natural powers, each as opportunity occurs, to do good with them.' Much the same idea is expressed in his *Leben Jesu*, p. 220.

God, who is come into the world? Is not on that very account the Lord's power of working miracles at once both conceivable and probable? In what respect should it be *made* probable to them? We do not wish to withdraw from our former declaration, that in our whole exposition we have in view such minds as, though inclined towards faith, assure us that they find a stumbling-block in the miracles of our Lord; but we seek to answer more decidedly. Even to those who see not the least difficulty in Jesus' power of working miracles *in itself*, because they know that the Son of God is in possession of divine powers, and thus qualified for divine actions, even to them on close deliberation weighty thoughts must arise. This is not very plain in the form in which Schleiermacher has expressed it (*Leben Jesu*, p. 227): 'The continuity and the unity of the human being and working of Christ must not, however, be annulled.' It is expressed more to the purpose by M. Baumgarten (*Geschichte Jesu*, p. 171): 'If it is thought that almighty power was indwelling in the person of our Lord while working miracles,—a power which was indeed always present in Him, but which did not always come into action,—the life of Jesus is thereby injured, so that to no one can the connection between the performance of miracles and their non-performance be made plain; or if this almighty power is thought to be always existing,—but that in miracles it is evident, while at other times it remained concealed,—the whole human life of Jesus is made nothing but an appearance. In both cases, all true interest in the miracles of Jesus is lost, and we ask with reason why He had not done many more and much greater miracles.' The question is this: If it is as the Apostle Paul wrote of Christ: 'He thought it not robbery to be equal with God; but made Himself of no reputation, and took upon Him the form of a servant, and was made in the likeness of men,' so that He, born of woman and made under the law, was also especially subject in its fullest extent to the laws and ordinances of life,—He was hungry, He was thirsty, He was tired by a journey, required to sit down for rest, fell asleep from necessity, sent His disciples to buy food and order lodging;—if so, it cannot possibly be said that working miracles was natural to Him, that miracles came from Him as spontaneous outflowings of His peculiar nature. But it is quite indispensable that it should be considered as an act of the will preceding it, of determined resolution to work in that manner.[1] Even on the supposition of a divine almighty power being in Christ, the working of miracles by Jesus can thence only be found conceivable and probable, if it is acknowledged that there is a satisfactory motive. It has already been shown, in the words of Twesten, how essential in a miracle is the teleological point of view. If, in order to comprehend the *gubernatio miraculosa* of God, we need to see the divine purpose, there occurs also a similar desideratum in regard to the working of miracles by Jesus. Christ Himself has expressly asserted the resemblance of the point of view from which should be judged the working of miracles of the Father, and that of His own. John v. 17: 'My Father worketh hitherto, and I work.' 19. 'What things soever the Father doeth, these also doeth the

[1] It needs no proof to show that the most cursory glance at the miracles of our Lord, related in the Gospels, justifies this view. We always see Jesus, as it were, rise up to prepare for a premeditated action, and one full of importance. Not to mention the most important cases, which are overpoweringly convincing from this point of view, such as the raising of Lazarus and the curing of the man born blind, we may take into consideration the instructive example of the woman who had an issue of blood, who, by merely touching His garment without His knowledge, as it were behind His back—in fact, without His *will*—wished to get cured by it. We know that she did *not* succeed. The question of Jesus, Who touched me? testifies to His knowledge that a power had gone out from Him—that His will, His intention, had been the preliminary to each miracle.

Son likewise.' 21. 'As the Father raiseth up the dead, even so the Son.' And thus we approach the question of the motive of the wonder-working of Jesus.

We cannot consider it either as a sufficient, or even as any, reply to this question, if it is answered, that a request addressed to Him, and the pity awakened by it, caused our Lord to use His miraculous power. Granted that Christ did numerous miracles in consequence of the call for His help; and further, that He never withstood a request for release from suffering (in the end He showed compassion even to the Canaanitish woman); lastly, let it be allowed that He performed all His miracles, as stands to reason, on account of His love; still this interpretation only applies to the very limited number of those cases with which Schleiermacher was able to agree.[1] To the rest it does not apply. No one will assert that Jesus performed His miracles on nature in consequence of being requested (even in several healings of the sick, John v. and ix., Luke vi., xiii., and xiv., we miss any previous request). Still less will one judge that He was always moved to do so by pity; He did not procure the 'piece of money,'[2] nor did He curse the fig-tree out of pity. But apart from these subordinate reflections, even to

---

[1] This theologian, from his illustration of the present question, arrived at the proposition that Jesus never performed a miracle for the sake of show. This has been admitted much too easily. It is only true in so far as the word ἐπίδειξις is used in the sense which is meant in Scripture by the expression μετὰ παρατηρήσεως; otherwise it is wrong. The effect of the miracle at Cana which 'manifested forth His glory, and His disciples believed on Him,' was one intended by Jesus. The awakening of Lazarus, which was nothing less than a work of mercy, and which had quite a different motive than the raising to life of the young man at Nain, was expressly introduced with the intention, 'that the Son of God might be glorified thereby.'

[2] Στατήρ, the word used in the original, as also in the Latin and German translations, was a silver coin of the value of four drachmas.—St. Jerome, quoted by Freund.—TR.

say nothing of the *cause* and *motive* being often confounded with one another, we do not at present wish to treat of the motive of Jesus in a few single miracles, but of the motive of His working miracles in general. This last is not at all affected by the issue we have refuted.

We should receive a more satisfactory answer if we were to pursue still further the analogy we have pointed out between the miracle-working of the Father and that of the Son. In Church dogmatics this has always been asserted, as Twesten (*Dogm.* ii. p. 178) thus expresses it: ' In reality, the chief biblical miracle is the origin of the kingdom of God, and that in its twofold evolution: first, the preparation for it in the Israelite theocracy; and then the fulfilment in the origin of Christianity.' *Other miracles are only presented as its accompanying phenomena*—yes, in fact, *all* others. Let us look at the miracles in the Old Testament. Where do we first meet with them in the history of Holy Scripture? Some of the older theologians are certainly wrong in pointing out the creation as the first miracle; for as a *miracle* and a *law of nature* are correlative conceptions, we cannot put in the former category the act of God by which the latter was first laid down. On the other hand, those who consider the birth of Isaac to Abraham and Sarah as a miracle of God have the Apostle Paul as their authority (Rom. iv. 19-21). We know that by the election and call of Abraham, and by the promise made to him, the path of the history of redemption was laid down. We meet further with the miracles of Moses, but the connection in which these stand to the foundation of the Old Testament kingdom of God cannot easily be disputed. Later we meet with the miracles of Elijah and Elisha. They happened at a time when the falling away from the Lord was very great, when the theocracy was coming to an end, and when it was important to keep a band of such who had not bowed the knee to Baal. Lastly, those miracles which the Father with His own hand performed on His only-begotten Son,—the miracle by which He introduced Him into this world; the miracle by which He raised from the dead this great Shepherd of the sheep,—bear quite unmistakeably on their face the teleological relation we have pointed out. For if the wonder-working of God stands in this relation to His kingdom, we must also in the very same way seek for the end in view of the wonder-working of Him whom the Father sent into the world to found the 'kingdom of heaven.' How expressly and in what manner Christ Himself has brought out this point of view, will be seen directly. At present we will only remark, that the Lord has explained in the same way the endowment of His apostles with miraculous powers;[1] that even the apostles themselves never understood otherwise the endowment of the gracious gifts they received.[2] Thus the wonder-working of Jesus can be conceived in its connection with the kingdom of God.[3]

---

[1] Compare His instructions to the Twelve in Matt. x. 7, 8: 'The kingdom of heaven is at hand. Heal the sick, cleanse the lepers, raise the dead, cast out devils;' as also in Luke ix. 2, x. 9; Acts x. 36-39.

[2] Notice especially the manner in which Peter speaks of the miracle performed on the lame man at the gate of the temple. In Acts iii. 12-26, he shows it as a manifestation of Christ by the Father, as a call to repentance, to faith, to enter into the kingdom of heaven, to which the Jews are called as children of the covenant; and in chap. iv. 8 and foll. he places the fact in its relation to the circumstance, that the builders have rejected the chief corner-stone, but that at the same time there was no other salvation, but only in the name of Jesus of Nazareth.

[3] By this is explained the objection which was raised by Strauss (it has also already been used by Schleiermacher in his *Glaubenslehre*, vol. i. p. 101). Strauss declares (*Leben Jesu*, 147; Eng. transl. i. p. 196): If 'the Christian faith calls upon science . . . not indeed to disallow the miracle altogether, but to allow it to have existed within the circle of original Christianity, . . . it cannot indulge so narrow a pretension, and will say: I will recognise miracle as possible, either in all provinces of religious history, or in none.

Undoubtedly nothing is gained by this formula except a safe point of departure. For the present, we can from this ground only say, that a miracle of Jesus would be inconceivable to us, or would appear to us a monstrous phenomenon, if this connection was *not* recognisable; and that just as satisfactory an answer proceeds from this position, if it is asked why Jesus did not here and there employ His miraculous power.[1] But there occurs immediately the further question: In what, then, does the connection between the wonder-working of Jesus and the foundation of the kingdom of God consist? We cannot give a *simple* answer to this new question now, because we are only treating cursorily of the conceivableness of the wonder-working of Jesus in general, while our real task requires us to show it in each single miracle. But we cannot and may not assert that *all* the miracles of our Lord are to be reckoned *in like manner*, as having their purpose in showing the foundation of the kingdom of God, and also in like manner were really effective towards it, however confidently we may consider them collectively as 'miracula proprie et rigoroso

However,' he adds, 'in the alternative she does not intend to be serious, because to do so would be simply to abandon herself' with it in all these departments. This objection only occurs to those who will know nothing of a kingdom of God and a history of it in the world; but for those of the opposite view it completely disappears. A revelation such as the Apostle Paul claims for the heathen (Rom. i. 19, 20) excludes miracles, just as much as that intended for the foundation of a kingdom of God on earth includes it.

[1] The most extraordinary of this kind of questions is that raised by Schleiermacher, *Leben Jesu*, pp. 224, 242: 'Why did not Christ make use of His miraculous power when His life was in danger?' It also struck Strauss, and he justly declares that the attempt to explain it by saying that Jesus was obliged to acknowledge human authority, the Roman as well as that of the Sanhedrim, has failed. But when he himself informs us that Christ did not possess at all such a miraculous power (*d. Christus des Glaubens*, etc., p. 122), we certainly prefer the answer given by our Lord, 'It must thus happen, or how would the Scripture be fulfilled?' or how otherwise could God's kingdom come on earth?

sensu sic dicta.' Our answer must accordingly be arranged in different divisions, by the connection of which a complete one will be attained. For good reasons we proceed, keeping in mind the *expression* used in Scripture for the miracles of Jesus. The opinion is advanced, that in the New Testament several designations are employed for them. Our attention is called to passages such as Acts ii. 22, where Peter preaches that Jesus of Nazareth was proved a man of God by δυνάμεις, τέρατα, and σημεῖα. We have no reason to object to the distinction which Schleiermacher has made between these expressions in his *Leben Jesu*, p. 206, where he says, 'In σημεῖον the most prominent thing is the significance of what we should deduce from the result; in δύναμις, the chief thing is the nature of the actor—that he has in himself such a power; and in τέρας, the comparison of this result with other results.'[1] However, even according to this exposition, only one of the three expressions gives us any instructive light, and it is the one made use of throughout the fourth Gospel, particularly in order to illustrate the teleological point of view. It may indeed appear as if the σημεῖον characterizes the miracle simply as an appearance happening in a sense pointing to a higher supernatural region, that is, to the kingdom of God: τὸ σημεῖον σημαίνει. However, by examining the use made in Scripture of this expression, and by considering the elements dependent on it, we shall be led to

[1] It is, at any rate, more correct than that given by Ammonius, 'τέρας παρὰ φύσιν, σημεῖον παρὰ συνήθειαν γίνεται'—which was adopted by Theophylact and Valckenaer; it is also more correct than what has been proposed by later theologians—Reiche, Flatt, and Lücke. See the copious excursus on these expressions by Fritzsche, in his *Commentar z. Brief an d. Römer*, Th. iii. p. 270 and foll. Osiander agrees with Schleiermacher in his commentary on 2 Cor. xii. 12.

[An interesting article on the use of the word δύναμις will be found in Cremer's *Wörterb. d. Neutest. Gräcität*, 2d Auflage, p. 218; Eng transl., Edinburgh 1872, p. 200.—TR.]

more certain results. We find thereby that the use is fourfold.[1]

Firstly, The first signification of the expression σημεῖον is that it expresses a token, out of which something—that is, something not perceptible to the senses, or at the time not yet perceptible to them—should be deduced from it. The Apostle Paul gives the Church at Thessalonica a σημεῖον, that is, a token by which they should recognise the epistles really coming from him (2 Thess. iii. 17). It is in this sense that the phrases σημείοις τῶν καιρῶν, from which the character of the present, and σημεῖον τῆς παρουσίας, from which the nearness of the decisive future, are to be taken. Thus, if the miracles of Jesus are called σημεῖα, if they stand in the relation of tokens of the kingdom of God, they will in the first place be considered as *tokens of the kingdom of heaven which is at hand.*[2]

---

[1] By this we settle at the same time the question of the classification of miracles. We can here make no use of those classifications which have been made by the dogmatists,—as when Gerhard names them 'miracula primativa and positiva,'—because we are only considering the miracles of *Jesus;* that of Cotta (that miracles may have happened 'naturam rerum immutando, quantitatem rerum augendo, qualitatem tollendo') has no real value. If others have distinguished between 'miracula naturæ' and 'miracula gratiæ,' the conversion of St. Paul, given as an example of the latter, cannot convince us of the justness of the second class. Certainly we consider what took place on the road to Damascus as miraculous; but the miracle to us consists only in what appeared to the senses, in the dazzling light, in the clear voice, especially in the perceptible manifestation of the Lord. With regard to the effect, we cannot place that in the point of view of a miracle, just because the freedom of Saul had to concur in it. The attempt at division by Vitringa (*Betrachtungen über d. Wunderwerke Jesu Christi, Einl.* § vi.) is not worthy of consideration; that this grouping which is presented to us offers no very exact line of demarcation, stands to reason, because the boundary between the constitutive elements in the conception of a σημεῖον is a fleeting one. It naturally depends only on what in each single case is the most important relation.

[2] Even in the Psalms, especially Ps. lxxiv. 9, the σημεῖα of Israel, and among them in particular the miracles of the Lord, are shown as the *tokens* of the government of God, and complaint is made that, instead of *these* tokens, others, the signs of the enemy, have occurred.

It may be concluded from this, that the troublous time, the time of oppression and of waiting, is past, —that He who should come has appeared, and with Him the 'acceptable year;' the day of salvation has drawn near. 'The kindness and love of God our Saviour toward man appeared' (Tit. iii. 4). The rays of this light which breaks forth in the miracles, certainly strike directly only the surface; but just so much the brighter do they shine as *symptoms*. Now this is exactly applicable to the miracles of Jesus. Those in the Old Testament have preponderatingly a punitive character. In the miracles of Moses, the divine indignation is poured out on the cowardice and unbelief of the people, as well as on the obduracy of Pharaoh. In the miracles of Elijah we observe the rushing of the 'wrath,' rather than the soft whispering of the breeze. Our Lord Himself, in rebuking the 'sons of thunder,'[1] spoke in reference to the miracles of the Old Testament. On the other hand, concerning His *own* miracles, He preached in the synagogue at Nazareth, that by virtue of their healing and relieving effects they were the tokens of the coming year of salvation; and in a similar sense, He bids John the Baptist draw from it the conclusion that the Messianic time had really come.

This is the proper place to acknowledge the germ of truth which lies in Schleiermacher's assertion, formerly mentioned, that Jesus used His power of working miracles, as opportunity offered, in doing good. If we do not object to speak of a benefit or even of an alms that our Lord has miraculously given, there is not wanting biblical authority for it. When Peter and John (Acts iii.) went up to the temple, the lame man asked for alms. Peter answered, 'Silver and gold have I none; but such as I have give I thee: in

[1] Luke x. 55.—Tr.

the name of Jesus Christ, rise up and walk.' *That was his* alms. Certainly we must guard ourselves from representing miracles thus conceived as expressions merely of an individual compassion, but must conceive them rather as proofs of the grace of God visibly appearing, so that they give us a presentiment of the 'fulness' which through Christ became 'grace.' The remark is quite correct, that by far the greatest number of the miracles of Jesus may be judged as σημεῖα in *this* sense. At the same time, there are only a few cases where this method of consideration would suit. In many others it will not suit.

However, in the expression σημεῖον there are also other important elements. As a second one, we meet with that of a *symbol*. The Apostle Paul writes (Rom. iv. 11) of Abraham, 'he received the sign of circumcision, a seal of the righteousness of the faith which he had yet being uncircumcised.' In what sense has he called circumcision a σημεῖον? Are those expositors right, who understand this only as an external sign? (Bengel and Fritzsche: 'nota corpori indita;' Philippi says: 'the sign which Abraham bore on his body, by which he was distinguished from the uncircumcised.') Then would be taken away from us the value of the apostle's apposition, σφραγῖδα, etc. For a purely external sign, which would of itself be without any significance, can certainly not be a σημεῖον σφραγιστικόν. Therefore the unavoidable supposition is, that the sign must be in *the first place* a *symbol*. We are directed to the symbolical signification of circumcision here so much the more, as the apostle has expressly brought it to view in the second chapter, vers. 28, 29. We have quoted these passages simply to establish the fact, that the use of the expression σημεῖον in the sense of a symbol is founded on the biblical use of the term. The express references of the evangelists, and especially of John, go to prove that, in fact, many miracles can be placed in this point of view; they cannot be conceived otherwise than as *symbols of the treasures of the kingdom of heaven now opened.*

They have in so far a relation to parables; for as a parable shows on earthly grounds the reflex of a higher truth, in order to serve as a means of explaining the latter, so a miracle which relieves an earthly pain is the symbol of the help within reach for a deeper need. Our Lord cures the sick of the palsy; but the first words of the narrative point most expressly to a higher region. He gives sight to him that was born blind; but the concluding words of the history exclude the thought of a mere deed of compassion. Even the healings of the sick are evidently those miracles of Jesus which become conceivable in the relation we have pointed out to the kingdom of God. However, our Lord also performed other works which surpass ordinary therapeutic power, and which cannot be brought under either of these classes. Are there not in the expression $\sigma\eta\mu\epsilon\hat{\iota}o\nu$ some other elements?

To find a third, we will again make use of an expression of the Apostle Paul. He writes to the Corinthian church (2 Cor. xii. 12): 'The signs of an apostle were wrought in you.' As these $\sigma\eta\mu\epsilon\hat{\iota}\alpha$ become individualized at the end of the verse into $\sigma\eta\mu\epsilon\acute{\iota}o\iota\varsigma$, $\tau\acute{\epsilon}\rho\alpha\sigma\iota\nu$, $\kappa\alpha\grave{\iota}$ $\delta\upsilon\nu\acute{\alpha}\mu\epsilon\sigma\iota\nu$, the expression in the former place must be understood in a wider sense than in the latter. There it can by no means signify a mere token, from which the Church should conclude that Paul must be more than a common teacher. But the '$\sigma\eta\mu\epsilon\hat{\iota}\alpha$ of an apostle' testify to him as an apostle, because only an apostle, and no other, was in a position to do the same. (In a similar sense is the expression, 'the sign of the Son of man,' in Matt. xxiv. 30.) In the σημεῖον there is also the element of a witness, of the authenticated proof; the miracles of Jesus are consequently substantial *witnesses of the power of the kingdom of heaven which has become active.* The casting out of devils and the awakening from the dead are those which come under this point of view. It cannot be denied that both kinds of the miraculous working of our Lord can also be considered as mere tokens of the new time which had begun; but even the immediate impression of their magnitude raises them above the level of being simple signs. What is especially to be regarded of the casting out of devils, is the fact that they have been placed by the immediate witnesses in a peculiarly high rank, as our Lord Himself has especially pointed out. While separating them from His other miracles of curing, He assigns them an independent position *beside* them. See Luke xiii. 32: 'Behold, I cast out devils, and do cures;'—thus the casting out of devils is on one side (and *primo loco*), and the 'doing of cures' on the other. The same distinction, and in the same order, is found in Matt. viii. 16, 'He cast out the spirits, and healed all that were sick;' as also, in the introduction to the instructions to the Twelve in Luke ix. 1, He gave them power and authority over all devils, and to cure diseases. Besides, whoever acknowledges that Christ 'was manifested that He might destroy the works of the devil' (1 John iii. 8), will be contented with no other way of considering them, than that they really testify in themselves to the powers of the kingdom of God which have become effective; as our Lord Himself has expressly stated (Matt. xii. 28): 'But if I cast out devils by the Spirit of God, then the kingdom of God is come unto you.'

In the same way the raising of the dead may also

be considered; they stand just as much in opposition to the view of their being mere signs, as having only a purely symbolical meaning. What we often hear expressed, that they are meant to represent allegorically the 'life' which the Son of God can give, is opposed by the decided explanations in John v. 20, 21, xi. 25, 26, 42.

In modern theology there has willingly been conceded a much closer connection between miracles and prophecy than its mere formal relationship,—a relationship on account of which, in Church dogmatics, prophecy itself has been called a miracle, and thus has been made the distinction of 'miracula potentiæ' and 'miracula præscientiæ;' in fact, prophecy and miracles are considered as both equally constitutive elements of revelation. Rothe has drawn the connection between them even closer; for he not merely acknowledges a *general* relation of miracles and of prophecy to revelation, but also a *reciprocal* relation of them, the one on the other. 'Without its connection with prophecy, a miracle would be a mute figure' (*Zur Dogm.* p. 83). But we may, and we ought to go still further, and maintain that there is a prophetical meaning *in the miracle itself.* We have to consider this in the expression σημεῖον. So much is evident, that אות in the Old Testament often represents a miracle, which is appointed to foreshadow a future event, and especially the certainty of its coming to pass; as in 2 Kings xx. 8-11, and other places.

Many of our Lord's miracles also are σημεῖα in this sense—in fact, those which He performed on the laws of nature. That in these there is room for a symbolical meaning is just as undeniable as natural. Only here it is not the prevailing one, much less the only justifiable one. The narratives in question are conceivable purely in the case that their prophetical character is acknowledged. Certainly we must guard ourselves from the idea that this prophecy relates to an uncertain something that will happen in the future; the relation to the kingdom of heaven is here self-evident. The *future* of the kingdom of heaven is, however, that of its victory, especially of its victory over the enemy, and its dominion over all powers. Thus the miracles of Jesus are, in the *fourth place, prophecies*, founded on fact, of *the future dominion of the kingdom of God* on earth. Thus we stand at the actual threshold of our problem. We now purpose to show the motive of each single miracle of our Lord, and to place it thereby in the full light of probability.

II.

THE MIRACLES OF JESUS.

FIRST GROUP.

THE MIRACLES OF JESUS CONSIDERED AS SIGNS OF THE KINGDOM OF HEAVEN THAT IS AT HAND.

THE number of narratives which can be placed under this point of view is inconsiderable; for how few miracles of Jesus can be considered as specially signs of the kingdom of heaven at hand! And here we wish to treat solely of those which come exclusively under this method of consideration, and which by its means alone become perfectly conceivable. Chronologically, these occur in the beginning of the public ministry of our Lord; and among them will therefore be found that miracle with which Jesus' power of working miracles commenced. It may be that we can thus explain the passage in John ii. 11, where the evangelist wishes to point out the turning of water into wine at Cana as the very first miracle which Jesus performed. We cannot, however, determine to which of the miracles of the class in question should be assigned the first place in point of *time*, with the same certainty with which we can decide on that which concluded the Lord's work.[1] The balance of probability will, however,

---

[1] It is customary to consider the healing of Malchus, who was wounded by Peter at Gethsemane, as the last miracle of Jesus; in one sense justly so. But we cannot reckon this event as part of His peculiar work of performing miracles, for the Lord had already concluded *this*, as well as His ministry of teaching. It seems significative that Jesus, in the last moment that His hands were still free and unbound, should have used them in stretching

incline in favour of the incident in the house of Simon Peter, if the improbability is considered in relation to the manifestly high value set on it by all three evangelists.

THE HEALING OF PETER'S MOTHER-IN-LAW.—MATT. VIII. 14; MARK I. 29; LUKE IV. 38.

The very humbleness of the occurrence deeply attracts us; it contains points of importance peculiar to itself. In the first place, there is the fact that this is the only case, in the whole extent of the working of the miraculous power of our Lord, in which He performed his operation silently and still. At other times, He always opens His mouth to say some words while He cures; but here He works without a word. Thus we have a sign in the strictest and most literal sense, and are therefore compelled to show what is the plain meaning of this sign. How is this deed conceivable? What was it that caused Jesus to employ in this case His miraculous power, and here perhaps for the first time? We are informed by Mark and Luke, that our Lord was made aware of the illness of the woman: 'They tell Him of her;' 'They besought Him for her.' But He who was in no way moved by the pleading of Mary at Cana, would also here have paid no attention to the remark, unless He had had His own motives for miraculous assistance. And these must have been quite special ones; for the sickness in question demanded *in itself*

---

them out to bless,—'Suffer ye thus far' (Luke xxii. 51), allow me still liberty until I have done this;—but His rebuke to His disciples, however manifold was the motive for it, contains also especially the important point that Jesus was compelled by this action to take up again a power which He had laid down. This miracle is therefore singular; it does not come under any of the groups we have pointed out, but is only to be seen in its true light, by its connection with the history of the Passion.

the interposition of the physician of Israel much less than any other which He cured. The mother-in-law of Peter lay sick of a fever. The 'sick of a fever' of Matthew and Mark, is expressed more distinctly by Luke as 'taken with a great fever;' but even if the case had been very severe, the condition was still a transitory one, and in such a case our Lord was not wont to bestow His help. All the physical sufferings which, according to the reports of the evangelists, He took away, presupposed a long infirmity, and were advancing slowly and steadily towards dissolution; at any rate, they mocked the art of a human physician. The remark in Luke viii. 43 applies in general to them all. Only in the narrative of one other is there the gleam of a supposition that a fever yielded to the absolute command of our Lord; see John iv. 52, 'At the seventh hour the fever left him.' The point of difficulty here lay in the power of Jesus working afar off, while the state of the suffering was purposely kept out of sight; but the healing of the mother-in-law of Peter remains the only case where an illness, which in the course of nature would soon have passed away of itself, was miraculously removed. It is a misinterpretation of the announcement which is added by all three evangelists, that 'she who was cured ministered to Jesus and to those who were with Him,' to conclude, as Schleiermacher does in his *Leben Jesu* (p. 220), that 'her ministry' was thus taken into consideration; 'and as she had become incapable on account of her illness, it was natural that Christ should remove it in order that she would be in a position to do her duty.' The tendency of this concluding remark (as also the 'anon' of Mark, and the 'immediately' of Luke) is merely to prove the *reality* of the cure effected: the sick person was now perfectly free from fever, and well; just as the return of the daughter of Jairus to life was shown by the circumstance that she at once took food.

The *motive* of Jesus must be sought for elsewhere. We are content with the supposition, that the Lord in this work simply wished to give a token of the kingdom of heaven which was at hand. According to the report of Luke, He was accompanied by several disciples, who had come directly from the synagogue at Capernaum. There He had taught, and (as at Nazareth) had announced the 'acceptable year of the Lord,' and had preached the gospel to the poor. Now, to Him whose mouth had just poured forth such a testimony, the view of the sick woman (Matthew says: 'He saw her laid, and sick of a fever') must itself have served as an impulse to make it shine forth as a sign that 'this day is the scripture of the promise fulfilled in the ears of Israel.' Is not also the fever— קַדַּחַת (Deut. xxviii. 22)—marked as a curse of the broken law on the head of Israel? This case of sickness did not come under our Lord's sight[1] on the road, but in the house which He entered, the house where He was lodging; further, in the house of one of His disciples, who had been called to announce with Him the time of salvation, without annulling, by the institution of this call, the household tie (1 Cor. ix. 5). All these are circumstances which must have strengthened that general impulse, and raised it to a constraining motive (conveyed also in the words, 'He rebuked the fever').

The impression of obscurity is produced at first sight by another narrative of the healing of a sick woman, which we place beside it, to be considered on

---

[1] Calvin says: 'Videntur evangelistæ miraculum hoc peculiariter narrasse, non quod per se aliis esset nobilius, vel memoratu magis dignum; sed quia in eo Christus *domesticum* et interius gratiæ suæ specimen exhibuit discipulis.'

the same grounds. The event took place 'as He was on the way,' as our Lord was about to proceed to a great proof of His almighty power. On the other hand, the receiver of the benefit carefully avoided looking up, while she sought to obtain help from Jesus, not by entreaties, but by taking it unobserved.

THE HEALING OF THE WOMAN WITH THE ISSUE OF BLOOD.
—MATT. IX. 20; MARK V. 25; LUKE VIII. 43.

The accounts of this event by the three evangelists are not in complete harmony with one another. Matthew relates it very shortly and summarily, while Mark and Luke have endeavoured to give it with remarkable explicitness and copiousness. Strauss, in observing this, has thought it right to give the following judgment (*Leben Jesu*, p. 456; Eng. transl. ii. p. 194): 'There is nothing here' (in Matthew's account) 'which might not have occurred as is stated. A sick woman may have touched Jesus in a spirit of faith, may have traced an amendment in herself in consequence of this touch, and may have been dismissed by Jesus with a comforting word. What the evangelist says, and represents Jesus as saying, is something which even we think reconcilable.' Soon he goes on to say this simple 'narrative ceased to satisfy the belief in miracles;' and the event is so amplified and embellished by Mark and Luke, that Jesus appears in the light of one in whom all the fulness of the divine powers of healing dwelt bodily. What we answer to this is, that the account of Matthew, which is certainly not very explicit, is completed by those of the two other evangelists, and that by them this miracle of Jesus is rendered conceivable.[1] Jesus was on His road to the

---

[1] If we here speak of an inexactitude in Matthew's account as compared with that of Mark and Luke, and later repeat this judgment in the narra-

house of Jairus. He was accompanied not only by His disciples, but by a great multitude of people, whose pressure on Him is indispensably presumed, in order to understand even the text of Matthew (that is, the 'came behind Him' of ver. 20). On His way He was detained (in a similar manner, as in chap. xix. 16, 'one came') by an incident. A woman (a fabulous tradition relating to her is very explicitly and particularly told by Eusebius, vii. 18) had 'heard about Jesus,' that is, she had heard that

tive of the daughter of Jairus, we do so while decidedly acknowledging the authenticity of the first Gospel, of which we are no less certain than we are of that of the fourth. Whoever has followed with attention and participated in the critical researches of the last few years, will have received the impression that the general opinion of the majority inclines in its favour, notwithstanding the judgments here and there expressed, 'that there can no more be a question of an apostolic authorship of the first Gospel.' One is not only tired of the constant reiteration of old and the starting of new hypotheses, but it is also to be remembered that nothing really well founded has been advanced against the authenticity of Matthew. What has hindered its acknowledgment so long, is partly the entirely unjustifiable signification which has been attributed to the testimony of Papias, and partly the synoptical manner of treatment which is adopted in the first Gospel. However, as soon as it is considered carefully by itself, there appears an order, a connection, a systematic plan, which is seen elsewhere in St. John's alone. Whoever keeps closely in view the introduction to the first period of the activity of Jesus in Galilee (from the imprisonment of the Baptist to his death, chap. iv. 12-25), cannot deny the fact that the evangelist has proceeded exactly in accordance with the plan here sketched out. Our present interest, however, demands simply the acknowledgment that Matthew was obliged to portray the Galilean miracle-working of Jesus (chap. viii. and ix.) as he has done, if he wished to solve the problem which he had made for himself (chap. iv. 23): 'Jesus went about all Galilee, healing all manner of sickness and all manner of disease among the people.' His intention was not to relate in strictly chronological order, nor particularly to give a complete picture of each individual case; but his expressly declared object (a very valuable one) was to trace out the most varied features of a comprehensive representation of the miracle-working of our Lord. The objection often made, that the indefinite formula with which the single narratives of miracles are arranged together excludes the possibility of the author being an eye-witness, hereby completely vanishes. We can thus acknowledge the greater completeness of Mark and Luke in *single* narratives, without calling in question the higher dignity of the first Gospel.

Jesus, as a man working miracles, had been asked to help and save a dying child, and thereupon resolves to take advantage of His presence for the healing of a peculiar suffering of her own that had lasted many years. On account of its nature, she was ashamed to come forward with a public request. But she hoped with confidence that, by merely touching His garment, she would attain her end. And the result appears to have justified this expectation.

A twofold supposition, which we express with marked emphasis at the threshold of our consideration, appears still more to heighten the difficulty which the event itself offers to the understanding; but by it the question is again clearly formulated, in the answering of which stands the solution of our problem. So much as this is evident, and there can be no question on the point that there is not the least dissembling on the part of the Lord. He has never sanctioned an appearance which would have hidden the whole truth; He has never represented Himself, never explained Himself, as if He were something which He was not. The opposite opinion cannot be maintained even in the history of the Canaanitish woman. Thus, when Jesus (Mark v. 30) asks, 'Who touched my clothes?' when He looked round about to see her that had done this thing (the feminine ποιήσασαν is naturally used by this evangelist in narrating the event, while Luke, citing the words of Jesus, writes τίς ὁ ἁψάμενός μου in the masculine), He wishes to discover something which was unknown to Him. The 'turned Him about' proves that He did know the side from which the touch came, but that the person touching Him still remained concealed. It is therefore not to be denied that the woman, unnoticed by Jesus, pressed near to Him, and that, unrecognised by Him, she had experienced His healing power. On the other hand, we still firmly hold to the conclusion we arrived at on a previous occasion, that the miracles of Jesus are to be considered, not as the result of an immediate natural power proceeding from His person, but as works for the performance of which, acting in the strictest sense of the word, He worked with a decided aim. Consequently we must not allow Schleiermacher's view (partly held also by Rothe), that in the case before us the result which took place rested on its purely physical connection (*Leben Jesu*, p. 214). Thus the question to be answered is, How can the circumstance that our Lord recognised the person of the woman only after the completion of the cure (not intended by Him), be reconciled with the proposition that every miracle must have been the fruit of His conscious, deliberate, intentional act? We shall arrive at the right conclusion if we sufficiently consider the very words of Christ. In the first place we take His explanation (Mark v. 34): 'Daughter, thy faith hath made thee whole.' The words refer to the 28th verse, where the sick woman said within herself (Matt. ἐν ἑαυτῇ; compare Luke vii. 39, εἶπεν ἐν ἑαυτῷ), or to herself, 'If I may touch but His clothes, I shall be whole.' A complete harmony exists between what *she* says in the sense of hope, and what Christ says in the tone of assurance. Faith has brought to her the way of cure. It is not difficult to comprehend the full value contained in this 'faith.' According to some authors, it was wanting in an important point. The text, however, gives us no right to charge the woman with the fancy that the healing powers of Jesus resided in the hem of His garment; for if she strove to touch the very hem, she only did so because it was the easiest for her to reach. There is certainly something superstitious in representing the garment as able to effect a miraculous work. Strauss has one-sidedly brought forward this meaning; he finds it, accordingly, as much in the representation of Mark and of Luke as in those narratives of the Acts of the Apostles, according to which the sick were made whole by the laying on of the handkerchiefs or aprons from Paul (chap xix. 12), or by the shadow of Peter falling on them (chap. v. 15). However, the other side of the question should not studiously be overlooked; it is, that the sick woman revealed an intensity in the confidence of her heart at the time, which completely puts out of sight its wrongful conception. For years she had borne her suffering, and fought against it by the use of the physician's skill. But neither the power of nature nor the endeavours of art had freed her from it. In fact, the last had not made any progress—'she grew worse;' and it had brought her nothing else but the loss of all her possessions (Mark says: 'she had spent all that she had;' Luke: 'had spent all her living;' she had therefore become extremely poor). Consequently she is convinced that only a miracle could effect her cure. Jesus appears; she will not merely *try* if His hand could perhaps do something for her, but she firmly believes that He is the right helper.

It does not appear to her a necessity that there should be an energetical movement on the part of our Lord, either by word or deed; but the minimum of means, the mere touching of His robe ('If I may but touch'—Matt.; if I may but, if only this), she considered quite sufficient to attain her end. That was a faith which He who discovers the pure vein in the dross knew how to value. Christ showed His goodwill even by the choice of His expression. 'Daughter,' He says to the woman. (In the whole of the New Testament we meet with this expression here alone, and in the Old Testament but once or twice in the book of Ruth. Our Lord was generally accustomed to say '*Woman*' even to His mother and to Mary Magdalene. The expression *son* (υἱέ) He never uses in a similar sense, and τέκνον only occurs once, in Matt. ix. 2.) But let us thoroughly examine the meaning in these assuring words: It is her *faith* that helped her. What is there in this? Jesus does *not* say that His *clothes* had done it; that would be in contradiction to the strongly expressed 'thy faith.' And just as little does He say that *He* did it; the expression 'thy faith' denies *this* no less decidedly. It is certain that the woman was cured *while* she seized the Lord's garment; this is testified by the term 'immediately,' the εὐθέως of Mark and the παραχρῆμα of Luke. She was not made whole by simply touching the garment of Jesus, but rather by doing so *in faith*. It is told us that a thronging multitude surrounded our Lord, and consequently the disciples were astonished at the question of their Master, 'Who touched me?' Let us suppose that among this thronging people there may also have been sick persons, who, being perhaps still nearer and closer than this woman, touched the clothes of Jesus as much as she did, but *they* were *not* cured in this manner. Thus also, on the part of our Lord, it was not the movement itself, but that perfected by the hand of faith, of which He became aware. Many touched Him in the throng without His considering it, or even being conscious of it; but this one touched Him in the spirit of faith, and in such a manner that He could have had no physical sensation of it; and yet He felt it *in Himself.* This expression (only contained in the text of Mark) does not mean simply the sensation of Jesus in Himself, as of one 'perceiving in His spirit;'[1] but the object of the context goes directly to prove that the cause of this sensation (by reason of the 'virtue that had gone

---

[1] In John xi. 33 and 38, the forms of expression, 'He groaned in spirit,' and 'groaning in Himself,' are used alternately, without any difference of meaning.

out of Him') is to be ascribed to a spiritual factor, the faith of the woman : for faith *alone* can render available the promise made from everlasting of the divine powers of grace. By this alone can a perception of it have been caused also in the inner soul of Jesus. An analogous incident will exemplify this 'knowing in Himself' on the part of our Lord. The disciples at Emmaus, after the revelation of the Risen One to them (Luke xxiv. 32), ask: 'Did not our heart burn within us while He talked with us by the way, and while He opened to us the Scriptures?' They had not recognised Jesus in the stranger, and had been far from thinking Him in any possible way near; yet they experienced a very decided perception of His presence,— a perception, however, which did not amount to a clear recognition. In the same way our Lord perceived, but His feeling was at once a sure knowledge (therefore it is 'knowing' in ver. 30), that faith had approached Him, and had received thereby His power of healing.

Let us, on the strength of the words, 'Thy faith hath made thee whole,' maintain that the cure of the woman was the fruit of her faith; we need not on that account have any solicitude to evade the question of the process of the cure. By considering this permissible, we do not in the least contradict the assertion we formerly justified, that every attempt to *explain* a miracle is wrong. We willingly agree to what Strauss states, that the experience which the woman had, considering her state of mind, appears nothing less than inconceivable. Still the account in Mark (ver. 29), that the sick woman, after she had pressed with the most intense exertions, physical and mental, to the person of Jesus, had experienced at the longed-for moment a decided effect on her organism, may give room for a psychological solution. But *is* the miracle which the evangelists wish to tell us thereby effected?

We have not yet penetrated into its true extent; we are still on the threshold. At present it is faith alone that has done something. What that can accomplish in the region of the natural life, has been pointed out in Scripture, especially in the eleventh chapter of the Epistle to the Hebrews, thirty-third and following verses, and its power is proved here also.

Our Lord Himself has, in the portions of the narrative already considered, remained passive. We have now to look for *His* miraculous power; and thus, even in this case, will be justified the proposition, that in every miracle He comes forward and appears as active in the strictest sense. He says: 'Thy faith hath made thee whole;' that relates to the past. But we read further: 'Go in peace, and be whole of thy plague;' and that certainly does *not* point to a past. Let us suppose the case, that the woman succeeded in stealing away, and in taking from Him the cure as a theft: what might have happened? That day, and perhaps for a more or less length of time, she would have been well, but she would not have remained so for any length of time. She had gained the cure by faith. The former would have lasted just as long as the latter; its effective factor was in existence. Her cure needed an objective reality; and this real extirpation of her sickness her faith was not able to *make*—the will of Christ could alone assure it to her. How much our Lord would have been inclined under these circumstances to use *this* gift of His power, we can estimate from the value which faith—especially 'such great faith'—has in His eyes. But it was first necessary to see the person who had touched Him in such faith. The success with which He looks about for this end ('He looked round about')—a common expression of Mark's to show the look of Jesus to discover and expose what is hidden (chap. iii. 5, x. 23, xi. 11)—**must** have increased still more His already existing readiness. The public acknowledgment which the woman, laying aside every consideration, makes (Luke says: 'She declared unto Him before all the people'); her bending the knee in fear and trembling, as if she had committed a wrong;—all denoted a resolute will which (as in the later case of the Canaanitish woman) grace could not refuse. And so Jesus says to her: 'Be whole.' By the power of these words He completes in her His miracle of healing; by it He makes her whole. In consequence of her touching His garment she *felt* herself whole, but now she *is* well. To her mere *feelings* of being cured, is now given the surer objective basis. The reality of her recovery lies also primarily in the *condition* in which (εἰς) our Lord leaves her; henceforth she shall remain free from the plague of this suffering. This 'peace' (just as the 'salvation' assured at the same time) does not even here lose the wider meaning which specifically belongs to it in the New Testament.

We will now refer to the text of Matthew. However briefly and summarily he relates the whole event, he leaves no doubt how the real miracle was performed on the woman. It is in Matthew that the effect accomplished is shown undoubtedly as the consequence of Jesus' declaration of His will; for, after reporting the words of Jesus, 'Daughter, be of good comfort, thy faith hath made thee whole,' he makes the results follow: 'And the woman was made whole from that hour.' It may be asked whether, according to this, the result seems the fruit of the woman's act of faith, or not rather the effect of a miracle wrought by Jesus Himself.

We conclude by referring to a parallel case, which will contribute somewhat to recommend this view. Luke tells in chap. vii. 37 of a sinner who anointed

Jesus. The conduct of this sinner is (taking into consideration the difference of intention in both cases) completely analogous to that of the woman with the issue of blood. She heard that Jesus was staying in the house of the Pharisee (as in Mark v. 27 it is said, 'she had heard of Jesus'); she presses in, and takes her place behind our Lord at His feet, 'stood behind Him'—she in moral shame—the woman with the issue of blood (Mark v. 27: 'came behind'), in natural female modesty. She wishes to take from Jesus the grace of the forgiveness of her sins, and for this end she completes the anointing of His feet, as a symbol of her repentance, just as the woman with the issue of blood will carry away the cure of her sickness by the touching of His garment. Our Lord certainly knew not the latter; and with regard to the former, the Pharisee Simon only imagines that she must be unknown to Him; but in both cases, Jesus at first keeps quite passive. Notwithstanding this, the sinner had experienced a *feeling* of the forgiveness of her guilt,—for the Saviour suffered her conduct,—just as the woman with the issue of blood was penetrated with the sensation of her cure. But what does our Lord do? After the dispute with the Pharisee, He says to the bending woman: 'Thy sins be forgiven thee.' It was by means of this declaration that she first received the forgiveness of sins, just as the woman with the issue of blood was first placed in the real possession of her health by the 'Be whole.' Both narratives therefore continue in the same concluding words: 'Thy faith hath saved thee, go in peace' (comp. Luke vii. 50 with chap. viii. 48). The three other miracles which belong to our first group form a striking contrast to the narrative which we have just considered. We perceive in the woman with the issue of blood a peculiar energy in her striving after a cure. She had sought the means of the medical art even to the exhaustion of her property, and at last, with intense exertion, she forces her way to the person of our Lord. On the other hand, in the cases now to be considered, Jesus has cured in advance, before any wish either in word or in sign has been made to Him. At the same time, He had in these very miracles a real *motive*, which is shown with peculiar expressiveness by the word 'answering,' apparently without a cause (Luke xiv. 3). This rested on the misapplication of the commandment of the Sabbath which He found existing, and which He combated. In fact, He wishes to uproot a pernicious error, and to bring to light an important truth. In this we agree somewhat with Strauss, when he says (in his *Leben Jesu*, p. 434; Eng. transl. ii. p. 162) that one being placed 'immediately after the plucking of the ears of corn on the Sabbath, shows us that they are less concerned with the miracle itself, than with its having been performed on the Sabbath-day.' But his further assertion, that 'when men were accustomed to expect miracles of Jesus,' in the formation of myths this event was seized as 'a suitable occasion,' is arbitrary and violent. For, besides including the design of an instructive lesson, these deeds of Jesus have also at the same time, or rather at once and chiefly, their end in themselves; they are signs of the grace, proofs of the mercy of Jesus, and they must be conceived as tokens of the kingdom of heaven which was at hand. Our Lord Himself has taught us the correct way of considering them, by the expression: 'Go ye and learn what that meaneth: I will have mercy, and not sacrifice' (Matt. ix. 13 and xii. 7, 8). Whoever 'goes and learns' in this sense, will above all recognise them as works of His mercy, which thereupon will also illumine with brighter light the commandment regarding the Sabbath.

THE CURE OF THE WOMAN WHICH HAD THE SPIRIT OF INFIRMITY EIGHTEEN YEARS.—LUKE XIII. 10-17.

The manner in which the evangelist St. Luke introduces (ver. 10) this narrative, which is met with in his Gospel alone, prepares us for the instructive lesson contained in it, just as remarkably as the continuation (ver. 11) brings to light the divine compassion from the point of view of a token of the kingdom of heaven which is at hand. Our Lord is in the synagogue on the Sabbath-day for the purpose of teaching. The sick woman has also entered the place, not because she had heard of the presence of the miracle-working Jesus, as the woman with the issue of blood had done, but to celebrate the Sabbath. There is certainly here *no* infraction of the fourth commandment.

But the description of the sick woman entering prepares us to expect that He, through whom the 'time of refreshing,' the true 'Sabbath rest,' had appeared, should interfere with His assistance. She had a spirit of infirmity. The expression infirmity, ἀσθένεια, is used in Scripture for every sickness, and in the case before us, where the sick woman wants the power to lift herself up, is certainly justified. However, as the question is of a *spirit* of infirmity, and as the Lord in the 16th verse speaks of a Satanic cause for this infirmity, commentators (Meyer and Bleek) have considered themselves necessitated to think of a demoniacal state. But no case occurs in the New Testament of a purely physical suffering, which simply took away the voluntary use of the limbs, being considered as having such an origin. The possession which always enters into the spiritual life, controls at the same time the power of the *senses*—of the eye, the ear, or the tongue. It is also not likely that a demon would drive any one into the house of God, but rather (as we shall see later) into the deserts and among the tombs. The spirit ($\pi\nu\epsilon\hat{v}\mu a$) has a much simpler meaning. The evangelist wanted, (it is known that he likes to characterize exactly the infirmities of those miraculously cured, as he alone speaks of a $\dot{v}\delta\rho\omega\pi\iota\kappa\acute{o}s$; he alone has the technical expression from Galen, $\pi\nu\rho\epsilon\tau\grave{o}s$ $\mu\acute{e}\gamma as$)—he needed a technical designation for the sickness, as it was manifested in visible symptoms. He therefore chooses a very common expression to show the hidden seat, the concealed state of the suffering; but he no more meant a demoniacal origin by the declaration of Jesus in the 16th verse, 'Satan had bound this woman,' than is meant in the passage in which the adversary of the pious is said to have laid chains on Job.

However, it is not the spirit of infirmity, but the manifestations of the sickness, on which the interest of the narrative rests. The 'behold' of the 11th verse points *them* out purposely to the reader, just as they attracted the eye of our Lord (He saw her, 12th verse; see also John v. 6, 'when Jesus saw him'). The woman went bowed down to the ground, totally ($\epsilon\grave{\iota}s$ $\tau\grave{o}$ $\pi a\nu\tau\epsilon\lambda\acute{e}s$) unable to raise her head; and this condition had lasted already eighteen years. It was truly such as to call forth the most sincere sympathy; at any rate it awakened the compassion of Jesus. And our Lord knows what He will do. He addresses the sick woman (the 'calleth' in relation to the woman), and says to her: Thou art loosed from thy infirmity. The 'art loosed' points to the cure which happened immediately on this word; and the laying on of His hands can only have had for its object to awaken the feeling of it in the cured woman, to encourage her to use the strength which she has again received. And so she then raised herself up, and gave

God the glory and praise. The weak objection made by Strauss (*Leben Jesu*, 436) on psychological grounds, even in this case fails at once. Apart from the fact that a proceeding which appears reasonable when we consider the energy of the woman with the issue of blood, becomes inadmissible in a case of a resignation which was felt in an appointed lot, the psychological solution is certainly not applicable when our Lord Himself appeared prepared to act.

If this miracle is in itself conceivable as a work of the compassion of Jesus, as a token of the divine grace in Him, it is in this point still more evident, by means of its connection with the conversation following. The sense of this will certainly be proved. It is conceded that all these three narratives of miracles which were performed on the Sabbath are intended to place the fourth commandment in its true light; but in the case before us, this tendency evidently is secondary to another interest. We must consider the cause of the conversation of our Lord with the ruler of the synagogue. The dislike of the latter was as little simulated as the similar indignation on the part of the disciples in Bethany, Mark xiv. 4. The man prejudiced by the law, really did take offence at this 'working' of Jesus on the Sabbath. The hypocrisy with which our Lord accuses him was therefore expressed not so much against that, but rather against the disordered government of his mind, in which the most forcible contrasts were mingled together. The rebuke ranges with the similar reproach raised against the Pharisees in Matt. xvi. 3. For just as these latter did in one case what they would certainly consider guilty in another, so the ruler of the synagogue finds a proceeding offensive *in Jesus*, which *in himself*, and others like him, he would consider natural. "Ἔκαστος ὑμῶν, each one of you (without exception), even thou, yea, the strictest Jew. And you permit it not only now and again, but on the Sabbath; that is, it is your regular Sabbath business. Yea, *what* do you do? you just look after your animals. The accompanying description, λύει, ἀπαγ. ποτίζει, points to a real work not less than to one passing quietly. This was an inconsequence, which had its roots in a secret though not clearly conscious impurity of heart; therefore, as soon as it was discovered, there appeared the silence of shame on all who had taken offence ('all His adversaries were ashamed,' ver. 17),—a silence by which the address 'hypocrite' became perfectly justified. But is this punishment in the interest of their souls, the whole, the real intention of the Lord's answer? In considering it as *such*, do we not lose the rich contents of the 16th verse?

The judicious though familiar comparison of Scripture between man and beast may in other places (as in Matt. vi. 26, x. 31) also express simply the higher dignity of the man made after God's image, over the creatures without reason; but in its present connection we are forbidden this line of consideration, because 'the ox or the ass' are not here placed in opposition to the 'man,' but to the 'daughter of Abraham;' and much more by the fact that it is not the value which the objects mentioned have in *themselves*, but rather the different estimation which their lords and possessors assign to them, which is taken into consideration. The animals named in the 15th verse are valuable to man just so much as he gains from them, otherwise they are indifferent to him. The question which St. Paul raises, 1 Cor. ix. 9, 'Doth God take care for oxen?' might also run, 'Doth man take care for oxen?' At any rate man takes care of them not for *their* sake, but purely for his own. On the other hand, the daughter of Abraham (however little she might be valued by her fellow-men,—as, for example, by the ruler of the synagogue, who grudged her the benefit she had received, and even seems to blame her because she received her cure on the Sabbath) had in the eyes of Jesus a high value, and one estimated upon very different grounds.

The title 'daughter of Abraham' in itself puts us in mind of the 'son of Abraham,' Luke xix. 9. But this parallel is still more remarkable, if we compare the call given to the publican, 'To-day I must abide at thy house,' with the question addressed to the chief of the synagogue, 'Ought she not to be loosed from this bond?' We have in both cases the $\delta\epsilon\hat{\iota}$, with which it is customary in Scripture to show the obligatory action of Jesus, as ordered from above (John ix. 4, etc.). He *must* visit the house of the son of Abraham, because He was come to seek and to save all that was lost in Israel. He *must* cure the daughter of Abraham, because He appeared in order to destroy the works of Satan in all the children of promise (1 John iii. 8, 'that He might destroy the works of the devil'). This $\delta\epsilon\hat{\iota}$ broke through all bounds, even that of the Sabbath. To that which self-interest, to that which *selfish* love (Prov. xii. 14, 'A righteous man regardeth the life of his beast') *permitted* (ver. 15) (whether rightly or wrongly remains undecided), *true* love (ver. 16) had a *right;* and whoever had in any wise learned love (Matt. ix. 13), would acknowledge willingly this right, would answer the question of the 16th verse with a decided 'yes.'[1]

Lastly, if the work of this love is not derived from

---

[1] We ought not in this view to overlook the sufficiently opposing relation of the particulars in the 15th and 16th verses. The being bound of Satan refers to the ordinary binding of the animal to his crib; the eighteen years to the short time during which the water is kept back from the animals; and the 'this bond' to the bearable privations which the creature must suffer in this case.

the individual sensibility of Jesus, but is considered to have been accomplished by Him in consequence of the call which came to Him to reveal the divine promise, what is this but a brilliant sign of the kingdom of heaven which is at hand? And it is this which we wished to prove.

It is certainly unmistakeable, that in the second miracle performed on the Sabbath, which is also narrated by the evangelist Luke alone, there is decidedly the same intention of a lesson in opposition to Jewish prejudices, as in the first which we have just considered. The light in which this work of Jesus becomes conceivable shines forth here also, not from this secondary object, but from the symbolical point of view already referred to.

THE HEALING OF THE MAN WHICH HAD THE DROPSY.—LUKE XIV. 1-6.

We find ourselves now not in a synagogue, but in the house of one of the chief Pharisees. Jesus was invited by him to his table with a very ambiguous motive (they watched Him, ver. 1). The time is that of His entry into the house ('as He went into the house'); for it is remarked only in the 7th verse how the guests had taken their places at the banquet. Just at this moment a man with the dropsy stands before Him. His appearance in connection with this 'watching' on the part of the Jews causes our Lord to demand (hence the 'answering') of the teachers of the law, and of those looking on, some declaration regarding it: 'Is it lawful to heal on the Sabbath-day?' Their silence (not to be confounded with their dumbness following it in the 6th verse) is caused by a real perplexity they are in for an answer. It must be understood that they did not consider every work on the Sabbath to be wrong—that, in fact, the assistance of physicians in severe illnesses was held to be admissible on the day of rest. But on the other hand, it appeared doubtful to them whether the suffering before them belonged to the exceptional cases which were justifiable or not. Jesus gives them an answer by His actions.

The chief interest now evidently centres on the question which He asks the circle of Pharisees after the completion of His deed, and after the dismissal of the man that was healed. The comprehension of its meaning is not so simple and easy as at first sight may appear. The common mode of understanding it is consequently excluded; but, for the same reason, the way to the more correct one is opened up, viz., that instead of the reading as in the received text, ὄνος ἢ βοῦς, there should be substituted for it that offered by critical scholars, and recommended by them on convincing internal grounds, viz. υἱὸς ἢ βοῦς. According to this method of reading the text, the whole field of view in the present case becomes different from that before considered in Luke xiii. 15. *There* it was the selfishness which made them take care of the animals, but here in its place is that immediate impulse which compels one to hasten to the assistance of a life in danger. No one can see a child, nor even an animal, in danger of drowning, without taking immediate steps to save them. The Sabbath would hinder one so little in such an event, that no thought of it even enters into the consciousness; for the immediateness (see 'straightway' in the 5th verse) and the strength of the impulse experienced, exclude totally all such reflections. Certainly, in our general experience, the power of this natural impulse is shown only in a moderate degree; and there are indeed some who coolly pass by a life in danger, as in the instance of the priest and the Levite in the parable. Christ therefore puts His question only specially thus: 'Which of *you*, having a son or an ox.' But within this limit He can reckon on its absolute acknowledgment. 'From saving from danger a life which is valuable to you, let it be that of your child, or even only of your animal, no Sabbath would keep you back; the consideration of it vanishes before the power of the natural instinct.'

By this foil alone our Lord's own conduct appears in its right light. Jesus experiences the impulse to save, not only when He appears compelled to it as a bystander, but at the sight of *every* person in danger, —as, for example, of this man with the dropsy. And what He then feels is more than the mere natural instinct which would proceed from the narrow human breast. What then is it? 'Is it not lawful to do good on the Sabbath-day?' Thus asks He who is come as a physician to cure the sick. He had said: 'The Spirit of the Lord has anointed me . . . to preach deliverance to the captives;' therefore, when He sent away this man with the dropsy (ver. 4, He healed him, and let him go), He by this Sabbath work, performed on account of this call, evidently announced 'the acceptable year of the Lord,' and gave thereby a sign of the kingdom of heaven which was at hand.

We turn now to the third miracle of healing performed by Jesus on the Sabbath, which occurs in the synoptical Gospels, and is this time recorded by all three evangelists; and again we acknowledge the truth of Strauss' remark, that here also the eye of the narrator is directed less on the deed in itself, than on the circumstance that it was performed upon the Sabbath. This is evident partly from the historical connection, which is strongly and studiously shown by Mark;[1]

---

[1] St. Mark has related the history of the disciples plucking the ears of corn, and reported the answer of Jesus, that the Son of man is Lord also

partly from the position in which the incident is found in the first Gospel. Matthew does not relate it in the part of his writing where he collects into one rich picture so many instances of the miraculous working of Jesus, without any regard to the chronology of the events, but in *the* part in which he observes thoroughly the real sequence of events, and the interest connected with which is especially to show the commencement of the conflict between Jesus and the Pharisees.[1] In this case also we must keep in sight the point of view, that our Lord by His deed has given a sign of the coming kingdom of heaven. Moreover, this is the condition by which it becomes really conceivable to us.

THE HEALING OF THE MAN WITH THE WITHERED HAND.— MATT. XII. 9-14; MARK III. 1-6; LUKE VI. 6-11.

We attempt the solution of our problem by endeavouring to understand this miracle of Jesus on the ground of the twofold interest attached to it, viz. that its object is in the first place to destroy the Jewish dogma of the Sabbath, and secondly, to present to view a token of the time of grace just begun. If we succeed in this, we can the better cast aside the assertion of Strauss, that the narrative is based on the ground of a Hebrew prophetic legend,—an assertion which is founded merely on a casual coincidence of single expressions. What are we to think, when, from

of the Sabbath. Thereupon, he continues, the Jews watched Him, to see if He would act on this principle even in the use of His healing work.

[1] This is one of the numerous points where the first and the fourth Gospels coincide; compare Matt. xii. 14 ('Then the Pharisees went out, and held a council against Him how they might destroy Him') with John v. 16 ('Therefore did the Jews persecute Jesus, and sought to slay Him, because He had done these things on the Sabbath-day'). The manner in which Strauss has misused this coincidence does not shield him, as by his specious arguments, from the reproach of arbitrariness and fantastic combinations.

a comparison between 1 Kings xiii. 4 ('And his hand which he [Jeroboam] put forth against him was dried up') and Mark iii. 1 ('And there was a man there which had a withered hand'), the conclusion is drawn, that 'the origin of the evangelical narrative cannot be doubtful,' 'the imitation can hardly be mistaken?' 'Stand forth,' says our Lord before He proceeds to action; for He wills that this deed should attain the highest publicity, and especially on that account determines that it shall be correctly understood, by preceding it with the question, 'Is it lawful to do good on the Sabbath-days, or to do evil; to save life, or to kill?'[1] The words are at first sight obscure. All would have been clear if Jesus had simply put the question, as He did in the history of the healing of the man with the dropsy, 'Is it lawful to do good on the Sabbath-day?' But now the ἔξεστιν relates just as well to the 'do evil,' which can never appear right, either on the Sabbath or on the working day.

We must take into consideration the peculiar character of the fourth commandment. It is peculiar only in a limited sense. The Sabbath was presented to man as a gracious gift of divine philanthropy. 'The Sabbath was made for man, not man for the Sabbath,' Mark ii. 27. On this day he was released from the duty of work, which had been laid on him on account of his sin. It does not stand thus: Six days shalt thou work, on the seventh thou shalt not; but the true

---

[1] We have already remarked, that an acknowledgment of the genuineness of the first Gospel, and the consequences flowing therefrom, does not exclude the assertion that Mark, and even Luke, are the more complete narrators of details. The question of our Lord, as Mark relates it in chap. iii. 4, bears in itself, in the plainest manner, the stamp of originality; but in thus stating it, he is supported by the text of Matthew, where in fact the conclusion (chap. xii. 12) does *not* follow, as we should expect from the 10th verse, where it says, 'Is it lawful to heal on the Sabbath-days?' But instead of so doing, there is written an unexpected 'to do well.'

state of the matter is this: Six days thou *must* work, on the seventh thou needest not do so. The ἔξεστιν at the head thus reduces the question to this: How is it about the liberty which the Sabbath grants? about the festival, the holiday which it authorizes? Has man on the Sabbath so extensive a freedom, that he can also do evil then? Or is it so limited, that he cannot even do good? Our Lord wishes evidently to point out, that the fourth commandment cannot be taken away from its connection with the others, and that the duty to do good and the prohibition to do evil stand *above* it, and self-evidently take effect even on the Sabbath-day. Thou must do good, thou must avoid evil, whatever day it is. The Sabbath does not loose thee from the duty of doing good, it does not justify thee in doing evil. Of the advice which some expositors give to the Pharisees as to how they should have contended with Jesus, they would with the best intentions have been unable to make any use; otherwise they would have been well enough satisfied with it. For in the 'doing good,' the question is not primarily that of curing the sick, but in fact of goodness in general. (If Bleek and others understand the former specially as the '*doing good*,' it conflicts even verbally, almost irremediably, with the just comprehension of the opposite proposition, the 'doing evil.') Now our *Lord*, in fact, at once makes a use of these general conceptions. But what use? He speaks of a 'saving' and of a 'killing,' without mentioning beside them a third as possible. Now if the Sabbath does not loose us from the duty of doing good, the 'killing' would be wrong (as at all times), but especially on the Sabbath; yea, it would be particularly a desecration of the feast day. Such a 'killing,' thus a contravention of the sixth commandment, does in truth occur on that day which is made holy by the fourth commandment, directly the power to assist (which is present) is denied on account of the tradition. The silence of the Pharisees on the question laid before them is made clear by the words in the 5th verse. There was a silence not on account of their embarrassment, nor of their shame, but because of their profound perversity. The hardness of their hearts hindered an acknowledgment which their reason could not deny; and by this is explained the anger not less than the grief on our Lord's part. He often at other times proceeds to work a miracle with a similar mixed motive. It may be disputed whether in the present case the simple command, 'Stretch forth thy hand,' would compel them to avow that *such* a cure could certainly not disturb the Sabbath rest. Still more doubtful is it to us, if this really striking[1] proof of the power of Jesus was not calculated to overcome the obstinacy of hardened minds.

However, we hold the opinion that our Lord by means of this deed wished to show before the eyes of Pharisees a sign, that the tradition over which they watched was antiquated and near its end, and that in Him the time was fulfilled when its oppressive and unbearable yoke was to be taken away. It had been carried so far, that the gift of divine grace had been changed into a heavy burden, and the Sabbath brought with it care and privation instead of refreshment; so that there was urgent need for a deliverance from its oppression, which was an object of longing with all the pious. 'Come unto me, all ye that labour and are heavy laden, and I will refresh you:' thus had our Lord spoken in regard to the pharisaic traditions; by means

---

[1] The cure in this case did not occur *on* or *by* the word of Jesus, but in consequence of His directing His will before the words. For the demand, 'Stretch forth thy hand,' supposes the cure of the hitherto useless and inactive member as already accomplished.

of the miracle before them He lets them see an evident token that the hour of refreshment is at hand—the kingdom of heaven is come near to them. In some sense, the Sabbath miracles which we have been considering prepare the way for us to our second group. For besides their general significance, which we have in each case kept in view, and proved, they contain in reality an instructive lesson—that which our Lord expressed in words full of meaning, thus: 'All plants which my heavenly Father has not planted, shall be rooted out.' But it is not our opinion that the narratives to which we are about to call attention do not *also* offer such a motive of instruction, one more outspoken, more studiously and more earnestly shown; but their intention is certainly not specially to *teach*, as we are accustomed to understand that expression; and if in a former place we have compared them to the parable, it was in the sense that the interest of the explanation always underlies the parabolic manner of teaching. Still less is it our opinion that these miracles of Jesus should not be considered as showing His compassion. This compassion is so much in the foreground, that those expositors who content themselves with laying exclusive emphasis on it, by no means hold an untenable position. We, however, maintain that these works of our Lord point beyond the region in which they are immediately performed; that they reflect a higher compassion than that which appears to the bodily eye; that they represent possessions as opened, as attainable, which belong to another sphere than an earthly one. From this standpoint they are conceivable; and it is our problem to place them in this light.

III.

SECOND GROUP.

THE MIRACLES OF JESUS AS SYMBOLS OF THE TREASURES OF THE KINGDOM OF HEAVEN OPENED UP TO US.

We are following the leading of a higher power, in placing at the head of the narratives belonging to this group, the one to the meaning of which our Lord Himself has provided a key, in the same manner as He has unfolded the first of His parables to the understanding of His disciples. The position thus allotted to it is, however, so much the more fitting, as it exposes as attainable a treasure in which all the other treasures of the kingdom of heaven are united together in their true value.

HEALING OF THE SICK OF THE PALSY.—MATT. IX. 1-8; MARK II. 1-12; LUKE V. 17-26.

The circumstance, that the representation of this event in Matthew is much more concise than is the case with Mark and Luke, has furnished Strauss with an occasion for making the same assertion that he had already done in the narrative of the woman with the issue of blood. He imputes to the third, but more especially to the second evangelist, the fact of having added to the original event, which must have been very simple, numerous and partly monstrous elements. This time, however, the text of Matthew also appears to him so made up, that he does not consider the actual facts which lie at its foundation to be distinguishable from the rest of the account. He finds it therefore more advisable to explain the history, in short, as a fiction which arose from a literal understanding of the prophecy in Isa. xxxv. 3-6. He appeals for this to the agreement of the prophetical passage with the expressions of the evangelists. 'Strengthen the feeble knees,'—thus it stands in the prophet, παραλελυμένα; but Luke speaks also here of a παραλελυμένος (chap. v. 18). 'Then shall leap as a hart the lame.' Now in the narrative before us none of these expressions occur, though they do in the somewhat similar one in Acts iii. 7. Really these are splendid grounds to stand on!

In order to form a due conception of this miracle of our Lord, we will simply follow the account which Strauss has in vain tried to make ludicrous, and in which all unprejudiced expositors have recognised the impression of truth. We are placed in Capernaum (Mark ii. 1), in the house which Jesus was accustomed to visit. He had been absent, for He had said to His disciples (i. 38), 'Let us go into the next towns, that I may preach there also.' After some days, He returned 'into His own city' (Matt. ix. 1). But hardly had He entered into the house, when a great multitude of people assembled on the report of His arrival, which made the entry into the house, and even the approach *to* it, impossible (Mark ii. 2). But our Lord taught in the house. Then four bearers brought near a paralytic on his bed; and as they could not make for themselves a way through the crowd, they let down the sick man through the opened roof into the room (the ὑπερῷον) before Jesus.

Matthew certainly tells us nothing of this; he *wishes*, as we have before repeated (chap. viii. and ix.), to relate everything only summarily. But the remark made by him, 'Jesus seeing their faith,' presumes some peculiar act of faith on the part of the bearers.[1] For the αὐτῶν leaves no doubt on this point, that the faith is recognised not only in the paralytic himself, but in his bearers. The conviction that the sick man would receive help, if they could only succeed in bringing him before the face of Jesus; and this in conjunction with the energy with which they knew how to overcome the hindrances,—that is the faith which they showed, and was just the same as that which our Lord had extolled in the woman with the issue of blood. And on account of this faith He could act as He was moved.

He does not proceed at once to cure, but thus speaks to the sick man: 'Son, thy sins be forgiven thee.' The irregular form ἀφέωνται compels our consideration. It matters little whether it be Doric, as Suidas and Phavorinus say, or Attic, according to the Etymologicon Magn.; for it appears to us, as to all grammarians, that we have here no conjunctive, but the indicative perfect. However, an emphasis *minime negligenda* is not sufficient as an explanation; it is rather shown by this, that the forgiveness announced is really already accomplished, just in the same way as the λέλυσαι shows to the bowed down woman that her cure is one already accomplished, although it has not yet appeared. We merely make this remark, as another question occurs to us.

The bearers of the paralytic had not brought him in order that our Lord might bestow on him the

---

[1] This 'seeing' (ἰδών) can certainly be understood also in the sense of a purely spiritual comprehension, for in the 4th verse the same expression is used in regard to the thoughts of the scribes. But when we consider that Mark and Luke only write 'seeing' in the former passage, and in the latter ἐπιγνούς (perceived), Mark adds, in His spirit; it is *certain* that the second and third, and at least *probable* that the first evangelist used ἰδών in the sense of observing an appearance occurring to the external eye.

forgiveness of his sins, but that the man might be healed of his sickness. Christ acts as if He was fulfilling a wish expressed to Him, and yet *this* request had not been made to Him. It is important to notice, that an expressly declared wish had not been uttered; but this circumstance *in itself* does not take away the difficulty, for the unspoken language, in the appearance of the person brought, was unmistakeable. Some expositors, as for instance Meyer, explain that our Lord knew that this sickness was the punishment of special sins, perhaps of voluptuousness, and on that account He first expresses forgiveness as the necessary condition for bodily restoration; but the representation of a forgiveness of sins as dependent on physical healing is quite unbiblical, and finds really no support in the passage (John v. 14) which is cited as a parallel. Others have accepted the idea, that the paralytic himself had no thought of bodily healing; that he as a truly repentant sinner had sought for nothing else but grace and forgiveness; and our Lord, who well knew his heart's desire, grants at once *that* on which his longing was directed. But to this arbitrary exposition the text gives not the slightest countenance. We will compare it to the analogous case in John iv. 47. Our Lord answers the nobleman, when he has 'besought Him that He would come down and heal his son,'—'Except ye see signs and wonders you will not believe.' He speaks as if the nobleman had come in order to learn how to believe, while his object was the healing of his sick son. If we pay attention to the result, as it afterwards appears in the 53d verse,—'and himself believed, and his whole house,'—it is evident that the reproving expression of our Lord ('that you always need a miracle before you believe') will point out the end which He strives after, namely, the faith of

F

the world in general, and that of this ruler in particular.

Let us now apply this reasoning to the narrative before us. While Jesus announces to the paralytic the forgiveness of his sins, He names to him and to all present 'grace,' which is the highest of the heavenly treasures which He came on earth (ἐπὶ τῆς γῆς, Mark ii. 10) to spread abroad. The bodily cure which He intended to work upon him, He wishes to be considered as only a symbol—here as especially a symbol, proving what was said before ('that ye may know,' Mark ii. 10),—that was its peculiar object. If He had done nothing else than simply cure the sick of the palsy, we should, from our present standpoint, say *also* that the complete cure symbolizes the *present* grace of our Lord, in fact, the unbinding of men from the burden of their sins; but *then* the significance of the sign should be expressly shown; and our Lord shows it,—not *in* the cure, nor *after* it, but *before*, in order that the unexpected light should shine out brightly to every eye.

Our conviction is, that Christ immediately on seeing the sick man intended to give him bodily help. If some expositors are of opinion that He was moved to this particular miracle by the διαλογισμοί of the Pharisees, this view is opposed by the fact, that in the whole range of the evangelical history no single case occurs in which He sent away a sick person with merely spiritual consolations. The actual proceeding of Jesus would have been the same, even if the thoughts of the scribes had not been remarked by Him. However, He makes use of this incident, by completing the healing, and thus refuting the suspicion which He observed, in order to place it clearly in the point of view which He had announced in His first expression, 'Thy sins be forgiven thee.'

This sentence certainly presents some important difficulties to expositors for its justification. We at once avoid endeavouring to find the suitable key in the Jewish exposition of the relation between sin and sickness. The opinion also held and applied, that he who takes away the punishment of the sin possesses also at the same time the power of freeing from the guilt of it, is one really satisfactory to no one. The evident trouble which Bleek takes (*Synops.* i. p. 379) to make it understood in this manner, was just as much in vain as the acuteness which Hofmann (*Schriftbeweis*, i. p. 601 and foll.) has applied to the same purpose. That the Jews have maintained a close connection between sin and suffering, is just as certain as that their method of exposition contains at bottom a real truth. But that this connection is intended to be referred to in the passage before us, we dispute on the ground of the teaching of Jesus Himself, who in John ix. 3 expressly wishes it to be left out of consideration. We must therefore seek it in some other way.

Whoever has remarked the change, not casual and indifferent, between the expressions λαλεῖν, εἰπεῖν, and λέγειν, must be inclined to pursue this line of thought, especially as the accusation of the Pharisees against Jesus consisted in this, that He had *spoken* out a blasphemy, λαλεῖ βλασφημίας (by the λαλεῖν is understood a thoughtless, frivolous way of speaking), and as our Lord Himself afterwards completes the cure by means of a σοὶ λέγω (the λέγειν being a manner of speaking with authority and power). Still on this the real point of difficulty cannot rest; for when the question of Christ runs thus: 'Which is easier to say (εἰπεῖν), Thy sins be forgiven thee; or to say, Take up thy bed and walk?' the one expression of the mouth is as easy to pronounce as the other.[1] The εὐκοπώτερον does not relate therefore to the speaking itself, but to the deed intended by the word, to the result happening in consequence of it. Which is easier to say with effect, 'Thy sins are forgiven thee;' or to speak with result, 'Rise up and walk'? But what answer could they make to it? The embarrassment which ensues necessitates us to examine more closely the expression εὔκοπος.

Even from the purely philological point of view, the present translation of it can hardly be acknowledged as sufficient. Εὔκοπος is something different from ἄκοπος. Ἄκοπος is, indeed, that which does not fatigue ('light work') (it is also used passively in the sense of 'unwearied'); but εὔκοπος forms rather in classical Greek (especially in Polybius), as well as also in the Old Testament Apocrypha, the opposite to ἀδύνατος, it signifies the *possible* (by no means the *easily* possible). Let us compare the instructive passage, 1 Maccabees iii. 18. Judas replied to the apprehensions expressed by his little company as to how they should fight with so strong an army: εὔκοπόν ἐστι συγκλεισθῆναι πολλοὺς ἐν χερσὶν ὀλίγων—that is, it is not impossible, a possibility does exist, that a few can conquer a great multitude. Further, in the New Testament—that is, in the gospel—we meet with the expression only in the formula εὐκοπώτερόν ἐστιν with a comparison following it. But even with this comparison it has in each instance a peculiar application. When our Lord, after meeting the rich young man, says to his disciples, εὐκοπώτερόν

---

[1] Bleek enters his protest against this. He asserts that there certainly is a difference in the expression of both enunciations. It would really be easier to *say*, 'Thy sins be forgiven thee,' than to *say*, 'Stand up and walk.' But it has happened to this exegetist, who usually sees so clearly, that he has unwittingly used the expression 'easy' in quite a different sense from the one applicable here,—in a sense which the Greek εὔκοπος cannot possibly have.

ἐστιν, 'that a camel should go through the eye of a needle, than that a rich man should enter the kingdom of heaven;' or when He (Luke xvi. 17) says to the Pharisees, εὐκοπώτερόν ἐστιν, 'that heaven and earth should pass away, than one tittle of the law should fail,' the comparison in each instance seems to fade from the sight, for the eye sees rather two impracticable things placed one *beside* the other; and it is in showing the impossibility of the one, that is manifested the impossibility of the other. But these things placed parallel to each other belong to two different regions: the one to the sensual, the other to the spiritual. The camel through the needle's eye, the passing away of heaven and earth, the walking of the paralytic,—all these occur in the sphere of nature, and would appear to the outward view. On the other hand, the riches of the kingdom of heaven, the failing of the law, the forgiveness of sins,—all relate to the ordering of God in the spiritual kingdom, and cannot be perceived by the bodily eye. From this, the conception of the question of our Lord, that He laid before the Pharisees an alternative on which they had to decide, 'How think ye, which of the two is most possible?' will appear unacceptable to us. But even the text itself opposes such a conception; for the words immediately following, ἵνα δὲ εἰδῆτε, exclude the supposition of a pause requiring an answer. We have, in fact, only the form of the question. Jesus in reality only demands them to consider; to consider, so as to be led immediately to the certain result, that both are equally impossible to *human* powers, and are *solely* in the power of God [1] Himself, and of *Him* to whom He has given the same

---

[1] In the parallel passage (Luke xviii. 25) we see therefore this 'it is easier' immediately followed by the expression, 'The things which are impossible with men are possible with God;' 'there is nothing impossible with God.' God is the God who doeth wonders.

ἐξουσία; to consider thereupon the force of the question,[1] whether He who performed before their eyes in the natural region that which was alone possible to God, did not at once thereby prove Himself the One who in the higher region could also act with divine power.

We see now the whole matter. The Pharisees had concluded that 'He spoke blasphemously in *saying*, Thy sins are forgiven thee; as He is not able to forgive sins, for God alone can do that.' And our Lord answers, 'You ought also in the same manner to judge, if I *say* to the sick of the palsy, Stand up and walk; for he does rise up and walk, that *also* God alone can effect. But in order that you may know that I have *announced* forgiveness of sins by my divine power, you thus see with what result I *speak*, Stand up and walk.' This result proves that His summons to the sick of the palsy was no empty phrase; but it proves also, further, that His former announcement to him had been in the name of God, from whom He had received the ἐξουσία to make both body and soul whole. By this is explained also the evidently emphasized clause 'on earth' in the 10th verse. If Jesus announces the forgiveness of sins by virtue of the divinely received ἐξουσία; the word, if even spoken on earth, is honoured before God and in heaven (Matt. xvi. 19, xviii. 18), the guilt is certainly and really taken away; there will be no more mention of it in eternity. However, we seek something still further in this clause. It seems to us as if it was intended to show the earth as just the *spot* on which the heavenly treasures hitherto promised will be spread abroad. The forgiveness of sins was under the Old Testament only an object of promise, the fulfilment of

---

[1] This question, so placed, we consider as the true contents of the 9th verse in an interrogative form.

which was looked forward to with eager longing: Now shall a race dwell on the earth who shall be freed from the burden of guilt. In Jesus this treasure of treasures is opened; this is what the narrative before us shows.

But thereby are we brought back to our former consideration. It has been said, that our Lord from the beginning intended the cure of the paralytic; and that even His first call to the sick man teaches us to consider the miracle intended by Him from the right point of view. At the same time, it is also to be remarked that He makes use of the incident of the suspicion of the Pharisees in order to place this point of view in a still brighter light. It will now have become clear in what sense this last assertion is meant by us, and with what justice we have used it. If the refutation of the scribes thus happens, so that they would feel themselves necessitated to follow on from what was perceptible to the senses to that which was spiritual, the conviction would lead to the effect in which the one appears related to the other. But this connection can here be no other than that resting on the relation of the symbol to the thing symbolized. If our Lord proves, by telling with effect the sick of the palsy to rise up and walk, His power to announce effectively and authoritatively the forgiveness of sins, He has thereby placed the healing of the sick man, the taking away of his lameness, as a symbol of the power which the Father has given Him to free men from the disabling pressure of their burden of sins. It does not matter as to the degree in which those immediately present acknowledged the true significance of the symbol. The account of the evangelist, that they acknowledged they had 'seen strange things,' that they were 'amazed,' does not exclude a deeper comprehension of the deed; but the narrative of Matthew,

'They marvelled and glorified God,' certainly seems to presuppose it. The miracle of Jesus is thereby quite conceivable to us if we understand the 'such power' for which the witnesses glorified God, of the power symbolized by the healing to forgive sin.

We have already shown the grounds on which He gave the narrative just considered its place at the head of our second group. We again express our opinion that it signifies the highest of true treasures, the foundation of all salvation, 'the salvation and remission of sins' (Luke i. 77) as revealed in Christ. All the other miracles belonging to this group move within a narrower circle: they relate to *single* treasures of the kingdom of God which are now attainable. A real condition of the solution of our problem will be to show correctly in the various cases the special treasures referred to.

THE CLEANSING OF THE LEPERS.

From various intimations of the evangelists, we may draw the conclusion that our Lord had repeatedly cured the sickness of leprosy, which often occurred in Palestine. At the same time, only two cases are expressly and fully narrated in which He manifested His power over this disease. The one is related by the first three evangelists (Matt. viii. 2-4; Mark i. 40-44; Luke v. 12-14), the other only by the third (Luke xvii. 11-19). John reports no miracle of that kind by Jesus.[1] Although Strauss cannot produce a prophetical passage which might have given occasion to

---

[1] The way in which Strauss arranges this circumstance (p. 444, Eng. transl. ii. 177)—'In the comparatively early Grecian world of Asia Minor, maladies of this kind were not so common, and they could not be so easily adapted to the symbolical system of the fourth Gospel, which consists in the opposition between light and darkness, life and death'—is in its first half unworthy of serious opposition; and as regards the second part, it

the composition of these narratives, he finds in them, nevertheless, 'prophetico-Messianic myths of the clearest stamp' (p. 442, Eng. transl. ii. 174). For instance, in Luke's account he believes that he recognises a palpable imitation of the healing of Naaman by Elisha. The resemblance between the one Samaritan who returned to give thanks, and the similar conduct on the part of Naaman, appears so much the more certain, since there is the express declaration in Luke iv. 27, that 'many lepers were in Israel in the time of Elisha the prophet, and none of them was cleansed saving Naaman the Syrian.' Besides, the connection between the *grateful* stranger and the *merciful* Samaritan, he says, is so evident, that the history of the miracle before us is thus recognisable as a later composition, written in a friendly spirit towards the Gentiles. We know no better way to oppose such violent arbitrariness than by showing the complete probability of this miracle of our Lord.

There is, in fact, some possibility that the healing of lepers by Jesus could be conceived as mere acts of His compassion, as simple tokens of the time of grace which had arrived. Was, then, leprosy such an evil as would at once have called forth that deep compassion which our Lord experienced at the sight of those smitten by it (moved with compassion, Mark i. 41), and which perfectly justified the urgent request of the ten (Have mercy on us, Luke xvii. 13)? Even the milder form of it, the λεύκη, *lepra Mosaica*, was so severe a suffering, on account of the pain connected with it; on account of the loathsome appearance which

---

can be considered only as the delusion of an ignorant man. For Strauss must know that in the fourth Gospel (chap. xiii. 10, xv. 3), as well as in the First Epistle of John (chap. iii. 3), the conception of cleansing takes a prominent place. We shall find further on an opportunity of considering why John has reported no healing of lepers.

caused disgust; on account of its course, slowly but surely leading to death, and on account of the depression caused by it on the spiritual life,—that the Jews recognised in it one of the hardest plagues, one of the severest punishments of Jehovah. At the same time, these cures only appear in their full light when they are placed in the symbolical point of view.

Before fully considering the subject, we will casually call attention to the following circumstance. Among the three miraculous signs which were entrusted to Moses, in order to attest his divine mission before the people, and to strengthen his own faith, the second was, as is known, his hand becoming leprous in his bosom, and again becoming cleansed (Ex. iv. 6, 7). Expositors do differ about its meaning; but they nearly all agree in this, that what Strauss calls 'only a divine jugglery,' is no mere τέρας, but a σημεῖον of symbolical significance. But then the conduct of our Lord in both cases in which He helped the lepers, demands consideration. He sends them cleansed to the priests (Matt. viii. 4; Luke xvii. 14). We will speak later of the peculiar, indeed almost violent, severity with which He does this (Mark i. 43, 44). As far as the general circumstance goes, we have to call to remembrance the legal ordinance in Lev. xiv. 2: 'This shall be the law of the leper in the day of his cleansing: He shall be brought unto the priest.' But if we consider the numerous symbolical acts by which this speaking of the cleansed to the priest is surrounded, this sending to him on the part of our Lord is just as certain a reference to the symbolical meaning of the healing of the leper, as the sending of the blind man to Siloam serves to the right understanding of the restoration of his power of seeing.

Now, when we consider the cleansing of the leper

from this point of view, the question arises, What higher gift has our Lord shown as manifested by these deeds? Vitringa is not alone in saying that the leper is a symbol of sin. The homiletical exposition of Scripture considers the point as settled. We should certainly blame expositors if they employed this view without sifting it and closely defining it. It is more than a mere want of taste to give an apparent precision to its interpretation, such as to liken the hereditary character of leprosy to hereditary sin, etc. It is certainly a view common to both Testaments to look upon sin as a sickness. Our Lord Himself interprets His assertion, 'They that are whole need not a physician; but they that are sick,' in this sense, 'I came not to call the righteous, but sinners to repentance' (Luke v. 31, 32). But what case of sickness which Jesus had cured could not just as well have been put in this point of view! Or had leprosy a special right to it? No, certainly not; for it is not in accordance with Scripture to consider leprosy as a sickness, and to include it under this general category! Let us compare the highly instructive passage in Matt. x. 8: 'Heal the sick, cleanse the lepers, cast out devils.'[1] Thus our Lord charges His disciples when He sent them forth. In this trial the sick proper, those needing therapeutic aid, are alone the ἀσθενοῦντες. The lepers are expressly distinguished from the sick as a special class of sufferers by themselves. The lepers are certainly sick in the general sense in which even the demoniacs can be so called. If therefore we wish to consider leprosy as a symbol of sin, we require a closer definition; and then from this closer definition we can recognise the gift of grace which

---

[1] Whether the clause 'raise the dead' is genuine or not is of no consequence. We leave it out here, because the settlement of the question which interests us is not really advanced by it.

our Lord wishes to point out in the deliverance from this suffering.

We call attention to a twofold circumstance. First, leprosy is an evil of which one is conscious absolutely by the appearance. A sick man is sensible of his suffering, he *feels* himself ill; the leper *observes* it, he *sees* that he is not clean. His eyesight, not his feelings, announce to him the alarming symptoms. In the first stage, according to Lev. xiii. 1–7, it needed even the sharp eye of the priest to diagnose whether the leprosy was really existing or not. And even the experienced priest might be deceived: he had to wait to observe until the appearances justified a decisive judgment. In leprosy there was a far closer connection between being and appearing than in any other bodily suffering; indeed, in this disease the one coincides completely with the other. In this view it is significant, that the help which was given to the lepers is constantly described as the καθαρίζειν. Hardly once (excepting, perhaps, Luke xvii. 15) do we meet in the Gospels with the expression ἰάσασθαι λεπρούς; in fact, the question is always of the καθαρισμός (Matt. x. 8; Mark i. 41; Luke iv. 27, xvii. 14, 17, etc.). If the appearance of the leprosy had vanished, the suffering itself was also taken away.[1]

It results from this, that leprosy can be a symbol of sin only so far as it relates to appearances, to its being perceived, and to its being observed with dissatisfaction as a personal disfigurement. And thus the gracious

---

[1] From this point of view the striking representation in Matt. viii. 3, 'His leprosy was cleansed,' is explained much more satisfactorily than by means of the supposition of an inexact method of expression. There is also no need to consider that καθαρίζειν means here (and Mark vii. 19), as in other places, 'to drive away.' If we bear in mind that it is in leprosy that the suffering and the appearance of it coincide; it can be said, 'the leprosy was cleansed,' with the same right and in the same sense which Naaman in 2 Kings v. 11 expected that Elisha 'would strike his hand over the place and recover the leper.'

act of Jesus pointed out by the *cleansing* of the leper will be this, that He takes away the sin which pollutes man's path. Just as the healing of the paralytic symbolized His power to put away the paralyzing burden of guilt by forgiveness, so the miracle before us brings to light His having revealed the open fountain to cleanse all unrighteousness. It is because this fountain is now opened in Him, that those in His kingdom are required to act as in the following passages: 'Lay apart all filthiness,' etc., Jas. i. 21; 'Cleanse your hand, ye sinners,' Jas. iv. 8; 'Laying aside all malice, and all guile, and hypocrisies, and envies, and evil speakings,' 1 Pet. ii. 1; 'Let us cleanse ourselves from all filthiness of the flesh and spirit,' 2 Cor. vii. 1.

We may compare the cleansing of the leper with the symbolical deed of washing of feet, which our Lord performed on His disciples at a later period; but the comparison must be made with care. Uncleanness was only attached to the feet of the disciples, otherwise (John xiii. 10, ὅλα) they were clean; while in the case of the lepers, they were unclean ὅλοι, in the sense in which the Pharisees said to the man that was born blind, 'Thou wast born in sin altogether' (ὅλος), John ix. 34. The uncleanness on the feet of the disciples was only on the outside, being caused by their walking in this unclean world; while in the case of the lepers, the uncleanness broke out from within.

Secondly, the disease of leprosy had a result with which no other bodily evil was accompanied. It excluded the person possessed with it from intercourse with others. The lepers could only associate with their fellows in affliction; they were bound to make themselves known by their dress, and other tokens; also, as a rule, they dwelt outside the towns. The ten (Luke vii. 12) therefore came not to Jesus, but stood afar off, and called out to Him for help from a distance (they lifted up their voices). The strictness in this was so great, that even when the disease was not yet proved, when the symptom observed was perhaps something quite innocent, a mere מִסְפַּחַת, a scab in the skin (Lev. xiii. 7), the suspected person was ordered prophylactically a seclusion for seven days, and under certain circumstances for seven days longer, from the community of the confederate people. The subsequent freeing from the trouble required to be just as much a really indubitable one, before he could be received again, and before the Levitical saying, 'he is pure,' could be pronounced. See Lev. xiv. But even from this view the symbolical meaning is not apparent. For there is this in the consequences of sin, that as far as it occurs in life it partly isolates, and at the same time partly introduces into the community itself a disturbing and hindering element. We will unite these two views, and say the cleansing of the leper exhibits *the* grace of Christ, in that it takes away from men the uncleanness of their lives, and thereby unites them in a common brotherhood; and then see how from this point of view all the details in our narratives are satisfactorily explained. As far as relates to the first of these miracles, we follow, for good reasons, the account of Mark. This evangelist shows (in agreement with St. Luke) more decidedly the urgency with which the sufferer who dared to break through the barriers of the law (he was even 'full of leprosy') beseeches the help of Jesus. The words in which he asks it are alike in all three accounts: 'If Thou wilt, Thou canst make me clean.' The fact that it was the cleansing from the *leprosy* that was desired, explains that the will is questioned; on the other hand, the power is presumed (in Mark ix. 21 the position is the exact opposite). As our Lord had shown, by the many miracles which He had already performed (Mark i. 32), Himself as He who *can* help; the conclusion was easy, that He was also in a position to cleanse even the lepers. But what was doubtful was *this*, whether He would be inclined to come into any personal relations with *such* sufferers, as all who had contact with them were rendered levitically unclean. It appears from the conduct of Jesus (ver. 41) that the phrase, 'if Thou wilt,' was really meant in this sense. He stretches out His hand and touches the suppliant. This must have been done with a special *intention;* for in the second case in which He meets with lepers (Luke xvii. 14), our Lord bestows His help on the suppliants by means of His simple word. But this intention could not have consisted *in* a designed opposition to any weakness of faith; for it was no Naaman, with the demand for a fulfilment of a heathen's wish,¹ who now lay at His feet. But the expression 'touched him' is the real answer of Jesus to the 'if' of the leper; just as His 'I will' (as Bengel says) is the echo of the 'Thou wilt' of the suppliant, and His 'Be thou clean' His answer to the 'Thou canst make me clean.' 'If Thou art inclined, that is, not afraid to come in contact with me, Thou canst make me clean.' And the Lord answered, 'I will,' by sign, by word, and by deed. The high significance of this feature in its allegorical application may be touched upon in a few words.

If it is a question of the forgiveness of sin in order to free from guilt, it is still entirely the power of Jesus which is presumed or questioned ('who hath power to forgive sins'). If, on the other hand, it relates to the cleansing from evil habits, the question

---

¹ Compare 2 Kings v. 11, 'Behold, I thought the prophet will surely come out to me, and stand and call on the name of the Lord his God, and strike his hand over the place, and recover the leper.'

is just this, as to whether the pure can take part in this matter. (Peter did not consider it right, John xiii. 6.) We saw Jesus justify the *power* in the history of the sick of the palsy; the *inclination* is here confirmed by assurance as well as by the result. But certainly a dissimilar and anxious interest is excited by the manner in which our Lord sends away the recipient of the benefit after his complete cleansing. The fact that immediately after the 'being moved with compassion' there follow the words 'straitly charged,' does not surprise us; we have perceived elsewhere a similar change from a state of tender feeling to the function of a judge in Jesus. But at first we do not see the reason why He so severely drives away from His neighbourhood the favoured person, and acts towards Him in the same manner as at a later period He acted to the moneychangers and those selling (ἐξέβαλεν, as in Matt. xxi. 12). How are we to understand His stretching out His blessing hand with mild compassion to the unclean, and with the same hand His thrusting him away when he has become clean?—that He allows the leper to draw near to Him, but will not suffer his presence when he is a leper no more?

Expositors have treated this question in such a way that they make the point of difficulty to lie on the μηδενὶ εἴπῃς. But the consequence of this view was a total misunderstanding of this last order. For it is an error to suppose that our Lord, by this repeatedly imposed silence on the recipients of His gifts, desired to prevent the running together of the people with their enthusiastic hopes of the Messiah. A command which was regularly broken (Mark i. 45, 'He went out and began to publish it much;' see also Matt. ix. 31); yea, which mostly had just the opposite effect (see Mark vii. 36, 'The more He charged them, so much the more a great deal they published it'), would not have been so often repeated by our Lord if He had meant it in this sense. With regard to the question in general, we must consider these instructions as *never* to be understood absolutely, but as always presuming a mere temporary value. The more particular definition which we see added in Matt. xvii. 9 ('until the Son of man be risen again') can in some sense be applied here as well as to all similar cases. We must not overlook how, in this view of the εἰς μαρτύριον αὐτοῖς, an absolute prohibition could be justly kept; but the reason of it must in each case be discovered by the context, as it is not everywhere the same (see particularly in Matt. xii. 17). As regards the passage *before us*, the emphasis evidently is to be placed on the positive motive, on the sending to the priest, which results evidently from the particle ἀλλά. Instead of relating to *others* the benefit received, he should *rather* go *himself* (therefore the word σεαυτόν placed before and emphasized), and show himself to the priest. The reason of the prohibition is thus to be found here in the urgency of the command which was to be first fulfilled,—an urgency which must be symbolized not by the ἐμβριμησάμενος, for according to Matt. ix. 30 this may become the simple μηδενὶ εἴπῃς, but rather by the ἐξέβαλεν.[1] But wherefore should now the person cleansed without delay hasten above everything to the priest (whether to Jerusalem or to a nearer place does not matter)? The fact that He similarly seemed to tell the cured demoniac (Mark

---

[1] Our opinion is by no means that the negative direction of Jesus should be completely taken away; it remains in its full force. It is only subordinate to the positive, and stands in dependence on the latter; it receives here its motive from it. There are cases where the position of affairs is the opposite. When our Lord says to Mary Magdalene (John xx. 17), 'Touch me not, but go to my brethren,' etc., the point of difficulty without question rests on the prohibition; and nothing would be

v. 18) to stay still, and to spread abroad in the town the grace he had received, only puts the question further back; it does not decide it.

The conclusive answer is obtained from the general considerations which we have made on these acts of Jesus. As our Lord wished by it to show His power and grace to lead back into society him who had been estranged from it by his uncleanness, so He must necessarily require that the cured person should first put himself in that position which would enable him to take again his place among the covenanted people. He hereby secured to His miracle at once that publicity which He himself intended. It was not that it should be spread abroad merely as a report; but the εἰς μαρτύριον αὐτοῖς should tend to make the deed known. The referring of αὐτοῖς to 'the people' is as little to be justified as it is admissible to conceive the μαρτύριον as a 'witness for them.' As often as the expression εἰς μαρτύριον αὐτοῖς occurs in the Gospels (and it certainly occurs often), it is always used in the sense of a conviction. This certainly should be taken into consideration, when we wish to recognise in it a fulfilling of the legal precept on the part of Jesus *Himself;* we may not adorn our representation of the Lord with such features. The observance of the ceremonial ordinances was, however, natural for the man that was cured; and that Jesus did not consider him freed from the fulfilment of a religious duty, is clear from the words.

However, it is not alone thus to be considered; but the real meaning of the text is, that Christ thus

more erroneous than to understand it as if it was declared, 'Instead of staying here, hasten rather to my brethren.' But also in this case we read no ἀλλά, but a δέ, which adds to the prohibition a charge in simple succession. This relation between the δέ and the ἀλλά comes out especially clear in the passage Rom. v. 13, 14, where we find both particles beside one another.

gives the priest the proof of the cleansing accomplished by Him, in like manner as He allowed the master of the feast at Cana to prove the goodness of the wine made by Him. They should themselves judge whether here the declaration ordered in the law and the prescribed offering could be performed; they should by it be convinced that in this case even a Moses would judge 'that the flesh of the man is again restored as the flesh of a young child.'

The second cleansing of lepers by Jesus, related in Luke xvii. 11, etc., also fully justifies the views already laid down. The Lord completed this work on His last journey to Jerusalem, in a village which was situated on the route chosen by Him, 'through the midst of Samaria and Galilee.' Our attention is naturally turned to a twofold fact. *First*, our Lord answers the request which was made to Him, not by the sufficient reply, 'Be clean,' but by the command, 'Go, and show yourself to the priests.' Now, although there was in this order the promise of help, the immediate cleansing thus promised was not yet observable by them; but only 'as they went' did it really appear to them. The Samaritan must have already proceeded some distance on the way ordered when he became aware that he was healed; otherwise there could have been no question of a 'turning back' in the 15th verse. As soon as the symbolical character of the event is acknowledged a difficulty occurs. Some have sought to remove it by saying that our Lord wished to try the faith of the suppliants. We shall, however, find another opportunity to call in question the opinion concerning such trials of faith which Jesus is said to have made before He allowed His miraculous assistance to take effect. In the present case, the view is frustrated by the fact that the faith (ver. 19) is only recognised in one, and wanting in all the others, although they also became pure 'as they went upon their way.'

The matter becomes plain, if we think on the spiritual effects which the Lord wished to symbolize by these miracles. In fact, the cleansing from sinful habits, which is accomplished by the grace of Christ, is by no means perfected immediately; it is a gradual work, it happens 'as one goes.' The *forgiveness* of sins can be embraced by faith and taken immediate possession of; the *purification* from sinful works is a gradual work. See Eph. iv. 22-32: 'That ye put off concerning the former conversation the old man, which is corrupt according to the deceitful lusts, and be renewed,' etc.; Rom. xiii. 12: 'Let us cast off the works of darkness.' While we walk in the way which Christ points out to us, we shall become purer and purer, until the whole body is light, and no manner of darkness remains any more in us. Secondly, at the end of the narrative we hear our Lord express His displeasure, that besides the one Samaritan there was no other returned to give glory to God. As we must at once deny that there is any connection of this complaint with the proverbial phrase which is in every one's mouth, there remains to us only one meaning. Our Lord points out the pain He feels that the real effect which He aimed at, and which He wished to show by this deed, was only attained by one and missed by the others. The nine gave no proof that they had become clean in a higher sense, as they were contaminated immediately by a pagan vice—ingratitude (Rom. i. 21); still less did they give evidence that the Church would have in them healthy and living members, as they had not attempted to have the commonest intercourse with Him who had been their physician. They *will* have taken care to obtain their rights as declared clean; they *will* have mingled with men; but the question, 'Where are the nine?' can also be made to include the thought as to what positions and in what circles can they move! In this view is the term stranger applied to the Samaritan. Although of a different γένος, he has entered into the community of the true people of God before the nine. His faith has procured him salvation. 'His faith has saved him.' We have met with this formula in the history of the woman with the issue of blood. It was there remarked that we should meet with it again in the account of the sinner who anointed the feet of Jesus (Luke vii.). We now add that it also occurs in Mark x. 52. In the present case, its connection with the narrative, according to our opinion, is by no means so unsuitable as Strauss (p. 443, Eng. transl. ii. p. 175) asserts. His opinion is, that Luke, in the 19th verse, has in 'Go thy way' imitated the parting words of Elisha to Naaman, 'Go in peace;' but that 'the concluding expression has been transferred by the evangelist from other miraculous accounts into this.'

These words will appear suitable if they are only rightly understood. The σωτηρία, which is in question here, cannot possibly mean the cleansing from leprosy, for the nine had also received this healing. Bleek's view, that Jesus has *confirmed* the cure of the Samaritan, will not do, for He has not taken it away again from the rest. What He has cleansed is, and always will be, clean. The σωτηρία can refer here to nothing else than to a higher κοινωνία, to which faith has helped the stranger. But this faith is different from that of the woman with the issue of blood. While that of the latter existed before the cure, that of the former only dated from his experience of the cleansing. It expressed itself in the 'returning and giving glory to God.' It is said with justice that the offering of this εὐχαριστία (16th verse) in its true value is above all the sacrifices which Moses ordered. But faith and giving of thanks do not on that account coincide. The Samaritan returned for the purpose of returning thanks; but as a consequence of the incitement received, his awakened faith in the Son of God also laid hold of the higher possession which our Lord had assured to him in His parting words.

There is certainly some sort of connection between the showing of grace by Jesus to lepers, and that kind of narrative which we are about to consider. But the chief interest in the latter rests on quite a different point. There is not here a certain treasure of the kingdom of heaven which is at hand, which is signified by the symbolical deed; but the point lies (as we will try to show) in the manner in which He rules who is the Lord in this kingdom. The chief objection which has been made against this event will show us the way in which we can conceive its probability.

THE CAPTAIN AT CAPERNAUM.—MATT. VIII. 5-13; LUKE VII. 1-10.

We should merely undertake a useless task, which for some time has had a satisfactory solution, if we endeavoured to establish the proof, that while the narratives of Matthew and Luke refer to one and the same event, that occurrence which is related in the fourth evangelist, chap. iv. 46 and following verse, is a different one. The means of proof are abundantly and convincingly brought together in Meyer's Commentary. It was not to be expected otherwise, than that Strauss would make use of the slight differences between the representations of the first and second evangelist on the one side, and the equally slight resemblance between the two and the Johannine narrative on the other, in order to give a character of probability to his view of the gradual increase of the narrative of miracles, first by repetition, and then, on reflection, by excessive elaboration. But in the present case we easily perceive the arbitrariness which he displays (pp. 459-462, Eng. transl. ii. 192-204), and which demands from his readers the adoption of the strangest conclusions;[1] so much the more, as he in this case even denies to the text of Matthew any fundamentally historical truth. 'We have not here a history, but a Messianic myth, which has grown out of the myth of the prophet in the Old Testament . . . the prophet Elisha has performed a miracle at a distance. . . . The Messiah could not be supposed to have fallen short of such miraculous power' (463, Eng. transl. ii. 204).

Even to Schleiermacher, an *actio in distans*, as it stands in the evangelical narratives, does not appear acceptable, because it is here apart from any and every analogue to human dealings (*Leben Jesu*, 218). We arrive at a different result. It is necessary that we should have a full account of the event. As we have observed before, Matthew never perceives the value of being explicit. For this purpose it is from St. Luke we shall receive the desired completion. We therefore follow his account.

A captain who was a Gentile, but favourable to Judaism and to the Jewish worship, probably in the service of Herod Antipas, hears of the arrival of Jesus at Capernaum at a time when his servant, who was very valuable to him (the παῖς of Matthew interpreted by Luke into δοῦλος; the ἔντιμος equivalent to the

[1] It is not the most difficult of these demands, that from the resemblance between the 'Trouble not the Master,' in Luke viii. 49, and the 'Lord, trouble not Thyself,' in Luke vii. 6, we should draw the conclusion that this feature in the history of Jairus has improperly been transferred into the narrative of the captain.

εὔχρηστος εἰς διακονίαν, 2 Tim. iv. 11), is, in consequence of general painful paralytic suffering (δεινῶς βασανιζόμενος, grievously tormented, as if it meant suffering from a diabolical pain), near to death (Luke, ἔμελλεν τελευτᾶν). He had by his benevolence gained the goodwill of the elders of the Jews, and at his request they hasten willingly to our Lord, and with a zealous advocacy for their sender, say, 'He loveth our nation, he hath built us a synagogue out of his own means; therefore he has a claim to a service in return.' That this account of Luke is not contradictory to that of Matthew, we assert with the same certainty with which we claim for the former the greater explicitness. Matthew only reports the general fact that the centurion had *turned* to Jesus, and that his request had been *spoken* in the ears of the Lord; while St. Luke adds to this the closer definition, that both happened by means of the Jewish elders. This closer definition, however, ranges itself so much the more naturally with the text of Matthew; as Luke also ascribes the request made to Jesus, as well as the subsequent request not to enter into the house, formally and expressly to no other than to the captain himself. See Luke vii. 3, ἐρωτῶν αὐτὸν (that is, the captain beseeching Him); also in ver. 6, λέγων αὐτῷ. Strauss, indeed, accuses the third evangelist of a contradiction in his using this ἐρωτῶν; but this apparent contradiction, which may be compared with that of Matthew's report, is not in Luke's representation itself, but only in the superficial consideration of the critic. In fact, the 'beseeching' in itself—that is, the request specially for help—is certainly from the captain, while the ἐλθών is purely a Jewish addition. To the elders the necessity of this 'coming' seemed evident; but the captain was far from thinking of it. *In so far*, they were false interpreters of his wishes. Therefore it is not as Strauss asserts, that the evangelist has afterwards corrected himself; but the captain himself rectifies the expression of the Jewish petition. On this ἐλθεῖν, which his advocates request, while the centurion has neither desired nor will suffer it,—on this ἐλθεῖν, which our Lord seems ready to do, without however accomplishing it, turns the point of the whole event: it forms the centre-point around which all the rest moves; it is the door to a satisfactory understanding.

'I will come and heal him,' Jesus is said to have spoken, according to Matthew, while Luke only relates that he went with the Jews on the way. He addressed these words to the pleading elders, some of whom will have hastily reported them to the centurion, while our Lord follows after with the rest. 'I will come and heal him;' thus He spake, to prove him, for He Himself knew what He would do (John vi. 6), and what would happen.[1] The advocacy of the Jews in no wise influenced Him; but while He accepted the request of the captain, His Father showed Him the work *which* He was to do, and the manner *how* to perform it. Therefore the message which He received from the house did not surprise Him *in itself*, and as regarded its general purport; but He was moved to marvelling (ἐθαύμασεν αὐτόν) at the faith of which the desiring Him not to come gave evidence. Τοσαύτην πίστιν, we read; the humility of the man, which is not to be denied, is here, as in the case of the Canaanitish woman, kept out of consideration. Τοσαύτην πίστιν it is said with emphasis; τοσαύτην, not τοιαύτην; this *measure* is according to the representation which the captain has formed to himself of the almighty power of our Lord. If he, although a dependent man, finds in his servants obedience to his word, how much more must Jesus, the

---

[1] The exposition of Fritzsche, who makes the words interrogative, 'Shall I come and heal him?' we cannot accept; however, it is the evidence of a fine sense, which perceived clearly our Lord's hidden meaning.

sovereign Lord, be able, by virtue of the simple declaration of His will, to bring the sickness to an end! However, the greatness of this faith is only brought fully to light by means of the particle οὐδέ of which our Lord makes use. Let us consider the passage strictly on that point. Jesus does not show His *grief*, but His *wonder*, that what He had hitherto looked for in vain in Israel, where He had a right to expect it, He should here meet unsought for at the hands of a heathen. The fact is this: The history of Israel related the testimonies of the God who doeth wonders, and told of the numerous heroes of the faith who, hoping against hope, had held firmly to faith in the Invisible One. But at the time of Jesus no fruit of it was to be seen. All faith had not disappeared; our Lord's help was in reality sought for with more or less strong faith, but they needed also to see the means. Jesus was required to lay His hand on the sick; He ought at least to come, at least to be present,—pure faith in the effective power of His will was not native to the Jews. In the instance now before us, it is in a surprising degree manifest in a Gentile; and it happens to him according to his faith. The account of Matthew (chap. viii. 13) resembles the relation of Luke, in spite of the fact that our Lord had caused the captain to be told of the word granting his request through his friends, who then, on their return to the house, found the sick servant already cured (Luke vii. 10). If we have correctly shown the 'so great faith' of the centurion, and found in it the foundation of 'the great recompense of reward' (Heb. x. 35) on the part of Jesus,—that is, the *healing* of our Lord 'afar off' is the blessing on that faith which sees 'afar off' (Heb. xi. 13),—we have then found in this latter passage the doctrinal significance of this miracle. We do not lay any stress on the manifold mediation through which the request reached Jesus,—the captain pleading for his servant, the elders for the captain (see John xii. 21, 22),—but merely on the circumstance that our Lord helps 'at a distance.' He does not see the sick man, and is not seen by him; nevertheless the cure follows. The stream of His power goes out from Him, and reaches the point which He wills it to attain— ὅπου θέλει. His beneficent power reaches to all afar off, where any one trusts in Him with longing, to wheresoever a cry for help goes up to Him; a power which certainly pursues higher interests than that of curing the body only. In so far, the narrative contains at the same time a prophetical import, and has, according to this view, a relation to the later history of Cornelius. We are especially strengthened in this view by the words in which Matthew's account continues, though at the time these words may have been caused by the phrase 'not in Israel.' But if the members of the kingdom should come from the extremest distances,[1] they must have experienced first a working of the power and grace on the part of Him who, on His part, can work on all afar off, and make a communication of the blessing which is not conditional on bodily presence. We direct attention, lastly, to the conclusion of Luke's account. If, according to it, a personal connection between the captain and Christ never took place, neither at the beginning nor at the end, so the help which was asked for from the absent Lord was also received from His invisible hand, and thereby a link purely immaterial, but on that account so much the firmer, was established between giver and receiver.

If the narratives of the healing of the sick of the

[1] That this is the meaning of the expression 'from the east and from the west,' is testified by the comparison of the passage in Luke xiii. 29. In this latter passage the whole four quarters of the heavens are named in order to signify the *whole* earth. Here, however, the *two* represent mere distance. In other places in Scripture it is symbolized in this manner, as in Ps. ciii. 12 (compare also with ver. 11).

palsy and of the cleansing of the lepers represented symbolically certain treasures which are offered to men in the kingdom of God which is at hand, the history of the centurion at Capernaum teaches us that these treasures penetrate and reach wherever a desire for them is present. It was necessary for this end, that He who could and would bestow them should be *acknowledged*, and that the well-spring of His gracious power, now opened, should be sought. How, however, would it be, if this acknowledgment and this seeking His aid did not exist? There would then be need for the manifestation of a new power of the kingdom of heaven,—namely, the opening of the eyes of the blind.

THE HEALING OF THE BLIND.

There is no division in the region of the wonder-working of Jesus Christ where so many results have been attained by Strauss as in the one before us. He has with success directed his criticism against those who consider the cure of him that was born blind, narrated in John ix., as not meant by the evangelist in the sense of a real event. With similar ability has he shown that the history has also an ideal significance; perhaps in the interest of the latter, he should have drawn special attention to the penetrating force of the section, vers. 35-38. The result which he then draws from his generally successful exposition (pp. 420–432, Eng. transl. ii. 149–159), 'Thus the miracle in John is penetrated in all its features by the ideal spirit; it is throughout symbolical, and at the same time throughout real,' is a perfectly impregnable one. When he declares, notwithstanding this acknowledgment, that the narrative is an offshoot grown up from the root of the words of the prophet Isaiah

(xxxv. 5), it was certainly possible for him to do so with regard to the *fourth* Gospel, if he still maintained his supposition that it was only a novel with a special tendency. But the healings of the blind contained in the *synoptic* Gospels must cause him so much the greater difficulty, the more decidedly he on one side denies that the first three evangelists had devised their narratives in a figurative sense, and the more he loses on the other in these cases the weapon of harmonistic differences. There remains therefore to him only a very general reference to the miracles of Elijah and Elisha, as being similar to those which Jewish popular prejudice would expect from the Messiah. But from want of more certain materials, an attempt of this kind must fail most decidedly.

There would certainly be nothing to say against those who consider the healings of the blind, on the part of Jesus, as deeds of His compassion. Blindness was among the Jews felt as a heavy suffering. Compare the complaint in the book of Tobit, chap. v. 12: 'What joy shall I have who must sit in darkness, and cannot see the light of heaven?' Also the humane institutions which the law has provided for those deprived of sight (Deut. xxvii. 18). As Jesus had now appeared; as Simeon thankfully said, 'Mine eyes have seen Thy salvation;' and as our Lord Himself held those eyes blessed which saw *what* they saw; blindness presupposes the most sensible deprivation. At the same time, it is not alone the Johannine narrative, which by its commencing words, 'While I am in the world, I am the light of the world,' and by means of the sentence, 'I am come into the world for judgment, that they who do see shall be blind, and the blind shall see,' places it on a symbolical standpoint; but also the writings of the three first evangelists require us to view it in a similar manner. However painful the suffering of blindness was even in an earthly point of view, however much the fact so far symbolically entered into a higher region, that the blind man was not able to see the Christ that had appeared, it is quite another eye, it is the φῶς τὸ ἐν ἀνθρώπῳ, which looks upon our Lord as a Saviour. If this *inner* eye is not light, the sharpness of the bodily one avails nothing; if the former is bright, the want of the latter is supportable. After God had again spoken in Christ, 'Let there be light,' after the darkness and its power was broken, and the 'true light' had appeared in the world, 'that it may light every man,' it would be bright for all who had the spiritual eye open. But the rising from on high with its streaming light had visited those in vain, whose blind or crafty eye is not fitted to accept it; Matt. vi. 23, 'If the light that is in thee be darkness, how great is that darkness!' Thus the appearing light is a blessing only where 'the eye is single.' In the opposite case, a work of grace is needed to open the eyes of the blind. And our Lord *will* open them. He who *is* the Light, *makes* even the organ for its perception healthy. And for this work of His, His bodily healings of the blind are the symbols. The synoptic Gospels report to us three of this class of miracles. One is found only in Mark viii. 22-26; the second in Matthew alone, chap. ix. 27-31; while all three Gospels narrate the third, Matt. xx. 29, Mark x. 46, Luke xviii. 35; and lastly, we read in John the history of the cure of the man that was born blind.

The history of the cure narrated in Mark viii. 22 and following, draws attention to itself in a higher degree than the rest. The evangelist places us at Bethsaida Julias, lying on the eastern shore of the lake of Gennesareth. A blind man is brought to Jesus, in order that He may touch and heal him. Jesus is ready to do so. The preparations for the deed as well as its accomplishment are manifold and peculiar. The simple touching of the blind man had been asked for, but our Lord takes him by the hand and leads him out of the village. The taking by the hand and the leading out is easily explained as such, for the blind needs a leader; and here has he found a masterly one, as Israel saith to Moses, 'Be thou our eye in the desert.' Our regard rests with pleasure on the picture, as He who is the true light leads by the hand the man walking in darkness. But why now specially this leading out? Why did Jesus not heal him on the spot? On what grounds must He be with him alone? We should be in an evil plight if we had to make our choice between a twofold issue. Bengel's supposition is the best of any which has been considered: 'Cœco visum recuperanti lætior erat aspectus cœli et operum divinorum in natura, quam operum humanorum in pago.' On the other hand, Strauss sees in this transaction the exposition of the mystery, which was not to be performed before the uninitiated (p. 429). But we need not decide between these alternatives. There is a better answer possible. In fact, we meet with the same or at least very similar conduct of Jesus once, but certainly only once, besides—in the narrative of the deaf and dumb man (Mark vii. 33, 'He took him aside from the multitude'). Now, as we find in both these cases the use of the spittle on the person of the sick, we may seek in that alone the cause of the leading out; but in how far the use of the medium formed a motive for seclusion, is more easily felt than explained. As Jesus does not here, as in John ix., spit on the earth in order to make clay with which He anointed the eye that was extinguished,—as He rather spits in the eye of the blind man, as well as on the tongue of the deaf and dumb,—every one will feel that there the presence of witnesses would have been disagreeable and inconvenient. We shall certainly plead guilty to being unable to answer very exactly the further question, why our Lord this time used spittle for the cure. We know that this practice was not unusual in eye diseases among the Jews. But we also know that our Lord cured *other* blind men by His mere word, and that He had no necessity for this medium to attain His object. Therefore we are in a position to oppose the assertion of Strauss, that this feature is not to be understood from the history of medicine, but from that of superstition (his quotation in support of this, from Tacitus, he must have valued very highly, as he uses it twice to the fullest extent); or we can at least make a conjecture which will have some claim to our consideration. It is this: in the 23d verse the evangelist narrates that Jesus spit on the eyes (ὄμματα) of the blind, while in the 25th verse he writes that our Lord put His hands on the eyes (ὀφθαλμούς). This spitting on the ὄμματα, and putting His hands on the ὀφθαλμοί, must not be overlooked. Ὄμμα is not quite the same as ὀφθαλμός, but both have the same relation one to another as ἀκοή has to οὖς. Ὄμμα is more the inner power of seeing: on the other hand, ὀφθαλμός is the organ of which this power makes use.[1] The spitting thus signifies an energetic influence, which restores the power of seeing which was extinct, while the hands

---

[1] The expression ὄμμα does not occur in any other place in the New Testament (for the reading ὀμμάτων of some MSS. in Matt. xx. 34 has no claim to be acknowledged; its origin is not difficult to recognise). It is rare even in the Septuagint; we find it only in a few passages in the Proverbs. In classical Greek there may be no difference between the more poetical ὄμμα and the ὀφθαλμός (used by prose writers), as both are derived from the same ὄπτομαι, the former in the perfect, the latter in the aorist form. But when the New Testament this once makes use of the expression other-

only make the organ correct. If this supposition is not unfounded, it makes us disposed to consider the whole event as symbolical. This inclination increases, however, into a feeling of necessity when we consider the striking manner of the cure, which we will further dwell on. While usually in the cures by Jesus the complete result is accomplished at once, in this case it is after a repeated act of touching on the part of our Lord that the suffering is completely relieved. At first the blind man could see only *something*. After Jesus asked him 'if he saw aught,' if he perceived the power of sight again returning, he answered, 'I see men as trees walking.' Thus he sees forms, but only because they move can he conclude that they are men; otherwise he might think they were trees: he is still wanting in clearness of recognition, and in just means of measurement. He is subject to optical delusions. The antithesis of it, the τηλαυγῶς in connection with the ἀποκατεστάθη; the restoration pointing partly to the healthy normal condition. It is evident from the expressions, as well as from the circumstance that the blind man knew the form of a man and of a tree, that he was not born blind. The etymon of τηλαυγῶς leads to the conception of distance, 'shining in the distance.' But even in the Old Testament the expression is used simply to show clearness and plainness; see Isa. xix. 9. In fact, it shows the lightning flash shining brilliantly in the eyes, Ps. xviii. 14. The question is now: Why did our Lord cure so *gradatim?* why did

---

wise foreign to it, ὄμμα, and when we see here the ὀφθαλμός follow soon after, there can be no question of an exchange of significations without intention, or in the mere interest of change. If we compare the narrative akin to it in Mark viii., it is said also there that our Lord put His finger into the ὦτα of the suffering one, while we read afterwards that the ears (ἀκοαί) were opened. As here, ἀκοή must signify the sense of hearing, and ὦτα the organ for it; thus it resembles the relation of the ὄμμα and the ὀφθαλμός.

He not here, as in other cases, let the complete result immediately appear?

That this blindness was more deeply rooted than was generally the case, we willingly grant; but it is impossible for us to acknowledge that these deeper roots necessitated a greater expenditure of power on the part of the helper. Even here, the suffering would have been taken away by a mere εἰπεῖν λόγῳ on the part of Jesus, if this had been His intention. Strauss speaks of an 'endeavour which failed' of Mark to bring the miracle down to the lowest conception; we speak of an action of our Lord purposely intended which the evangelist has truly narrated. Scripture testifies often of a blindness which hinders men from perceiving the benefits and the objects of salvation in the kingdom of heaven that is at hand. Thus St. Paul complains of the blindness of Israel, of the veil that is before their eyes, so that they cannot see clearly God on the face of Jesus—2 Cor. iii. 14; Rom. xi. 25; Eph. iv. 18; and the presumption is forced on us, that the gradual action of the cure of the blind man before us is meant to signify the similar course in the taking away of that spiritual blindness,—a gradual course which it takes, if not in all, yet generally in most cases. It may occur that our Lord will with one stroke take away the veil from their eyes, so that the man can see all things clearly on the spot.

We have a striking example in the apostle himself, in whom the opening of the spiritual eye happened in a marvellous manner with a temporary bodily blindness. When in Antioch he again opened his bodily eye, he was able to see all things clearly in the higher region; in him there is no question of a development of perception; suddenly it was as if scales had fallen from his inner sight. However, that was not the rule, but an exception,—an exception which we understand in him who was thereto called, that he should 'open the eyes of the blind, and turn them from darkness to light' (Acts xxvi. 18). As for the *light in general*, that is seen immediately on the blind eye being opened; but that all things should be recognised in this light clearly and justly, without deception or error, as it is stated in relation to the man cured in the narrative before us, 'he saw all things clearly,' everything which came within the reach of his vision, all things in the world of appearance, thus the adoption of all objects, relations, ordinances in the kingdom; to do this much was wanting. 'In Thy light we see light;' that is, as a rule, the result of the gradual process. In a certain sense, it does not in general attain its perfection during earthly life. St. Paul testifies, 'Now we see through a glass darkly . . . now we know in part' (1 Cor. xiii. 12). But in one aspect, there is a clear acknowledgment of heavenly things even in the present time; in fact, the Son of God can be seen with uncovered face. See John ix. 38; 2 Cor. iv. 6: 'God hath shined in our hearts, to give the light of the knowledge of the glory of God in the face of Jesus Christ.'

The representation which we have just made is strikingly justified by the context which follows in St. Mark. There it is said, in ver. 27 and following, that after Jesus had left Bethsaida with His disciples, He asked them what people thought of Him. And they answered Him that some considered Him as John the Baptist, others as Elias, others as one of the prophets, but that they themselves acknowledged Him as the Christ. Can a more suitable representation of the gradual process of the healing of the blind be wished for than is given here? Those who imagined in Christ John the Baptist; or Elias, or one of the prophets, saw something of the truth; but it was only *something* of it,—they saw men as trees, while the disciples saw clearly, when they saw in faith the Son of God. But before this even *they* had not recognised Him, but had only then *learnt* to know Him as such, and that was through Him, Jesus Himself. He made *them* also see gradually. And even in them, until the last moment of their earthly communion with Him, we still find deficiencies and obscurations of vision; their question in the hour of His ascension to heaven gives testimony to this. Lastly, in order to express the concluding recommendation to our criticism of the miracle of Jesus before us, we would point out the remarkable coincidence between the conclusion of the history of the healing (ver. 25) and the end of the conversation with the disciples (ver. 30). In both cases the command is to be silent, and to possess in advance a quiet joy in the light which has now been manifested to them.

This commandment to be silent we find not only in the narrative just considered, but also in the similar one given by Matthew (chap. ix. 27-31). We proceed now to this latter, with the conviction which we have already sufficiently justified, that *it* also can be conceived from the symbolical standpoint. Our Lord was in the way when two blind men called after Him with the petition for compassion. But only after He was in the house does He let them come before Him, and their cure results from it. The prominent point is their address, 'Son of David.' This was by no means in such use as is commonly supposed. In the evangelical history we meet with it very rarely. It is not to be found in the fourth Gospel; and in the first three only in the third healing of the blind, in Matt. xx. 30,[1] then in the mouth of the Canaanitish

---

[1] An opinion has been founded on the strength (in itself weak) of the same expression occurring in both accounts of Matthew of healings of the blind (chap. xx. 30 and chap. ix. 27), that the one narrative is a mere

woman, and lastly, in the jubilant cry of the people at the triumphal entry of Jesus into the town of Jerusalem. In one sense the Apostle Paul has justified it; in another Jesus Himself (Matt. xxii. 41) has rendered it doubtful. How did the blind men understand it? It is just to effect this, to bring it to their consciousness, that our Lord lets them wait until He has entered into the house; and as there was now an opportunity for conversation, He asks them, 'Believe ye that I am able to do such a thing?' and they answer, 'Yea, Lord.' On this follows the granting of their request: 'According to your faith be it unto you.' We can only understand this 'Son of David,' which is changed into a 'Yea, Lord,' and the question of our Lord, with the declaration following, 'According to your faith be it unto you,' from a symbolical standpoint.

This long delay, this proving the meaning of their address (we compare this proof with the proof of the meaning of the address 'Good Master' on the part of the rich young man), and the granting of their request after it had been proved,—all this points to the similar process at the opening of the spiritual eye too evidently for us not to look into the deed through the symbol. To purely grammatico-historical exposition this result will be doubtful; but it is really no secret that this interpretation, in its onesidedness and arbitrariness, rather conceals than unveils the true sense of Scripture.[1]

variation of the other. It is not, however, perceived that the evangelist, in the 8th and 9th chapters, wishes to report an unchronological but rich painting of the Galilean miracle-working of Jesus, while the collected miracles recorded by him later are arranged partly in strict chronological order, and partly according to the interest which arises from them.

[1] Even in this case we cannot explain the strict commandment of Jesus in Matt. ix. 30, 'He strictly charged them, saying, See that no man know it,' on the mere intention to avoid a possible tumult of the people. How-

It is the same with the third narrative of the healing of a blind man, which is common to all three evangelists, and which also all refer to one and the same time, immediately before the entrance of Jesus into the capital. Mark calls the name of the blind man Bartimæus, son of Timæus.[1] On the way, in which our Lord walked from Jericho to Jerusalem, he sat and begged. Instead of troubling ourselves about the unimportant discrepancy that Mark and Luke narrate only about this one blind man, while Matthew speaks of two (which is even reconciled by the circumstance that Bartimæus comes out as the one specially known), we would rather observe the difference of the conduct of Jesus in this and in the case just considered. Here our Lord lets the blind man—whose unwearied repeated cry, 'Son of David, have mercy on me,' the bystanders sought in vain to stop—come immediately before Him, and asks him, What *wilt* thou that I should do to thee? 'Rabboni, that I might receive my sight.' And Jesus said, 'Thy faith hath made thee whole;'

---

ever, it is brought into a satisfactory light by means of the supposition that our Lord, by His miracle, partly showed allegorically, and partly manifested in reality on these two blind men, His power to open the inner eye. He who immediately spreads abroad the recognition which had just dawned on him, that Jesus is the Christ, receives from this spreading abroad neither a blessing to himself, nor does it spread this blessing on others. As is known, our Lord, after the acknowledgment of Peter, expressly prohibited the disciples from telling any one that He was the Christ (Matt. xvi. 20). We would strive no further with those who think they are able to explain even this commandment (understood solely from the standpoint which we have shown) on the understanding that it was to contradict the fanatical expectations of the Messiah.

[1] The explicitness with which the evangelist has designated the blind Bartimæus as the son of Timæus has not prevented Strauss from expressing the wonderful conjecture that the root of the name must be sought for in the ἐπετίμων of the 48th verse. Some expositors have started the question whence Mark knew the name, and on what grounds he specified so designedly the father of the blind man; but in a similar manner they would have to settle why he, Mark, and he alone, shows Simon of Cyrene to be the father of Alexander and Rufus.

and he followed Him. For the third and last time we meet here with this formula; but as we, in the history of the ten lepers, were compelled to an interpretation other than the literal one, so even here we must do similarly. If we connect closely the question of Jesus, 'What wilt thou that I should do to thee?' with the explanation following, 'Thy faith hath made thee whole,' we should perceive that the thoughts of our Lord were directed to something else than merely bodily help. Even the term σέσωκεν does not suit exactly the reattainment of the physical power of sight. We have here neither a freeing from a torturing pain, nor even the taking away of the peril of death; and one could hardly resolve to speak of the σωτηρία of a blind man that is healed. Involuntarily one thinks of a different kind of salvation. And to that view we are most decidedly prompted, when we read in ver. 52 that this blind man followed Jesus. We surmise the σωτηρία is the following of Him who has said, 'Whosoever follows me will have the light of life.' The 'that I might receive my sight,' which follows the question, 'What wilt thou,' is considered by our Lord in a higher sense; and in this He assures him that his faith has obtained for the suppliant a σωτηρία which he will find more and more complete in the faithfulness of his following after Him.

With the miracles of Jesus on the blind, there is another work of His hand which stands in the same close connection,—a supposition strengthened by the saying of the prophet: 'Then shall the eyes of the blind be opened, *and* the ears of the deaf be unstopped' (Isa. xxxv. 5); yea, even as is to be presumed from the explanations themselves of our Lord (Matt. xiii. 16): 'Blessed are your eyes, for they see; and your ears, for they hear;' and Mark viii. 18: 'Having eyes, see ye not? and having ears, hear ye not?' Here also the subject is the restoration of an organ for the reception of the revealed treasures of the kingdom of heaven.

THE HEALING OF THE DEAF AND DUMB.—MARK VII. 31-37.

If we are quite prepared to hear this narrative considered as a myth which has arisen out of the word of the prophet, 'that the deaf should hear, and that the tongue of the dumb should be loosed,' it will still surprise us to hear that it is the true sample of an account of a miracle in accordance with the taste of the second evangelist. 'Here,' says Strauss (p. 445, Eng. transl. ii. 178), 'Mark was performing a task in which he took particular pleasure . . . the mysterious taking a part . . . the Aramaic word used as a sort of talisman . . . the description full length . . . lastly, the depicting of the effect.' Enough, he wishes to show that Jesus has herewith done all which was to be expected of the Messiah, according to the passage in the prophet. We gain by this a complete definition for our problem. Before, however, we commence our attempt to solve it, a twofold remark is needed. First, it is certain that we cannot in the very least consider this deed of our Lord as a mere proof of His mercy. This sufferer had no conception of the misery in which he was imprisoned. He did not know his deficiencies, because he had borne them from his youth up, and consequently had not the power of reflection. If, on this very account, he appears so much the more a fit object of pity,—of a pity which led him to the Helper,—it is because the root of his suffering grew principally in the spiritual region; and even the witnesses of the miracle seem to have felt this, when they afterwards acknowledge, 'He hath done all things well.' They see Jesus not only as the helper in earthly need, but as a

Saviour in the most comprehensive sense. Secondly, they are not two self-existing wants, by the side of and independent of each other, which have been united,—on one side deafness, and on the other dumbness,—but are in this case especially inseparable. The general connection between both sufferings is indeed shown by the circumstance that κωφός (dull, from κόπτω), in classical as well as in biblical Greek, signifies 'dumb' as well as deaf. In the case before us it is called 'deafness' only. But when it is asserted of the deaf man that he was μογιλάλος, it is not said that he was *also* dumb; but the κωφός shows the primitive want, of which the μογιλάλος was the natural and necessary consequence. Μογιλάλος does not mean 'stammering' of a heavy tongue, but it signifies (the Septuagint rendering of אִלֵּם) the inability to express articulate words, so as to be understood by others; and this was just the result of the deafness.

We must allow that there is sometimes a dumbness, in which the faculty of hearing has been intact. Later we shall meet with a case where the *mere* being dumb occurs (see Luke xi. 11): 'And Jesus cast out a devil, and it was dumb. And it came to pass, when the devil was gone out, the dumb spake.' But this was only a temporary deprivation of the power of speech, which was effected in this case by *Satan*, just as the tongue of Zacharias was placed by God beyond the power of use, until the circumcision of the child John. Here, however, we have an absolute binding of it, and its significance is seen from the preceding closing of the ear. In fact, *hearing* cannot be learnt by man; he is born with *this* faculty, as with the power of seeing. But he must *learn* to speak; he can of himself only utter sounds, not speak words. And by what means does he learn the latter? By the hearing alone. Whoever is born deaf cannot learn to speak; he only possesses the inborn faculty of pronouncing sounds, but as to speaking he remains μογιλάλος.

The method of our Lord's healing takes full account of the origin of the dumbness. First, He lays His finger on the deaf ear, then He spits on the tongue. In the same manner we read of the sufferer: first his ears were opened, and then 'the string of his tongue was loosed, and he spake plain,' that is, he spoke really; he uttered words. No one will object that, according to this view, the opening of the ear had been alone necessary. It was not the intention merely that the sufferer should be placed in a position *to learn* to speak. No; this learning was to be spared him; he was to *be able* to speak at once. Consequently, then, the result also appears connected in a double sense: ἐλάλει, he *spoke*, what can be called *speaking;* and ὀρθῶς, quite normally, as if he had always been able to do so. No one, on hearing him, remarked any deficiency; he gave no impression that he was bringing into use with difficulty a power only just received; but his speech was at once plain and articulate,—the ὀρθῶς corresponding with the τηλαυγῶς in the case of the blind man that was healed in chap. viii.

There is, however, a still deeper sense hidden behind this double action of our Lord on the tongue as on the ear of the sufferer,—a sense which we discern only by recognising the symbolical side of the miracle. It must be here borne in mind, that the apostles, although for a long time they had heard aright, experienced at the same time a special dedication of their tongues by the fire of the Holy Spirit.

We pass on to the main point, and commence by pointing out what is related of Jesus,—for it stands isolated, and occurs nowhere else in Scripture,—' that He, sighing, looked up to heaven,' *after* touching the sufferer, and *before* His commanding word. That 'Jesus sighed' we are told in other places, and that 'He raised His eyes to heaven' occurs still oftener; but a sigh *before a miracle* is peculiar to this passage. We must not think that we have a parallel in the passage (John xi. 35) where our Lord weeps before the raising of Lazarus. Weeping and sighing differ widely. In accordance with Heb. xiii. 17, we can oppose *grief* to *joy*, but joy itself is a conception with many meanings. There is a psychical χαρά and a χαρὰ ἐν πνεύματι ἁγίῳ. As to what the 'sighing' signifies, we must oppose those expositors who explain it in a pathological sense. Meyer praises unjustly the solution of Euthym. Zig.: ἐπικαμπτόμενος τοῖς πάθεσιν τοῦ ἀνθρώπου; and Bengel errs greatly in judging *suspirium est* πάθος *cordis*. Holy Scripture points to a very different result. We read also in Mark viii. 12 of a sighing of our Lord, when the Pharisees tempted Him, and demanded a sign from heaven; but the evangelist expressly adds, 'in His spirit.' Even the groanings in Rom. viii. are by the Apostle Paul referred to the Spirit. They are not witnesses of the weakness in which the πάθη sink, but expressions of the Spirit—of the Spirit πρόθυμον (which excludes the ἀσθένεια of the flesh).

When James (in chap. v. 9 of his epistle) writes, 'Grudge not one against another,' and strengthens his command by pointing to the day of judgment, it is evident that he judges the sigh as the strongest accusation that could be pronounced before the Judge. We have therefore, in this case, not to think of a pity of Jesus for the misery of the individual standing before Him (and so much the less so, as in the 33d verse the healing has already been completed); but His sigh is the most expressive picture to place symbolically before our eyes the appearance of this κωφός. And, in fact, there was here before Him the most speaking, the most impressive picture, not of the spiritual misery of man, but of the persistency with which men remain in its bonds, and pass by Him who can loose them from the evil magic. Still more is it a picture of the opposition which our Lord found to His work, from the want of receptivity for His gifts, and for the object of His appearance on earth.[1]

We say the *most speaking* picture of it. It *appears* indeed to be a mere, at least an unimportant variation, when by the side of the complaint of blinded eyes that of insensible hearing is also heard; but in reality there is a discernible difference. In fact, if we are asked as to the higher significance of the one or the other, the balance unquestionably leans in favour of the hearing. All honour to the eye, but the ear is more important. The superiority of the latter over the former is fully recognised in the region of the senses. We can close the eye if we wish to do so; it is so formed that it can be closed, and in sleep it closes of itself. On the other hand, we can only stop the ear by means of mechanical and unnatural force (Acts vii. 57); even in sleep it stands open, and is therefore at all times the ready medium to banish sleep. (There is much food for thought, according to this view, in the passage full of meaning in Eph. v. 14.) But still more evident is it that the spiritual perception is effected more through the ear than through the eye. The gospel directs itself to the ear. Blessed are they who hear the word. Where there is no hearing there is no salvation, for *faith* comes by *hearing*. Thus, when our Lord sees the deaf man, whose spiritual life is stagnated in conse-

---

[1] Meyer reproaches Hofmann for reading between the lines the thought that 'Jesus sees in the deaf and dumb a picture of the people incompetent to hear the faith and to speak the confession.' But really Hofmann has considered the work of Jesus from the right point of view. The only thing we are doubtful of is, whether he has not laid an unjustifiable stress upon the ὀρθῶς λαλεῖν. The point of difficulty is manifestly the hearing.

quence of this want, it is to Him a symbol of the closed ear of the world, which does not perceive His word, and therefore does not receive it. And if He comes forward and opens his ear, this is for *us* the symbol of His power to effect the spiritual hearing, and to open the heart for His gift. But for Him who did this sign, there remained still cause enough deeply to sigh. Then, if in *this* case His Ephphatha meets with no hindrance, He knows that He will often have to sound it in vain in a higher region; for even almightiness is powerless before unwillingness to repent.

Only in this view of the case is the narrative conceivable by us. But certainly we must not extend this explanation beyond the boundary which we have drawn. It is unwarrantable to say that Jesus sighed over the sins of the tongue which would still be committed by men, and more specially by him whom He had cured. When we take into consideration the circumstance that Jesus at the same time ordered silence, thus teaching that the tongue should be held in check; it has been on one side overlooked that this silence was imposed in no way on the healed man himself, but on the *people* standing around—'He charged *them*,' ver. 36;[1] and on the other, that it stands as such in no other connection with the deed, but as impressing that the stress is here to be laid not on the tongue, but on the ear; for there is certainly no question as to the right use of the tongue.

We close with a consideration which will certainly

[1] The command in the 36th verse, 'not to spread abroad,' has here another motive, and is to be understood otherwise than in the similar cases in which we have hitherto met with it. In the earlier cases it was each time directed to the *receiver* of the benefit; it must therefore be considered and understood always under this point of view. But here, where our Lord turned to the *people*, to the witnesses of the miracle, another key to the understanding of the prohibition must be used. And which? Now no other than that which Matthew supplies us with in chap. xii. 16-21.

contribute something to recommend our view. It is that the Gospel of Mark is especially the one which narrates the most numerous and the most urgent exhortations to hear aright in the spiritual sense. Compare chap. iv. 23 ff. The apophthegm with which this passage commences, 'If any man have ears to hear, let him hear,' does occur also in the other evangelists; even Luke has the following words, βλέπετε τί ἀκούετε. But in Mark alone is found the parable immediately connected with it, that the earth of itself brings forth fruit after it has received the seed. The pith of the parable is this, that by hearing all salvation is communicated; that what is heard is to be heard aright,—that is the beginning of all wisdom. To this it is well to add that the same evangelist gives us a narrative which declares the same truth symbolically.

The sighing of Jesus is caused by the fruitless endeavours of the sower, caused by the closed ear of the people, to sow the seed of the word. His miracle, however, shows His power to open the ear in case no pride of self withholds him. Even as to what concerns the hearing and the being deaf, He has come for judgment into the world. And as in John ix. He attacks those blind to the word, saying, 'I have appeared for judgment, in order that those who see not shall see, and those who see shall become blind;' so we have a perfect right to form a similar explanation of the history of the healing of the deaf and dumb: 'that I am come for judgment, that those who do not hear may hear, and that those that hear may become dumb.'

If, in all the narratives in the group which we have been considering, we have placed in the foreground this symbolical intention, our meaning was not that our Lord in these miracles always *represented* those higher treasures He could and would bestow. But if not in all, in many cases, what He showed *allegorically*, He gave also at the same time in reality. In the history of the sick of the palsy this is evident; the sick man receives in reality the forgiveness of sins—what was shown symbolically in his cure. However, we must maintain that in all the cases of this group the symbolical meaning is the predominant one. Quite otherwise is it with those miracles of Jesus in the group on the consideration of which we are about to enter.

IV.

THIRD GROUP.

MIRACLES OF JESUS CONSIDERED AS WITNESSES OF THE POWER OF THE KINGDOM OF HEAVEN WHICH HAS BECOME EFFECTIVE.

We have already pointed out the sense in which we use the expression 'witness.' A witness is more than a mere sign, more even than a symbol pointing beyond itself. It bears testimony to something already existing. Those miracles which we include under this category are *real proofs of Jesus as the Redeemer*. They do not show what He *can* and what He *will* do, but they manifest Him in the fulness of His glory, as the Lord of the kingdom, who, as such, acts with majesty.

The kingdom which was come near in Him, could not simply take *any* place on the earth; it must fight and must gain by force its *real* position there, and this in a combat against him who rules in the darkness of this world, and who (Matt. iv. 9) said to Jesus, that the world with all its glory was his, for he could both promise them and present them. Our Lord did not now receive it from his hand as a fee, wishing to take it from him by the overpowering of its prince; thus a fight must necessarily break out, which will grow more and more intense, and at last become decisive. We know that not until the moment of the death of Jesus does the concluding decisive combat occur, as our Lord Himself, in John xiv. 30, says, in view of His departure, that the prince of the world cometh, although he has nothing in Him. But this last decisive act not only does not exclude, but in reality *presupposes* that movements on the other side have taken place, where the scene of action was not in the centre, but merely on the outskirts. Scripture shows the victory of the Son of God over the prince of this world in a double view, the one *negative*—He has overthrown him, has taken from him the reigns of government; see John xii. 31: 'Now shall the prince of this world be cast out'—and the other positive: He has on His part now brought life and incorruptible being to light (2 Tim. i. 10). It ascribes the negative side more to the account of His death; the positive to that of His resurrection 'through death.' It says in Hebrews ii. 14, Jesus 'had destroyed the power of him who had the power of death, that is, the devil;' and since He has arisen from the dead, it is taught that He gives eternal life to all who believe on Him. Now, if there should have been given some real *witnesses* of this working of His death and resurrection during His earthly appearance, these can only consist in the fact that He at one time accomplished deeds by which Satan was cast out (Luke x. 17, 18); and at another, deeds by means of which his effective power was taken away, and that of his opponent substituted. The former are the drivings out of devils; the latter, the raisings from the dead.

THE LIBERATION OF THOSE POSSESSED.

It is this class of miracles within which Strauss has made the most concessions. Just as Schleiermacher (*Leben Jesu*, p. 219) most willingly lets them pass, Strauss declares (p. 446), that if Jesus has really cured the sick, it must have been chiefly demoniacs; at least, among all the cures which have been ascribed to Him, *these* have in themselves more of natural possibility and historical probability than others. He adds, indeed, to settle the question, that he will not say that even any single one of the narratives related gives a true historical report, and thus he leaves to each one only so much reality as his psychological views allow him.

But here we have not to deal with Strauss alone; others, who in nowise share his views on other points, have represented the persons on whom our Lord has performed these deeds, in such a manner, that we must at once express our dissent from it. It is said that the so-called demoniacs are persons with a characteristically natural illness, whose sufferings, according to the view of the time, were supposed to be founded, not in an abnormal physical organism, and also not in natural disturbances of the psychical habit, but in devilish possession; that, in truth, there lie here before us only forms of mania, epilepsy, melancholy cases of contraction, temporary dumbness, and blindness. How these theologians can explain their position as to the positive side of the question, that is, how they can believe that they are able to put aside the difficulty, that they are contradicting the plain meaning of the evangelist himself, they give us no information. But it will certainly be acknowledged that the biblical writers knew very well when they saw natural sicknesses, and they were quite able to distinguish them from cases of demoniacal possession. They speak *also* of natural blindness, dumbness, paralysis; they also knew of a natural mania, as was the case in the Old Testament (Deut. xxviii. 28), שִׁגָּעוֹן, where such madness is referred to. If they narrate of blind, of dumb, of lame, who were possessed, they will have had good grounds for believing them to have had no mere natural sickness.

But let us see how it stands with the negative side of the opposite assertion. There are four arguments which have been used against the reality of a demoniacal possession. In the first place, it is remembered that in the whole of the Old Testament there occurs no single example of the kind; and secondly, stress is laid on the fact, that in the present time nothing similar is known. We will stop for the consideration of these two points. The facts stated are both right; the question is, whether a sufficient examination would not destroy the force of the argument. Let us try all the cases where possession by demons appears in our Gospels. Where are they found? It is marvellous that they never, not even once, occur in Judæa, the centre of the theocracy, but always in the extreme borders of Palestine; partly in heathen countries, partly in those strips of land of Palestine which bordered on a heathen region where the inhabitants dwelt among the heathen, in Galilee of the Gentiles, high in the north, or in the extreme east. Let us examine this closer. Those castings out of demons which have been reported in detail to us, are performed partly on real Gentiles, partly at least on Gentile ground and territory.

The daughter of the Canaanitish woman is characterized by this definition as a Gentile; the chief narrative of the possessed at Gadara has a purely Gentile stage, for Josephus expressly tells us that only a few Jews lived there, as in the Diaspora; that the real inhabitants were Gentiles. But the other demoniacs also with whom we meet are found in Upper Galilee, mostly in the country of Capernaum, on the road to Damascus. Hence the 1st chapter of Mark, which especially describes the working of Jesus performed in this part of Galilee, frequently mentions His driving out demons. See Mark i. 27, 32, 34, 39. In Jewry proper, we do not meet with any appearance of demoniacs. It is well known that the Jews considered the whole of the Gentile world as subject to Satan, while they looked upon themselves as the peculiar people of Jehovah. And this was no presumptuous view, as it had the truth at its foundation, that the Lord had really chosen Israel as a 'peculiar people,' and that it was to be from Zion that the 'shining light' should be extended over the Gentiles.

The kingdoms of the world which Satan, in Matt. iv. 8, shows to the Saviour, were the Gentile countries. Here only he reigned with undisputed power, while in Israel Jehovah was acknowledged and worshipped as the Lord. Thus it is that these manifestations, by means of which Satan announced his right of possession (see the significant expression *possessed*), only occurred on Gentiles, and only in those places where heathenism possessed more or less influence over Judaism. This latter could (especially at the time of its strict exclusion from heathenism under the Old Testament dispensation) show nothing of these manifestations. That they did not occur later, that they in fact never occurred any more in after times, will not be remarkable to those who believe with the apostle that Jesus was come that He might destroy the works of the devil, and who are convinced that He has attained that end. In the first centuries of the Christian Church, we still continually meet with demoniacs. There was, it is known, an ecclesiastical office of Exorcists, who drove out the unclean spirits.[1] The

---

[1] The remark of the *Apostolic Constitutions* (chap. viii. 26), that an Exorcist cannot be chosen, as it is the gift of the free grace of God in Christ, hardly places the office in question (it is not much different with the catechetical work); at any rate, it *justifies* the otherwise assured acceptation of a complete exorcising of possessed on the part of the Church

fact that this appears especially in the Gentile Christian communities, and disappears when the Church has overcome paganism, casts a confirmatory light on the view we have just taken.

In the *third place*, objection is taken against the reality of demoniacal possessions, from the fact that cures of such evils were performed at the time of Jesus by others as well as by Himself and His disciples; for in Matt. xii. 27 our Lord asks the Pharisees, 'By whom, then, do your sons drive out the demons?' This fact is undenied. Apart from the passage just quoted, it is attested by Josephus. This historian reports, in the 8th Book of the *Antiquities*, chap. ii. par. 5, in the history of Solomon (Bekker's edition, vol. ii. p. 163), 'God gave him to know the art against demons for the service and advantage of men.' And he continues to narrate of a certain Eleazar, who, in the presence of Vespasian, cured in the most convincing manner by means of a magic ring, and of Solomonic magical formula, a man that was *possessed*. But it is difficult to comprehend how any earnest doubt can be founded upon this. The sons of the Pharisees in the passage in St. Matthew are Jews, who devoted themselves to the driving out of demons, made a profession of it, perhaps made journeys for the purpose, just as other Pharisees, according to Matt. xxiii., gave themselves up to the hunting up of proselytes. But that there were such Jewish exorcists, professional or privileged ones, is of no further significance than that there were Jewish *physicians*.

It would enter in the mind of no one to doubt the miraculous cures of Jesus on paralytics, dropsical

---

and in its name. If the demoniacal, as such, is taken out of the Bible, the view held by the ancient Church of the continuance of such like appearances must be explained as superstitious; in fact, we must decide that it, with its Sunday prayers for the Energumens, was founded in fundamental error.

people, those with an issue of blood, or sick with fever, on the ground that even the Jews had combated these diseases with *their* means, perhaps now and again with a good result; therefore no conclusion should be drawn against the reality of the driving out of demons by Christ, from the fact that we hear of similar endeavours on the part of the Pharisees. At the same time, we do not perceive in the least any *result* from them. We put aside the account of Josephus: every one perceives what he aims at. But even the passage in Matt. xii. 27 does not assert that the scholars of the Pharisees had really driven out devils; the ἐν τίνι ἐκβάλλουσιν may really only signify the endeavour; the ἐκβάλλειν, in fact, points to the act, not to the effect. However, we are often told in Scripture of *fruitless* attempts which have been made in this region. We leave on one side the passage, Mark ix. 18. For if it is here said of the disciples of Jesus, 'they could not,' they *were not able* to heal the demoniacal son of the beseeching father, we must seek for the cause, according to the explanation of our Lord, in their 'want of faith.' However, we point so much the more confidently to Acts xix. 13. There it is said that by the hands of the Apostle Paul many great deeds had been done in Asia; in fact, at his command the 'evil spirits' went out. In consequence of this, some of the neighbouring Jewish exorcists, namely, seven sons of a chief priest Sceva, on their part, said to the demoniacs, 'We adjure thee by Jesus whom Paul preacheth;' not only did they receive the surly answer, 'Jesus I know, and Paul I know, but who are ye?' but at the same time the person possessed leapt on them, and so ill-used them, that they fled away naked and wounded.

Fourthly, as the most striking argument against the reality of the driving out of demons, is pointed out the silence which John observes on this point; which silence is so much the more expressive, the more the fourth Gospel is considered to give the conquering of Satan as the Messiah's special object. When an exegetical writer like Meyer gives this opinion, we wonder that he has not appreciated better the passage in Mark ix. 38. Here it is in fact John who makes the complaint to Jesus that some one had driven out devils without being His disciple. He had thus entered on a work to which only the Messiah and His disciples were called. From this it follows that John also considered the driving out of demons as a specifically Messianic problem which Jesus solved. Undoubtedly the fact that the fourth Gospel narrates no driving out of demons is explained, and that sufficiently, by the generally accepted fact that John is especially sparing in the relation of miracles, and that he reports no cures of lepers, of dumb or of deaf persons. It needs this explanation so much the more, as the fourth Gospel uses not unfrequently the expression 'to have a devil' (chap. vii. 20, viii. 48-52, x. 20), but always merely in the sense of 'not being right in the understanding,' and never in the sense of the synoptics. Wherein lies the explanation? The fact that in this Gospel no demoniacal cures occur, is to Strauss a sure sign of its unauthenticity. To a disciple of Jesus, he continues (p. 454, Eng. transl. ii. p. 192), the driving out of demons which really and undoubtedly occurred, could not possibly be unknown. But it may be conceivable that the author of the fourth Gospel did not wish to know anything of them, as it would not have been in good taste to have mentioned 'demons, and expulsion of demons, at the period, in the district, and the state of cultivation in which and for which he wrote.' 'The whole thing had come into such discredit, by means of magicians and impostors, that it appeared most desirable to keep Jesus aloof from the whole of their department.' This treatment of Strauss is strong, but still stronger does the intelligence appear that between the 5th and 6th chapters of the fourth Gospel ' a portion has been lost, in which would have occurred the account of an expulsion of a devil.'[1] The want of demoniacal cures in John can be cleared up more satisfactorily. In fact, the fourth Gospel also represents Jesus as engaged in a fight against Satan. And in reality, no other Gospel testifies to it so often and so designedly as this. But it keeps in sight a certain side of the combat—the hidden one, that which does not appear, and which cannot be represented by deeds. John does not speak of the subjection of the power of Satan, but of his moral overthrow; he does not depict the combat which is waged on the outskirts, but that which occurs in the centre. First, our Lord appears in this fourth Gospel, not as He who fights with the *ministers* of Satan, but as the combatant against the very person of the adversary himself. Ἔρχεται ὁ ἄρχων τοῦ κόσμου . . . νῦν ἐκβληθήσεται ἔξω. On the other hand, the demoniacs in the synoptics are never inhabited by Satan himself, but always by his ministers only. The battle against the kingdom of Satan appears here only in its beginning; our Lord is revealed solely as He who *will once* give the deathblow to the prince of this world. *Then*, in the fourth Gospel we see Christ, not as Him who annuls the outer workings of the power of Satan, the outer witnesses of his power over men, but as Him who destroys his *real* power.

John relates how Jesus designates the Jews, to their surprise and deepest embitterment, as children of Satan, who do according to the lusts of their father, and resemble him in lying and in murder. They,—the

[1] Ewald quoted by Strauss.—Tr.

Jews, who thought that Satan was only powerful among the Gentiles, that they, on the other hand, are not ignobly born, that God is their father,—they must have felt it an inconceivable and unbearable assertion, that they could stand in a real connection with the devil; that thus Christ, when He combats Satan, combats them, and when He strives against them, He thus strives against Satan. Our Lord replies to them (John viii. 37 and foll.), that Satan does not certainly possess a visible dominion over them, but that he can gain and has gained a moral power over them, and that the Son of God must free them from it. It is just this side of the matter that the fourth Gospel brings forward; therefore it is silent on the cures of demoniacs. For *these* latter are not such as have stood under the moral influence of Satan; his power over *them* concerned the physical and psychical life alone. Therefore also the early Church acted similarly in handing over the demoniacs to the exorcists to be cured, while it excommunicated those who had morally given themselves up to Satan. Ananias and Sapphira were demoniacs just as little as Alexander and Hymenæus, but they were the children of Satan.[1]

The considerations which we have advanced will be sufficient to weaken the arguments against the reality of the indwelling and of the expelling of

---

[1] It has surprised us to remark, how Meyer, in the latest edition of his Commentary, represents the circumstance that the demoniacs do not appear godless and wicked, as a *fifth* argument (this is thus the fruit of his latest deliberations) against the reality of the indwelling of demons. A more searching examination of this would have infallibly led him to the opposite result. Church dogmatists (Gerhard, Quenstedt) have with perfect justice most decidedly made a distinction between an obsessio *corporalis* and an obsessio *spiritualis*, and with equal justice have declared the latter the more dangerous. They have only erred in this, that they have confined the obsessio to the physical region, and not at the same time extended it to the psychical. On the other hand, Delitzsch goes too far in judging that the demoniacal powers had any dominion over the *spirits* of men.

demons. However, we have thereby gained little for the positive understanding of the matter. We know not yet how we should demonstrate to ourselves that evil spirits, δαιμόνια, πνεύματα πονηρά, πνεύματα ἀκάθαρτα, can in a manner take possession of a man, so that they have dominion over the whole region of his physical and psychical life, deprive the consciousness of its clearness, of its freedom of movement, and especially become in him the moving principle. Insight into the matter is rendered especially difficult by the circumstance that we cannot pursue the history of the demons as we can that of Satan himself. We know the latter from the Old Testament, as he meets us almost in the first page, and in the whole history he is never quite out of sight. On the other hand, as far as the demons are concerned, they come before us suddenly and unpreparedly in the evangelical history. Former traces of them are mentioned in the Apocrypha, even if not in the canon of the Old Testament (for the passage, Isa. xxxiv. 14, where, in the prophecy of the wasting of Edom, between the ὀνοκενταύροις and στρουθοῖς and σειρήνοις, there occur also demons, as companion-inhabitants of the state that has become desolate, belongs as little to this as the kindred passage, Baruch iv. 35: πῦρ ἐπελεύσεται τῇ Ἱερουσαλὴμ παρὰ τοῦ αἰωνίου εἰς ἡμέρας μακράς, καὶ κατοικηθήσεται ὑπὸ δαιμονίων τὸν πλειόνα χρόνον). In fact, the book of Tobit seems to know demons as scourges, who took up their abode in man (see chap. vi. 8): ἐάν τινα ὀχλῇ δαιμόνιον ἢ πνεῦμα πονηρόν; and the view of Josephus harmonizes with it, who, *De bello jud.* Book VII. chap. vi. § 3 (ed. Becker, vol. vi. p. 141), narrates of a wonderful plant, 'whose root, besides other virtues, possessed the power to cure demoniacs. With regard to demons, those spirits which came out of dead men and entered into living ones, so that they would perish without help, it (that is, this root) will drive them out by merely being brought near them.'

But these scattered traces do not render us the least service, and we find ourselves referred solely to abstractions, which are to be drawn from the evangelical narratives themselves. Even if these be only rays of light, the solution of our problem—how to conceive these miracles of Jesus—will not really suffer. For this purpose, we assume the acknowledgment, not only of a Satan, but also of a kingdom of Satan, which continues until the fulfilment of the prophecy, 'of the everlasting fire prepared for the devil and his angels' (Matt. xxv. 41). What we assume, however, will receive its stamp in some degree from the narratives before us. As Olshausen, more than thirty years ago, daring timidly to acknowledge his faith in the reality of these demoniacal possessions, and in the existence of a Satan, anticipated astonishment by calling to remembrance the word of the poet, '*From the* wicked they are released, the wicked ones have remained,' and then pointing to an undeniable present world full of devilish men. He is wrong in this remark, for demoniacs are certainly not devilish men. We infer otherwise; for if the narratives before us *evidently* allow no other meaning than that demons are powerful over men, and that they must yield up their power to Jews, and if all endeavours to take another view have completely failed, confirming light is thereby made to fall on what we place in this connection as a *supposition*.

The evangelical history does repeatedly assert that Jesus cured demoniacs (see Matt. viii. 6; Mark i. 39; Luke iv. 41, viii. 2, and foll.); but detailed narratives of them are found only in six cases. They are nearly all common to the synoptical Gospels; only one is found in Matthew alone, and another in Mark and Luke. We certainly do not think them of *equal*, but still each has its own *particular* value. The narrative from which we learn the least with regard to the being of demoniacs, is the history of the Canaanitish woman. The very opposite is the case with the complete report of the possessed at Gadara. Between them stand the narratives of the dumb who was possessed, of the dumb and blind man *possessed*, of the lunatic, and of the possessed at Capernaum. In none of them have we quite the same appearance. Sometimes we see how single organs (tongue, eye, ear) are affected; sometimes how the whole bodily organism is demoniacally seized; lastly, how sometimes man, ὁλοτελῶς, physically and psychically, has become the abode of evil spirits.

THE CANAANITISH WOMAN.—MATT. XV. 21–28; MARK VII. 24–30.

We come to the narrative, with the renewed remark that it teaches us to understand less about the demoniacal condition than any of the other histories of cures. But that there is really such a state here there can be no doubt; for not only does the mother complain, 'My daughter is grievously vexed with a devil,' and prays our Lord to cast forth the devil out of her, but St. Mark says expressly, 'Her daughter had an unclean spirit;' and Jesus says, in finally granting her request, 'The devil is gone out of thy daughter.' But the child is not brought before our eyes; Jesus cures her without seeing her. And Strauss is wrong, both in judging that the deed is to be considered chiefly as a cure effected at a distance, and in asserting that the prevailing tendency of the relation is not directed to the communication of a miracle. At the same time, a double result may arise from the case; for even if it should give no ray of light, it does confirm the views formerly brought out.

Thus, in the *first* place, if it is a child who is seized by the demon, the possession cannot be connected with any ethical relations, but rather with the physical-psychical ones; *secondly*, When our Lord speaks of the dogs to whom the children's bread must not be given, this harmonizes with the supposition that this suffering only belonged to the Gentile world, for that figurative designation of the Gentiles was the current one among the Jews. No one will deny the fact, that there is truth in the meaning which Strauss has given to our narrative. He says (p. 220, Eng. transl. i. 300) that it is to be considered as an antitype of the progress which the announcement of the gospel would afterwards make. 'The stiff-necked Jewish prejudice against the admission of the heathen world to Christianity had been overcome by its faithful perseverance in the effort to obtain it. Thus Jesus Himself, after repeated refusal at first, must have been persuaded, by the persevering and humble faith of a heathen woman, to pour out His blessing upon her.'

But true are mixed up with erroneous elements, and the fundamental error in Strauss' statement is this, that a history which bears in itself the highest internal probability of its *reality*, is explained as a mythical fancy.

We should destroy the necessary basis of the event, or at least annihilate the frame which encloses the picture, if we conclude from the expression, 'in the borders of Tyre and Sidon' (Matt. xv. 21), that Jesus had gone over into the Syrian country. Apart from the fact that we have no instance of Jesus going beyond the boundaries of Palestine (He did indeed visit regions where the majority of the population were Gentile, but we never find Him outside the promised land), if He had been standing on heathen ground, He would never have been able to speak to the woman in the tone which He did here. Entering a Gentile country, He would have had to cause the riches of His blessing to follow His footsteps; and it would have been hardly possible for Him sternly to refuse pleading Gentiles. We therefore consider Mark's representation (ch. vii. 24) the better, where we read, instead of μέρη, rather μεθόρια. Thus Jesus left the heart of Galilee, where the Pharisaic plots became more and more troublesome, and visited the bordering district which separated Galilee from Syrian Phœnicia; therefore He was still on Israelitish ground. With this exposition alone does the text of Matthew agree: 'She came out of the same coasts,' that is, she crossed the boundary; she came out of the Phœnician region into the Palestinian, in which our Lord was found, even although close to the borders.

The slight difference, that according to Matthew the woman found Jesus in the way, and uttered her request in the open air, while according to Mark she entered the house in which our Lord tarried, and falling at His feet indoors, brought her cares to Him, is explicable without our having to decide between the two narratives. The two blind men (Matt. ix. 27) called out their request after Jesus by the way, and in the following verse it is said: 'And as He came into the house, they came to Him.' Thus also the woman accompanied Him for a time weeping, and then followed Him into the house, where, kneeling down, she repeated her request. A thorough comparison between Matthew and Mark, moreover, *necessitates* this view; for Mark, who lays the scene at once in the house, begins immediately with the stern expression which Jesus used in answering the woman, while Matthew reports the explanation directed to them—the disciples—that He was only sent to Israel. Thus the account of Mark comes in at the middle, just between the 23d and 24th verses of the text of Matthew, and it is explained by this that Jesus hastens into the house, in order there to be concealed. But He does not succeed; for already a Syrian woman had heard of Him; she had already gone after Him, beseeching Him on the way, and now pressed into His immediate presence, where she more urgently renewed her cry for help. As regards the woman herself, she is called by Matthew 'a woman of Canaan;' on the other hand, by Mark, 'a Greek, a Syrophenician by nation.' Both mean the same. In the Septuagint, the Canaanites are the names of the inhabitants of Palestine whom Joshua found there, and partly rooted out, partly drove up into the extreme north. Consequently in this expression is included the 'Greek,' a Gentile according to the religious view, as the 'Syrophenician by nation,' a Phœnician woman from her country. According to Matthew, the woman had for a long time followed Jesus with her requests: 'O Lord, Thou Son of David, have mercy on me.' Bengel says: 'suam fecerat pia mater miseriam filiæ.' The motive of her request was κακῶς δαιμονίζεται, she is very ill from demoniacal possession; but Jesus is silent, quite contrary to His usual custom. The disciples become impatient, and request Him to put an end to the matter, certainly, in the sense that He should grant her request. If our Lord is silent, He has still patience with their cries, in the beautiful sense in which it is said of God in the parable (Luke xviii. 7): 'He bears with those crying after Him day and night.' It will not be burdensome to Him to listen always to their renewed requests; but He will least fulfil it *in order* to gain rest. However, He has *grounds* for His negative conduct; and He explains it to His disciples, Matt. xv. 24. This saying is directed to those only who addressed Him, *not* to the woman; on the way He has given the explanation, not in the house. (The scene is changed to the house by means of the ἐλθοῦσα in the 25th verse.)

In order to understand the 24th verse, we must emphasize the expression ἀπεστάλην. By this our Lord refers to the instructions which He has received from above; and we know that He was sent εἰς τὰ ἴδια. He was indeed come for the whole world, as the 'Light of the world;' still, as far as regarded the planting of the kingdom of God on earth, He should work exclusively in Israel. It is quite conceivable that the Jews, in John vii. 35, should break out into the wondering question, 'Will he go unto the dispersed among the Gentiles, and teach the Gentiles?' The μαθητεύειν of all things to the Gentiles was the task of the apostles, although even they were not to leave out of sight the 'first to the Jews;' and they did not.

It is an untenable representation, and one contrary to truth, to say that our Lord only appeared as if disinclined, in order to prove or raise their faith. To accept of such a dissimulation, would be to mar the holiness of His picture. Once for all away with this worn-out and really impious view, which gains the appearance of edification at the expense of truth. Never ought Jesus to be judged according to our own, even though well-meant, practice. But certainly, two dark questions present themselves. First, our Lord seems not to act consistently with the proposition advanced by Him. The centurion in Matt. viii. was also a Gentile (by no means a proselyte, for he is spoken of in opposition to Israel), and yet Jesus fulfilled at once his request, without raising difficulties. But it must not be overlooked that this centurion lived in the midst of Judaism, that he had shown his predilection for it, and in the sense of the apostle, was a Jew in spirit.

A benefit shown to him was therefore no μετάβασις εἰς ἄλλο γένος. Secondly, the conduct of Jesus against the Canaanitish woman does not appear quite reconcilable with the assertion which our Lord made, Luke iv. 24, etc., after the sermon in the synagogue at Nazareth: There were many widows in Israel at the time of Elijah, and to none of them was the prophet sent, save unto a woman that was a widow in Sarepta of Syria. How then? Would he not see therein an intimation for him on his part to be ready to bestow a higher benefit than that merely of increasing the meal in the barrel and the oil in the cruse? But we again call attention to the ἀπεστάλην in the 26th verse. Of Elijah Jesus Himself says (Luke iv. 26) ἐπέμφθη, that is, he had received a special divine command to do so. He, the Saviour, had not this task, but He was to move within Israel, in order to save the lost sheep of this fold; *thus* was the historical beginning of redemption to be. He knew that there were still other sheep which were *not* of this fold, and He would also ἀγαγεῖν them, only not during His personal work on earth, but, according to our supposition, when all the scattered ones were collected together at the fulfilment of His death (John xi. 52). And thus His silence had a good motive, but He was not by this placed under an inflexible law; He had power and right to break through the restriction in a given case. Only there must be a good reason for it. And here there is one.

Let us seek it in the right place; let us *not* seek it in the renewed request of the woman in itself. That our Lord allowed Himself to be persuaded, that the repeated blows opened the door, and that the more fervent, uncontrollable weeping conquered His opposition; against this there arise more important considerations than the expressions of the promise: κρούετε καὶ ἀνοιχθήσεται ὑμῖν. It requires another answer. The supposition that Jesus has determined otherwise than had been His original intention is not astonishing; there is at least no cause for fearing the consequences which arise from it.

In some sense the ordinances of our Lord must be changeable, from the fact that His kingdom has a history. Only His ethical laws are eternally unchangeable, and can neither grow old nor become superannuated (that which decayeth and waxeth old is ready to vanish away. Heb. viii. 13). No one can move Him to give something evil,—to offer a stone, a serpent. On the other hand, with regard to the ordinances of His kingdom, He can in given cases anticipate what was to become the rule in a later phase. The time was to come in which the heathen also should be drawn, out of the fulness of His grace, into grace. This time was not yet fulfilled, therefore He turned away the beseeching Canaanitish woman. But *when* the woman showed herself in this sense as an ἔκτρωμα, by which a Paul has thus distinguished himself, ἔρχεται ὥρα could become in her a καὶ νῦν ἐστίν. It will be asked, perhaps, by what means the claim for such grace before the time was justified. We renew the protest we have already made against the fancy, that the intensity with which she cried at the feet of Jesus, 'Lord, have mercy on me,' conquered His opposition. Nothing that has grown out of the soil of nature, no maternal love, no maternal anxiety, even though it had arisen from the tenderest emotions, from the deepest and best sensations, could have done this; it required another and more effective factor. We see that Jesus answered her renewed 'have mercy on me,' even though there lay in the cry the whole yearning of the mother's heart, with renewed refusal. What changed His determination? In order to find out an answer, we must consider more thoroughly the answer which contains the refusal. We keep to the account of Mark. Not that it differs from that of Matthew, but it contains a clause before that of the latter which bears in itself the guarantee of originality. According to this, Jesus *thus* commenced: 'Let the children first be filled,' and after that He added, with the word 'for,' what Mark has in common with Matthew (Mark vii. 27). We set a high value on this clause, that is, on *one* word of it, the word *first*. This it is which the apostle brings forward in the Epistle to the Romans, not only by means of the repeated 'first to the Jews,' but it lies also at the root of a complete exposition of the 15th chapter, that the Jews received salvation for righteousness' sake; the Gentiles, on the other hand, for mercy's sake. Our Lord says, therefore: I am come for the children of the kingdom, that is, for the Jews—these must *first* be satisfied; I may not take their bread 'and cast it to the dogs.' And by this stress is laid on two points. In the 'cast it to the dogs' is considered the despising of the bread, a misuse of the noble gift designed for better receivers. In the 'take the children's bread,' on the other hand, is shown the *claim* which the children have on it; it is *their* bread (the children's bread, as in Matt. vi. 11: 'Give us this day our daily bread'). It should be given to no one not authorized to receive it; and on both points was our Lord in complete earnest.

He does not wish simply to see if the woman will be humble enough to hear this speech, if she will be pleased with the comparison with dogs (a comparison which was, besides, a very general one, and in no way surpassed the very similar expression τελώνης καὶ ἐθνικός). He says to her really nothing more nor less than what He has before publicly said to His disciples: 'Salvation is first for the Jews; if I bestow it on the Gentiles, if I take from the former what is due to them, I should be no just householder, who divides to each what cometh to him.' And what does the woman thereupon answer? Yes, Lord, Thou art right. The following καὶ γάρ makes a difficulty. The mere philological interpretation does not sufficiently explain it. Meyer is on this point quite right when he rejects Luther's well-known translation, and explains it rather: 'Yes, Lord, Thou art right; for not only do the children satisfy themselves at the *family* table; it is so richly furnished, that even the dogs receive from it their portion; so much the more unbecoming would it be to take away this the children's bread and cast it to the dogs.' But to the reply of the woman thus understood, the praise of Jesus following it would stand very strange.[1] Luther has shown great tact by his 'aber doch' (but still). We must make an addition after the 'Yes, Lord.' 'Lord, Thou art right; however, I still persevere in my request; Thou canst indeed grant it to me without breaking Thy rule; for (to speak in the tone of the symbol) even the dogs eat,' etc. The woman acknowledges that she in no way enters into the category of Israel, in whose *rights* she wishes a share; she does not demand to *sit at the table* with invited guests; but, as Jesus has Himself now come to the outermost boundary of Israel, a crumb of bread can fall from this edge of the table, and be re-

---

[1] It cannot be called explaining the New Testament out of the classics, but rather obscuring it by them, when Köster (in the *Theol. Studies*, 1862), on the ground of a passage in Xenophon (*Cyrop.* viii. 24), thus explains the words: 'If it be as you say, just on that account I repeat my request; for as masters accustom their dogs to dependence by bits of food, so will you also not refuse me, the Gentile, a benefit of little cost to you, for which I shall be so thankful.'

ceived by those not originally entitled to it; 'let me have it' makes for once an exception. And on this our Lord answered, according to Mark, 'For this thy saying, go thy way;' according to Matthew, 'O woman, great is thy faith! be it unto thee even as thou wilt.' If we are to decide between this double account, our choice would be difficult. In no case should we be willing to give up the account of it in Mark. But it is quite probable that both came from the mouth of Jesus, that He said, 'O woman, great is thy faith! for this thy saying, be it unto thee as thou wilt.' In fact, the reply of the woman contained a truth so striking, that it was able to disarm the opposition of Jesus. *She* said, Yes, Lord, in this Thou art right; but she was *also* right in what she answered in reply. We do not wish to say that our Lord was moved by the suitable answer, as such, to be gracious to the woman; but He certainly yielded to her on account of the disposition of her heart, which was manifested in her reply. He calls it a great faith. It is not the τοσαύτη faith which He extolled in the centurion at Capernaum. While the latter acknowledged the great power of Jesus, to which nothing is impossible, the Canaanitish woman relied on a love which could break through the fixed barriers, and allow a beam of light to fall also on those originally unentitled to it. The humility, also, is in both cases different. The one humbly avoids the immediate neighbourhood of Jesus, for he considered himself unworthy to receive our Lord under his roof. The other acknowledges humbly that she had no claims; but on the basis of her want of claims, which she allows, does she ground her renewed requests; she puts back the consequences of the humility by her victorious faith, without her humility in any manner suffering by it. Just herein consists the great faith which Jesus extols, on which He compliments her, and which He praises.

Only by the concluding words of Mark are we again reminded that it is the cure of a demoniac which has been laid before us. In opposition to this narrative, a real contrast is furnished for the one next to be considered, in which the demoniacal condition is placed immediately before our eyes with all its horrors.

THE POSSESSED AT GADARA.—MATT. VIII. 28-34; MARK V. 1-20; LUKE VIII. 26-39.

Let us say a word as to the scene of the event. The manuscripts differ between Gadara, Gerasa, and Gergesa. As nothing is known to us of a town of Gergesa further than that Origen calls it a πόλις ἀρχαία, without giving any further account of it; as, besides, the town of Gerasa lies in Arabia, and has near it neither a sea nor a lake; the reading Γαδαρηνῶν (the Sinaitic Codex has also Γαζαρηνῶν) will certainly be considered the correct one. Gadara was the chief town of the province of Peræa, situated on a mountain south-east of Gennesareth. From it the whole of the country lying about it is called Gadaris (Strabo), Gadaritis (Josephus), or, as in our text, the country of the Gadarenes. The town to which the shepherds (Mark v. 14) brought the news, was Gadara itself; the sea in which the swine were drowned, the sea of Galilee; and the scene of the miracle was the part of the Gadaritis lying on the sea-shore. The fixing of this spot is so far important to us, as the heathen population is here the preponderating one; since the death of Herod the Great, the town of Gadara belonged to the province of Syria. Jesus had gone over with His disciples, after a long period of activity in Galilee, to the other side ('which is over against Galilee,'

Luke viii. 26), and as soon as He left the ship ('immediately,' Mark v. 2) and had entered the country ('forth to land,' Luke viii. 27) the curtain rises. Strauss, p. 448, Eng. ed. 183, has allowed himself to be led into making the following *useless* remark: 'This, among the evangelical stories of possession, is the show-piece richly embellished with every accessory, possible and impossible.'

It *is* indeed a picture full of the majesty of our Lord, full of divine wisdom and divine power. The critic has felt himself necessitated to question the view developed by Baur, that the narrative is an allegory of the conversion of the heathen world and the establishment of the Gentile apostleship; and, moreover, is ready to acknowledge a foundation of truth in the representations of the evangelists, only that it has, indeed, been 'worked up into the monstrous and strange.' But, in truth, there is only one point to which he takes a real objection, a point which will be shown to be perfectly unobjectionable.

We pass quickly over the unimportant difference of number in the reports. According to Matthew, Jesus meets two demoniacs; according to Mark and Luke, only one; Luke calls Him expressly a man 'out of the city,' that is, a man inhabiting the town of Gadara. The difference is explained here as easily as in the narrative formerly considered of the two blind men at Jericho. There Mark also spoke only of one man, because he knew his name; here was the fact, that one of these demoniacs belonged as a citizen to the town of Gadara, a sufficient ground to name him alone, even if he be not (as is probable) the one that was most powerfully seized, and who came out with the most violence. All three evangelists begin the scene with the conception of 'meeting;' thus a *meeting* had taken place between our Lord and the demoniac. We have not to consider this meeting as something happening by chance, though it was intended by neither our Lord nor by the sick man. The possessed man did not go out to find deliverance from Jesus; and our Lord, though after the perfected work He bids the person cured announce in his home the benefit that has happened to him, was not there for the object of Messianic work, but, as it seems, had come to Peræa for the sake of a period of rest.

The whole conduct of Jesus towards the Gadarites is singular. The man possessed feared Him, and still he is irresistibly drawn towards the Saviour. After his cure he desires to stay with his helper, and it was refused him. Again the Gadarenes themselves desire our Lord to leave their country directly. This peculiar mixture of an attractive and repulsive force, which has here proceeded from Jesus, will assist us to understand the occurrence. But at present the condition of the demoniac, as drawn in the narrative, has the claim to our whole interest. Mark and Luke, by their detailed representation, put us in a position to obtain a clear view of it. The demoniacal possession was in this case a perfected one. As it was not a single organ which was demoniacally possessed, so it was not only the whole body, but the soul also, as is shown by the significative manner in which this ὁλοτελές is designated by Mark (chap. v. 2) as 'a man with an unclean spirit,' that is, a man who was completely banished from his own sphere into that of the 'unclean spirit,' without being able to break through the tightly-drawn bonds of its dominion. And, indeed, Luke says he had been so for a long time, ἐκ χρόνων ἱκανῶν, or, as it is afterwards said, 'for oftentimes he had caught him,' that is, for years the demon had completely overpowered him, and snatched him away.

The prominent appearances are these:—*First*, The

condition was that of a savageness (in opposition to civilisation). The demoniac suffered no clothes on him; he could not endure to be in the dwellings of men; it drove him out on the mountains, where he stayed day and night, in desert places, in uninhabited regions. But this wildness was joined also with unnaturalness; he did what even an uncivilised man would avoid, for his favourite residence was among the graves (from such a place, according to Matthew, he rushed out to meet Jesus); thus, in places where no one willingly tarries; where, on the other hand, nature experiences a dread, and which were especially an abomination to the Jews (and he was one), on account of their power to make them unclean; yea, he even wounded himself, beat himself with stones, raged against his own flesh. *Lastly*, He appears full of malice and wickedness; he strives to do harm; it was necessary to bind him with cords and with chains; but the latter had been snapt asunder, and the former broken in pieces. The country where he abode was hence universally avoided; no one could pass that way; he was χαλεπός, a true plague to the country. We know that all these appearances, whether in the same individual or not we will leave aside, do occur in cases of insanity and madness. Psychiatry must be in a position to manage such cases. But although the appearances are shown as quite similar, their foundation may be quite a different one. They can be caused naturally and physically, but they can also have a demoniacal origin. If this last is not the correct conception here, the conduct of Jesus would appear as a delusion.

It is certainly a portion of the art of a physician of the soul to enter into the foolish conceptions of the sick; but our Lord was really no psychiatrist as a man is. And that here there is more than merely facing a madman, from an 'idea' overpowering him (Bleek, *Synopsis*, ii. p. 374), from a mad fancy, is undeniably manifest in the further representation of the evangelist. In fact, the sick man hastens to Jesus, falls at His feet, and asks Him imploringly, Spare me! Who would undertake to premise such a contradiction from a mere madness? Nothing prevented the suppliant from remaining in the μνήμασιν, if he really was afraid of Jesus, and expected torments from Him. Why did he not stay away? By earnest supplication he wishes to be preserved from what he himself can easily prevent; for it was not Jesus that pressed Himself on him, but *he* on Jesus. It *will* not suffice here to insist that it is a mere derangement of the powers of thought, a confusion of the imagination; here nothing will suffice but a real duality of the person and of the will. The sick man has still a consciousness of his true self; in this moment it flames up in him without his being able to retain it firmly to the end. While he casts himself at the feet of Jesus, the oppressed, imprisoned will acts for itself; it has restored itself, has freed itself a moment from the bands of the demon. But when he desires to translate the language of signs, in the bending of the knee, into explicit words, the demon makes his power over him available, and compels him to express another request than that which he harbours in the depths of his true consciousness. The *man* bends beseechingly before our Lord; the *demon* turns the request in his mouth into the opposite: Leave me in peace; cure, free me not. By the deliverance the man would be redeemed, but the *demon* would be bound. In fact, the words which Mark relates as proceeding out of the mouth of the demoniac (chap. v. 7), are solely to be understood on this supposition: 'What have I to do with thee?' In such a tone can no man in need of help speak to Jesus, the Saviour from misery, anointed and sent from God. Such a word our Lord could say to His mother, to show the difference of their mutual thoughts; but no sick man could advance such to the physician in the sense of aversion. It has truth in it only as spoken by the demon, who is separated from the Son of God by an impassable gulf. Again, the continuation of the speech does *not* belong to the demon; neither the acknowledgment that Jesus is the Son of the Almighty, nor even the 'I adjure thee,' the δέομαί σου. Indeed, the sick man could not know of himself that He who appeared before him was no other than *Jesus*, and that this Jesus was the Son of God Almighty; but only the demon.[1] But the demon could not as such acknowledge and conjure him, but only the sick man by his compulsion. The recognition, as well as the wish, is the affair of the demon; the acknowledgment and the prayer, that of the sick man. There might be some doubt with regard to the subjective definition in the request that 'thou torment me not;' but even for this there is good ground, for certainly the sensation of the torment would be experienced, not only by the demon, but by the sick person as well; by the former, because he saw the stronger one over the strong; by the latter, because he (with the longing after delivery in his heart) was obliged to express with unwilling mouth the opposite desire. In fact, there seems a

[1] The perplexities into which this view leads those expositors who persistently suppose a natural madness, is evident in the commentaries. According to it, the appearance of Jesus made so powerful an impression on the unhappy man in his excited state, that he looked on Him as a supernatural being. Either the evangelists Mark and Luke must be inexact narrators, in having arbitrarily added the speech in question, or it must be acknowledged that the madman had previously heard something of the person and work of Jesus. The very just remark of Meyer, 'Matthew represents the matter plainly thus, that the demons recognised at once and immediately, by their nature, that Jesus was the Messiah, their most dangerous enemy,' we cannot reconcile with his views expressed in other places on the demoniacs.

useless persistency in speaking of the confused utterances of madness, when, by simply accepting a demoniacal condition, every expression, every turn, becomes literally correct. At all events, He, to whom the 'confused' speech was immediately addressed, knew how to understand it. He is not as if He has met with unexplainable contradictions, but He knows the sense of the oppressed spirit, He understands its στεναγμοὶ ἀλάητοι, and He declares His resolution to take away the unnatural connection. We say, *He declares His resolution*. This is the real meaning of the words of Luke viii. 29: 'He commanded (παρήγγειλεν) the unclean spirit to come out of the man,'—a representation which, for greater completeness, is preferable to the account of Mark, that Jesus said, 'Come out.' If it had been a decisive *command*, the result would have taken place immediately, and yet it did not occur at once. The παρήγγειλεν (which is to be regarded neither as pluperfect, nor even as an act already proceeding from the request of the 28th verse) [1] points out the announcement to be made to the demon, that henceforth he was to stay no longer in this man. Just as the unjust steward was, by the declaration, 'Thou canst be no longer steward,' not yet really removed, was not yet dismissed from house and office, since he was in a position still to make arrangements, so here it is put to the demon only in a certain sense —Soon thou must depart from this man, thou hast been in possession of him as long as thou art to be; but by it he was not driven out, for there was still space for a discussion before it took place.

Our Lord asks, What art thou called? what name

---

[1] The particle γάρ comes, therefore, in its proper place; it is intimately related to the 'torment me.' This sentiment was present, was expressed: 'It was, *in fact*, the unconcealed resolution of our Lord that the demon should come out of this man.'

dost thou bear? The question, as well as the succeeding answer, 'Legion,' demands an explanation. With regard to the first, Olshausen has judged rightly in seeking for its object the strengthening of the consciousness on the part of the sick man: 'Bethink thyself who thou art.' If we consider how the utterances of the demoniac have betrayed just as much of obscurity as of a temporary brightening up of the clear consciousness of his personality, the question, 'What name dost thou bear? who art thou? appears thoroughly appropriate. But with regard to the answer and its reason (Mark says, 'For we are many;' Luke, 'Because many devils were entered into him'), we learn that not *one* demon, not even seven, as in the case of Mary Magdalene, but a whole band of them, had taken possession of the man. The expression λεγεών (it certainly occurs often among the later Jews to signify a great number, but it is foreign to the Old Testament, and dates from the Roman military language) is important to us so far, that we are thereby removed into the Gentile world. However, the *conception* of an indwelling of so many unclean spirits in one man, is disclosed to us by no analogy at command. The approximate consideration, that many vices can exist together in the one heart, we decidedly put aside, because we will not for a moment allow a relation between the demoniacal state and moral degradation. But the disclosure that our Lord makes in a narrative, which we shall consider further on, of a particular οἰκία of Satan, of a disciplined band who obey their head and leader, as well as the case which he gives as possible, that one 'unclean spirit' can bring in seven others into the careless man, strengthens not only the natural explanation which is immediately forced upon us, but also breaks the force of the statement of Strauss, that the second and third evangelist invented this passage, in order to gain by it a basis for the subsequent account, that the demons entered into possession of the whole herd.

With the answer which the sick man gives to our Lord's question, he joins a request. Before we discuss its import, let us consider the manner in which it is introduced by Mark and Luke, in order to confirm us in the views we have already gained. We read, in fact, in both Gospels, 'how he besought Him much,'—he, who was the he? The sick man! And what does he ask? 'That He would not send them away'—them, whom? The demons! But the sufferer would hardly have offered up a petition for his tormentor. No; only his mouth speaks out unwittingly, against his will, a request which is to serve another interest; and in the most melancholy sense is here fulfilled the saying, 'Thou art his mouth, he is thy God.' Soon after we find, therefore, the 'they besought' substituted for the 'he besought,' a change which is thoroughly explained by the request more fully given.

Now, as far as concerns the request itself. In Mark it is given in its general significance, 'That He would not send them out of the country,' while, on the other hand, it runs in Luke, 'That He would not command them to go out into the deep.' Both are in reality the same. The account in Luke contains the consequence of that of Mark. The expression (deep) ἄβυσσος is exemplified by the passage in the Apocalypse, chap. ix. 1 and foll. Here is, in fact, a mention of a bottomless pit, which an angel from heaven opened with a key given him. Although it may not be agreed upon that the expression occurs in the New Testament principally in the sense of שְׁאוֹל, the kingdom of the dead (see Rom. x. 7: 'Who shall descend into the deep? that is, to bring up from the dead'), we have in our narrative, on the strength and in the light of the apocalyptic passage, to think of the bottomless pit which belongs to the demoniac powers, on that which is elsewhere in the New Testament designated by expressions such as τάρταρος.[1] There is now a communication between this abyss and the earth. And, indeed, the powers of darkness can ascend *out* of the abyss (Apoc. ix.), just as they can be compelled to descend into it. This last applies to the case before us. The demons know that in the end they cannot avoid this fate; but it is only on the last day that they must be there, and now they consider it as untimely. Therefore their complaint in Matt. viii. 29, 'before the time,' that the tormenting in the deep, which was to happen to them certainly, should already commence; and just on that account their request 'that He would not send them out of the country.' Put in general terms, it was certainly not to be fulfilled; they themselves could not expect it to be possible that Jesus would permit them to take their dwelling in another man. But they also immediately gave this request a more limited application. There were on the neighbouring hill a herd of swine feeding (Mark gives the number of them as about two thousand), and they request our Lord that He will permit them to enter into these animals; 'and forthwith,' immediately and unhesitatingly, Jesus gave them permission. The difficulties which arise at this point, first, as to how our Lord could have granted the desired permission; secondly, how the demons could

---

[1] We certainly do not wish to speak of a special subterranean *dwelling-place* of demons. But when Hofmann, in his *Schriftbeweis* (vol. i. p. 453), refers the well-known passages in the Epistles of Peter and Jude, not to Satan and his angels, but to spirits who had sinned in quite a different way than Satan, and hence suffered quite different punishments: we regard the distinction as impossible. The kingdom of God stands in opposition to the *one* kingdom of Satan. πονηρά, spirits, demons who do *not* belong to this latter, who do *not* stand among this 'army of the demons,' cannot be accepted according to the New Testament.

have entertained and expressed such a wish, have received manifold explanations on the part of the exegetists and of the apologetists. So much industry and trouble would hardly have been expended on the former, if the question (completely settled on the authority of the Apostle Paul) regarding slain beasts had been asked, 'Doth God care for pigs?' [oxen] (2 Cor. ix. 9), and if, in reference to the loss of the possessors, commentators had considered the absurd consequences to which they would be led by considering the conduct of Jesus in relation to His divine power over the earthly possessions of men. The numerous attempts to preserve the integrity of the moral character of Jesus in the case before us, would therefore, however various the points of view, be proved to be as superfluous in their motives as unsatisfactory in their results. (The supposition of its being a punishment of avarice, is in accordance with the *evangelia infantiæ;* we never find in our Lord a zeal for the observances of the law; and the consideration that a man is worth more than many animals, is unsuitable, as the necessity of this price for the purpose of saving the man is not proven.) Bengel has exposed the uselessness of those apologetical endeavours by the remark, 'Damnum dæmonibus adscribendum, non Domino; quem quis cogeret, impedire dæmonas?' This is made *still* more evident from the circumstance that the Gadarenes themselves were *very far* from making our Lord responsible for the damage to their property. If they request him to leave their borders, they do so, not from fear of similar and greater losses, but from other and deeper motives.

The *second* point, however, demands more earnest consideration. This is the passage on which Strauss has based his attack on the historical probability of the incident. His case (p. 449 of his work; Eng.

transsl. vol. ii. p. 184) is this: Though some may find the *possession* of human souls by bad spirits conceivable, they could not easily imagine such a relation of them to the souls of animals; and even those who accept *this* representation as true, must still take objection to the contradiction which lies in the conduct of the evil spirits there stated. 'First they are said, in order to avoid the necessity of going down the precipice, or out of the country, to pray to be allowed to take up their quarters in the swine, and immediately after, when their prayer has been granted . . . they themselves destroyed the very quarters they had asked for.' He says that real devils would not have acted thus; only a myth or a fiction could have fallen into such a contradiction, which has occurred in depicting features with different aims and from different points of view. If we had only to upset this criticism, it would itself supply us with the most appropriate weapons for a hostile critique upon it; we prefer, however, to examine at once the event itself. The consideration of it does *not* start correctly if it arises from the question as to how the entrance of demons into animals is conceivable.[1] Instead of this, we must seek to find out the grounds on which the demons entertained their wish. On this view our Lord Himself has, in another narrative, given a most satisfactory explanation. He says (Luke xi. 21), 'If an unclean spirit is driven out of a man, he walketh through dry places seeking rest, and finding none.' What is there in these words? That it is unbearable for demons to be without a habitation. They certainly find *complete* satisfaction only in the possession of a

[1] To Olshausen the chief objection was, that human and animal appear here to be too much identified. He did not perceive that the demoniac condition did not belong to the ethical, but purely to the psychico-physical region. In consequence of this, his whole exposition (*Comm.* i. p. 306 and foll.) has become obscure and untenable.

man; but if this is taken away from them, they prefer, instead of being in the desert (that is, without a dwelling-place), to find their rest at least in animals; for then they have a domicile,[1] even though a despicable one. And Jesus grants their wish. The result is this, that the whole herd hasten into the sea, and find their death in it. The evangelists could not have expressed themselves more correctly and precisely, if they wished to represent that this catastrophe resulted from the entrance of the demons into the souls of the animals. Every attempt to ascribe it to the *demoniac* fails, even taking the words as they stand. But does this, the only suitable view of the Biblical account, furnish any just cause for surprise? We should rather feel surprised if the creatures had acted without opposition, if they had borne patiently their being taken possession of on the part of these powers. Their self-destruction seems to us to be the most conceivable feature. The demon can carry the *man* far; he can drive him to a wild life, to tear and damage his own body; but to suicide can Satan alone tempt him, or a natural frenzy blind him. It was different with the *animal*. This κτίσις is made subject to man, and submits to him only, even if often οὐχ ἑκοῦσα ... ἀλλὰ διὰ τὸν ὑποτάξαντα. But as soon as another than human power overcomes that of the animal, if a demon takes it in possession, it rids itself of its unbearable yoke by self-destruction. The fallacious conclusion of Strauss falls away with the false premises, that he considered what was the act of the animals as the intention of the demons.

[1] Schelling has recommended for comparison the passage in Peter, 'The devil goeth about as a roaring lion, seeking whom he may devour' (1 Pet. v. 8). Even here Satan appears thirsting after a reality, which he can only gain by means of the subjection of a foreign will. Against the comparison *as such* we have nothing to object. But we must again warn against the identifying of one tempted by Satan with a demoniac.

The evangelists, lastly, give a more or less elaborate report on the result of the incident. The shepherds of the drowned flocks make it known in the town and in the country. The inhabitants hasten out, and convince themselves immediately of the fact, that he who was once a demoniac was now cured. They find him, who formerly raved about without clothing or rest, calm at the feet of Jesus, and, according to appearance, rational σωφρονοῦντα (σῶς in regard to the φρήν, in the force of self-consciousness; not σώφρων in the ethical, but in the psychological meaning). They have it told them (Mark v. 16) by witnesses how the cure was done. But instead of being glad of it, and, like those Samaritans mentioned in John iv. 40, requesting Jesus to make a long stay with them, they beseech Him urgently to leave their borders. They were afraid (ἐφοβήθησαν, Mark; comp. Luke v. 8–10) of the holy and mighty Son of God. And Jesus goes. Within Judæa He would not have been able to grant the request; for, because He was ἐν τοῖς ἰδίοις, He must, as long as it was day, let the light shine among them. There does not exist any example of such a request being made to Him on the part of Israel. In the country about Gadara, however, He did not specially wish to work; at least He had not entered the country for that purpose. It would have satisfied Him by this one event, to have taken care that the Israelites dwelling there should hear of Him, in order that in the whole extent of the Jewish country in Palestine there should be no soul who did not know of Him. However, He does not leave the means to be only the naturally spreading reports, but He Himself chooses for this purpose an instrument. The demoniac (as Luke relates, 'the man out of whom the devils were departed'), the man formerly a demoniac (just as Simon the leper, who had been cured of his leprosy), besought Him that he might stay with Him. Mere gratitude did not certainly awake this wish. It is a fact, that previously other demoniacs had felt themselves drawn to a constant attendance on Jesus. Of Mary Magdalene we are told this expressly in Luke viii. 2. Only in His immediate neighbourhood did they feel themselves secure from the return of a condition which was not to be forgotten in its horror. But our Lord sends him away with a charge. He is to become the proclaimer of His name in the district of the Decapolis. And not only the result of this activity, but also more perfectly the event itself, has glorified the manifested Messiah, in that the 'oppressed of the devil' (Acts x. 38), and who 'had the legion' (Mark v. 15), has become changed into a pious, mild, and spiritual evangelist. However rich the gain the narrative just considered has been to us in obtaining a correct view of the demoniac condition, it was still more by way of abstraction that we attained the results, than by an instructive word proceeding from the mouth of Jesus Himself. But we are in possession of a case where our Lord proceeds with His own express explanations; He had been driven to it by repeated suspicions. No one could indeed deny that He really cast out demons; but it was said that He accomplished it by the help of their chief. Even once before (Matt. ix. 32-34) had the Pharisees dared to advance the similar reproach lightly; now they repeat it louder and more confidently, and Jesus enters on the charge fully.[1]

---

[1] It is very probable that this reproach to our Lord had been made repeatedly on the part of the Pharisees. We have said deliberately, that in Matt. ix. 34 it is said more *lightly*, as it is here spoken simply of 'a chief of the devils,' without the expression being '*Beelzebub*.' But even if we suppose that those expositors are right who (as Bleek does) declare the identity of both narratives, criticism gains not the slightest material for suspecting Matthew. In fact, if the evangelist had his grounds for arranging this case in the rich picture of the miracle-working of Jesus in chap. viii. and ix., and to place in its right light the high significance, by means of the re-

THE POSSESSED WITH A DEVIL, WHO WAS BLIND AND DUMB.—MATT. XII. 22–29.

Both Mark (chap. iii. 22-27) and Luke (chap. xi. 14-22) give a report of this event; but neither of these evangelists has specially characterized the suffering in question; we only discover that a demon has struck a sick man with blindness and dumbness, and by the power of Jesus it has come to pass that the healed man again spoke and saw. They thought so little of the incident, that Mark passes completely over the historical occasion, and Luke narrates only summarily of a demoniac who was dumb, to whom the gift of speech was restored. Instead of this, the *instructive* lesson which our Lord caused immediately to follow was to them of greater importance. It is after the astonished people had broken out in the words, 'Is not this the Son of David?' that the Pharisees bring forward the accusation that 'He casteth out devils by Beelzebub, the chief of the devils,' and Jesus refutes them.

We wish, however, not quite to pass over the grounds on which the one as well as the other rests. It must indeed have been a wonderful and striking result; otherwise the people would not have broken out in the question, showing budding faith; and then the Pharisees would not have considered it necessary to paralyze this impression. And in fact it was so; the man was both blind *and* dumb,—a case which, in the natural course of events, is hardly to be realized. Jesus has cured the blind, and helped the dumb; we

ported judgment of the Pharisees, he might in a later division of his writing, where he had other objects, and where he wishes to show the development of the hatred against our Lord, feel obliged to return again to an event which would be the means of showing a deep insight into the being, the growth, and the groundlessness of this enmity.

are perplexed at a union of this twofold defect from our want of experience. When one sense is wanting to man, it is customary for the others to be sharpened as a compensation, in so far as the one is not in the relation of dependence on the other (as speaking is to hearing). This anomaly is only conceivable on the supposition of a demoniacal cause. He who here takes possession to help, shows Himself thereby unmistakeably to be the stronger one over the demons, yea, even over the prince of them. It appears to us easy to be explained, how expositors since Jerome have given to the expression Beelzebub very wonderful and far-fetched meanings. If its meaning on linguistic grounds can be no other than 'dominus domicilii,' every other explanation is defeated from the connection in which it always occurs (see Matt. x. 25, 'master of the house,' 'Beelzebub,' 'household').[1]

We can perfectly conceive on what account a meaning signifying insult or affront was so persistently intended under this name. Supposing that this is the just view of it, the Pharisees appear to have shown not only the deepest malevolence, but also the most extreme narrow-mindedness. They say something absurd, which contradicts itself; they cannot possibly be of opinion that Satan would proceed to injure his own kingdom. And still they *must* have *expressed* this opinion, for it was just its untenableness which our Lord shows them as strikingly as forcibly. The interest for us does not now lie in this conviction, but more in the disclosures which we receive relating to

[1] As far as relates to the passage before us, the clause 'prince of the devils' (Matt. xii. 24) is evidently nothing else than the explanation of the word Beelzebub. The want of the article has justly been noticed. This want shows that the clause does not state anything new of Beelzebub, but is only to show the meaning of the name. In the account of Mark (chap. iii. 22) there *is* the article, but there 'he hath Beelzebub' comes first: 'he hath Beelzebub, and by the prince of the devils casteth he out devils.'

the kingdom of Satan, to demons, and the demoniacs. They are to us so much the more valuable, as the theory of an accommodation of Jesus to the Jewish prejudices is so completely exploded, that no modern expositor would venture any more to bring forward this impossible issue.

The words which Mark uses as an introduction to the speech of our Lord: 'He said unto them in parables,' may be understood, as is done by Meyer, as 'illustrating analogies,' and relate specially to the expressions 'kingdom, city, house;' but to consider that Jesus is speaking in mere pictorial language, without these pictures answering to realities, is decidedly in violation of the use of the word parable in the New Testament. The 'illustrating' is only for the demonstration as such; the conceptions themselves have, in the region to which they relate, the fullest truth and reality. Our Lord bears witness *first* to the existence of a 'kingdom of Satan.' Now, as we cannot realize the idea of a 'kingdom' without subjects, of a town without citizens, nor of a house without members of a household, we accordingly see through the words into a kingdom of evil spirits, 'spiritual darkness in high places' (Eph. vi. 12). And as, on the other hand, we cannot conceive of a kingdom without a king, the result is obtained, that the multitude of unclean spirits is directed by *One* will standing at the head, in whose name they go out, on whose commands they act, and whose interest they serve.

But our Lord also testifies, in the *second place*, that this kingdom of Satan, little as it may be divided against itself, is at present meeting its certain destruction; in fact, it is already as good as overthrown and broken. The particle ἤ (Matt. xii. 29) is by no means intended to add a new argument, in order to upset the doubts still somewhat remaining; to this is opposed not only the representation of Mark and Luke, but also even the text of Matthew. The context is based evidently on the sentence immediately preceding it, 'The kingdom of God is come unto you.' Our Lord does not speak in an apologetic tone, but He announces the kingdom of heaven approaching; and this He does no more in parables, but in the words of Scripture in the Old Testament. (He refers to Isa. xlix. 23 and foll.) In this passage Israel's future redemption is prophesied in the following manner. 'Thou shalt know that I am the Lord: for they shall not be ashamed that wait for me. Shall the prey be taken from the mighty, or the lawful captive delivered? But thus saith the Lord, Even the captives of the mighty shall be taken away, and the prey of the terrible shall be delivered: for I will contend with him that contendeth with thee, and I will save thy children. And I will feed them with their own flesh that oppress thee.' This prophetical passage contains the expressions which our Lord uses in such completeness, that the avowal of Bleek, that this passage must have been specially before the eyes of Luke, is not sufficient. Ὁ ἰσχυρός is not 'any strong man,' with whom the τίς has to do (Meyer), but *the* strong man, whom the prophet has in his mind, the *one* mighty tyrant, from whom all troubles and bondage, all oppression comes, and from whose dominion the kingdom of heaven approaching will deliver the captives. It has also its 'household,' or αὐλή, that is armed, and keeps a careful view over its subjects. All these are not pictures and parables, but vivid representations of real things in the 'kingdom' of the 'strong one.'

In some sense it can be conceded that by 'household' the world is to be understood. Is it, then, the question of a 'prince of this world,' and does the apostle say, 'The whole world lieth in wickedness'?

But not unintentionally is it a question of the οἰκία, that is, of the house and court, and thus of the dwelling-place in which the householder administers the law of the house. We have therefore to think of the sphere in which the strong one acts as the possessor, visibly, and in a manner apparent to the immediate perception. The demoniacs themselves are just those in this household, and are those prisoners of the tyrant to whom liberty is announced (Luke iv. 18); they are his σκεύη, ὑπάρχοντα σκύλα. Between these three expressions we cannot positively make any real difference. Paul does, indeed, once call σκεῦος ἐκλογῆς an arm in the service of God, and σκῦλον can also signify a weapon; but *here* the organs of the mighty one are intended just as little as are the means He has of using His power; in the present case the demons themselves are quite out of consideration. In fact, the *possession* itself is treated of; it is called ὑπάρχοντα as far as it still belongs to the tyrant, and σκύλα (שָׁלָל, בַּז) as far as it is taken from him as a prey.—From the circumstance that He leads the demoniacs out of the οἰκία of Beelzebub, that He gives again liberty, our Lord calls on the Pharisees to draw the conclusion that the kingdom of God is come. 'It is come unto you;' thus they see no mere sign or symbol that this kingdom is on the point of coming, but a *witness* lies before their eyes that it had already become effective, that the stronger one was already in the lists. He *has* already bound the strong one, otherwise He would not be in a position to take away his goods unhindered, to depopulate his house. There is an end of Satan's confidence in his armour. He is no more in peaceful and undisputed possession; it was no more in his power to say, Woe to him who attacks what is mine! Attention is principally to be drawn to the verb δήσῃ, which only Matthew and Mark have, while Luke substitutes for it the more general νικήσῃ. We must, however, guard ourselves from considering it, either here or in the passage in the Apocalypse xx. 2, as applying to a single act performed in a fixed moment. The casting out of devils by Jesus relates to the δῆσαι, just as the casting out of devils on the part of the apostles to the πεσεῖν of Satan from heaven (Luke x. 18). The force of the word δῆσαι lies in the person of the stronger one now revealed, who had become powerful. Because the strong has found a stronger, who has appeared in order to undertake the combat with him; because the latter possesses in his prevailing strength the guarantee of His final victory over the adversary; he is already bound; he can offer no real opposition, he must be contented with all restraints, must allow to be taken from him what he formerly possessed in peace, when no equal, not to say prevailing power was at hand, who would have been able to combat with him for it. Now he must look on inactive and helpless, while one or other of his subjects or σκεύη is taken from him, and becomes a weapon in the hand of a strange possessor; his means do not extend against the stronger one, against *Him* all the arms of his armoury are blunt and ineffective. He sees the gradual depopulation of his household, of his city, of his kingdom,—until he is completely put out of possession, so that the triumphal cry is, 'Now is come salvation, and strength, and the kingdom of our God, and the power of His Christ; for the accuser of our brethren is cast down,' Apoc. xii. 10.

The unprejudiced exegetical examination of our passage can absolutely lead to no other results. But would any one in earnest be ashamed to acknowledge and accept them? Such a shame might really meet a question to which the concluding relation of Luke (chap. xi. 27, 28) gives rise, namely, the question whether we would not rather be on the side of that woman, who, when our Lord had finished this discourse, breaks out in the deepest comprehension of His worth: 'Blessed is the womb that bare Thee, and the paps which Thou hast sucked;' or still more, whether we would not prefer to merit the beatitude spoken by Jesus Himself in beautiful and significant correction of the woman's words: 'Yea, blessed are they that hear the word of God and keep it.' Should we not find therein a greater satisfaction than if we allow ourselves to be referred by Strauss to the analogies in Josephus, or to the fables related by Philostratus of Apollonius of Tyana.

The short narrative of a casting out of a devil, which is found in the second and third evangelists, is of value to us in a very special way.

THE HEALING OF THE MAN POSSESSED WITH A DEVIL AT CAPERNAUM.—MARK I. 23; LUKE IV. 33.

This event took place while our Lord was engaged in teaching in the synagogue at Capernaum. What it really illustrates is not the circumstance that the demon acknowledges Jesus, 'I know Thee who Thou art, the Holy One of God,'—that it feared Him, and experienced His presence as a tormentor, and seeks to be let alone;—all this, after we have considered the history of Gadara, is nothing new; only from the 'I know Thee who Thou art' we are reminded again of the instructive parallel in the Acts, xix. 13-15. Just as little do we wish to rest on a point of which the narrative of the Gadarenes only gave us a slight signification,—that is, of the delight of the demon, even to the last, to wound, or at least to torment ($\sigma\pi\alpha\rho\acute{\alpha}\xi\alpha\nu$), the man whom he was forced to leave; for this feature will in another case be immediately and completely discussed, and more satisfactorily decided, than Strauss does, who this time says, quite rationistically: 'The faith of the sick man in Jesus at the moment of His commanding the demon to depart out of him, might have had the effect of producing a crisis amid violent spasms which put an end to the morbid condition.'

The *conduct* of our Lord in Mark i. 25 is especially manifest in the narrative before us. He speaks here no simple 'Come out of him;' He does not simply give the effective command that the demon should come out of the man, but He adds the rebuke, 'Hold thy peace.' This in no way refers to the 'calling out,' to the powerful demoniacal cry; for, if this had been the case, the 'crying with a loud voice' which followed in the 26th verse could not have taken place. It can therefore only refer to the *purport* of the demoniac's words. Our Lord does not wish that the demon should announce Him as the 'Holy One of God.' But this is not to be understood in the *same* sense in which He had forbidden His disciples and other believers to spread abroad that He was the Messiah; the intention is rather this, *demons* should not proclaim His rank. He will have no praise from *this* mouth. They, the demons, must tremble and yield to increase the glory of Christ, and not bear witness to Him with their mouth. Compare with this the striking passage Mark i. 34: 'He suffered not the devils to speak, because they knew Him.' Of men and of angels Christ will be acknowledged as the Being He is; the devils must *also* acknowledge Him, but *silently*.

The fact touched upon in this narrative by the use of the expression σπαράξαν, receives a thorough elucidation in the last occurrence which belongs to the present group.

THE LUNATIC.—MATT. XVII. 14, ETC.; MARK IX. 14; LUKE IX. 37, ETC.

We make use of the expression used above, only because it is once introduced, without on that account wishing to consider the suffering before us in the sense of the modern usage. The designation in the text has no further support, than that the father of the sick child (Matt. xvii. 15) explains that 'my son is a lunatic, and sore vexed.' He might have observed that the paroxysms were accustomed to appear at the changes of the moon,—an observation, however, also made in other, in fact in *natural* illnesses; for those 'which were lunatic,' which are introduced in Matt. iv. 24, in especial distinction from those 'possessed with devils,' have evidently only suffered a natural disturbance of the bodily organism. In the present case we lay so much the less value on the expression, as neither Mark nor even Luke (notwithstanding the latter's inclination for technical designations) use it. The former speaks of a 'dumb spirit' (in ver. 25 he uses also the expression 'foul'); in the latter we hear only of a 'spirit.' All the evangelists give the event one and the same very definite position, that is, immediately after the transfiguration of Jesus. Our Lord had taken with Him up the mountain His three favourite disciples, and there occurred the 'vision.' Descending with them, He speaks of the part which John the Baptist had taken, and of the similar fate which would overtake Himself in this world. But all these pictures of the future, with its terrors, and with its splendour, suddenly make room for the immediate duty of the present. Near to the place where He had left behind the nine, Jesus remarks, according to the complete account of Mark, a confusion among them, a dispute between them and the scribes. He asks the people, who, amazed,[1] saw Him coming, and drew near to Him with respectful homage, as to the cause. We consider the question spoken with emotion, though it is not so stated in the text, because it was not directed to the disciples themselves, but to those whom His voice could at once reach. 'What are you doing with my disciples?' thus demands He, who wished to give an account also of these nine,—ἐφύλαξα αὐτούς in the tone and in the haste of careful love. And there came forth a man, who shows the cause, and the further development of the present dispute. 'I have a son, an only son (Luke ix. 38); him have I desired to bring before you, in order that you might take a glance into his misery (ἐπιβλέψαι, vid. Acts iv. 29, ἔπιδε). But Thy disciples have not been able to put an end to this suffering.'

This is the point on which Strauss thinks he has discovered the motive for the invention of the narrative. He seeks to show (p. 451, Eng. transl. ii. 187) that its object is to bring to light the strength of the miraculous power of Jesus; the disciples seem unskilful to help what He Himself effected at once with ease. Such a mode of measuring the Master with His disciples 'was involved in the nature of the Hebrew legend.' Even Elisha once saved from death, by means of his superior power, the son of his Shunammitish hostess, whom his servant Gehazi had in vain attempted to wake up (2 Kings iv. 8 and foll.). But this issue does not seem to have really satisfied the

---

[1] Mark's representation (ix. 15), 'Straightway all the people, when they beheld him, ἐξεθαμβήθη,' describes the people as '*perplexed*' by the sudden presence of our Lord, by no means merely surprised, least of all as joyfully surprised by His somewhat unexpected appearance. The ground of this perplexity lies in the expressions which may have been used in the dispute between the scribes and the disciples about the *absent* Jesus, that is, about His power to drive out devils.

critic himself. He indeed felt that he must use the history of Elisha for his purpose, only to such an extent as would bring his theory into credit. While he therefore passes over the fact, that now and again Jesus had been able to accomplish what was impossible to His disciples, he has himself thrown away the key to the explanation which he had but just discovered; and that in relation to an incident which had for its result the amazement of those witnessing it, 'at the mighty power of God' (Luke ix. 43).

We now turn to the description of the illness before us. The spirit was called ἄλαλον, that is, the boy was under the power of a devil, who deprived him of speech. The stress, however, does not lie on this, but on other appearances. The presence of the devil did not assert itself constantly, but in fitful paroxysms (ὅπου ἂν αὐτὸν καταλάβῃ; that the periodicity is explained by the juvenile age is only provisionally used as a conjecture); but these were then of the most terrible nature. 'He suddenly crieth out' (Luke ix. 39),— the child suddenly raiseth an unnatural cry,—'and it teareth him that he foameth again;' that is, the spirit (the change of subject has been shown in the case at Gadara as a conceivable characteristic of demoniacs) tears him, he stirs up such convulsions that the boy appears as foaming; and when he unwillingly leaves him, it is only with wounds, συντρῖβον; this boy bears traces of the wounds, hurts,— not like the Gadarene who cut himself with stones, but from a fall or thrust. Similar, and still more evident is the description in Mark, 'He foameth and gnasheth with his teeth;' καὶ ξηραίνεται, 'he pineth' visibly, is sick near to death. The complaint of the father (which is connected with this description of his grief), that the disciples, notwithstanding their willingness to help, were unable to cure him, is satisfactorily accounted for in the representation of the second evangelist.

When our Lord gave the order, 'Bring the child unto me,' the 'spirit' seized him with special force, so that he 'fell on the ground, and wallowed, foaming.' Thus it probably happened when the disciples had made their attempts to cure. This frightful outbreak will have affected them in such a degree, that they lost their presence of mind, that psychical excitement repressed the power of their minds; in the face of such forces they mistrusted their power, and became disheartened and dispirited. This could only injure our Lord's cause before the people, and a gain would arise therefrom to the scribes. 'It is manifest from this that the evil spirits do not always depart at the name of Jesus.' Hence His regret. The words of Mark ix. 19, 'O faithless generation,' relate specially to the disciples. It is not to be denied that our Lord expressed His grief at the general unbelief in an unconstrained manner, so that the Pharisees also, and even the father himself, is included in His reproof; but this is only in general; the point of the complaint of Jesus is turned against the 'want of faith of the nine.' ' How long shall I be with you, that ye may learn to *believe;* how long shall I suffer you, have patience with your weakness of faith?' The reproof was well deserved. Our Lord had given His disciples power over evil spirits; they could have used it in faith, and therefore with success, so that they would have been able to rejoice thankfully 'that even the devils are subject to us in Thy name.' But in the present case they had not preserved their faith; they had thereby shown themselves as faithless, in that they had allowed themselves to be imposed upon by appearances, and had forgotten their *gift.* They showed themselves to be the same as they were before, at the storm on the sea. The sight of the rising billows, of the unchained powers of nature, had produced on them the same impression as in this case,—the picture of nature disfigured and distorted by the demon; therefore in both cases they experience the same reproach. 'How is it that ye have no faith?' is our Lord's question on the sea; and here He complains of their 'faithlessness.' The later conversation of Jesus with His disciples thoroughly justifies this view. There they ask Him how it was that they were not able to overcome the devils, and He replies, 'Because of your unbelief.' Ἀπιστία means *un*belief, not of *little* faith; yea, even 'the faith as a grain of mustard seed was awanting in them.'

At the same time, our Lord does not at all intend to identify them with those who faithlessly oppose Him, and who refused to acknowledge His name. Their 'unbelief' was expressly confined to the case before us. But in this they really acted as the restless, weak children of this world, who have forgotten their Lord, and the armour they had received from Him. This comes out in a still stronger light by means of the supplementary saying of Jesus: 'Howbeit this kind (that is, of devils) goeth not out but by prayer and fasting.' Strauss does not think that this explanation is in unison with the reproof before it. The semblance of a contradiction appears, however, only if the conception is understood merely superficially. It must be understood in the sense of the νήφειν, γρηγορεῖν, προσεύχεσθαι, as used by the apostles (1 Pet. iv. 7: 'Be sober, and watch unto prayer;' and chap. v. 8: 'Be sober, be vigilant'). It is sobriety in the disciple of Jesus that he should not allow himself to be prejudiced and intoxicated by the appearances opposing him; for as soon as he thinks on what he is or on what he has, they fail any longer to impose on

M

him. And this is the immediate effect of his prayer, that he becomes conscious of his Lord and his God, before whose power all the stormy waves must be still—'whatever the devil may do, however he may behave, however terrifically he may assert himself.' Our Lord points out to His disciples, 'Only have faith, keep it by prayer in soberness, and nothing will be impossible to you.'[1]

Our Lord first turned to His disciples—they merited the first word. Then only, after they had received the pastoral rebuke, Jesus turns to the complaining, beseeching father. That He does not immediately proceed to cure, although He had already promised it by His command, 'Bring him forth to me,' arises from the fact that He wishes not only to take away the *boy's* trouble, but specially to bestow a longed-for gift on his *father*. But at first the latter was by no means in the state of mind satisfactory to our Lord. The vain attempt of the disciples, the specially severe attack which the child had just that moment suffered (Mark ix. 20), must have made him completely disheartened and hopeless, and into such a faithlessly-closed hand Jesus cannot and may not lay His gift. He therefore first makes him fit to receive it, by holding with him a preliminary discourse, which appears in the event an unnecessary, but, from the pastoral standpoint, a searching one.

It is certainly incorrect to seek the motive for the

[1] Certainly the phrase 'this kind' limits it to one special kind of devils; the view of Euth. Zig., τὸ γένος τῶν δαιμόνων πάντων, contradicts thoroughly the text. But the view, that here a kind of spirits, difficult to be driven out, stiff-necks, is referred to, is just as incorrect as the supposition that a peculiarly lofty rule of faith, which could be obtained only by fasting and prayer, is needed for their overthrow. From the aforesaid circumstances we gain the view, that the driving out of devils, who assert themselves in such frightfully unexpected outbreaks, demands on the part of the physician an undisturbed presence of mind and confidence of faith, such, in fact, as is obtained by the 'watching and praying.'

question, 'How long has the child been ill?' to which the answer follows, 'From his youth up,' in the wish to illustrate our Lord's power to take away a suffering so deeply rooted and so old. As to the greater or lesser duration of a demoniacal possession, it cannot matter in the least. That an evil spirit can only be driven out by the divine power will be very generally allowed, whether it became powerful from infancy, or only since its subject had become a man. The object of the question of Jesus is therefore to be judged in the same manner we should consider the intention of His words addressed to the possessed man at Gadara, 'What is thy name?' The substance of the answer is of lesser importance. However, we do not wish completely to pass over the reply made by the father— 'Of a child.' It must serve us as a renewed guarantee for the assertion already repeatedly made, that those possessed with devils did not belong in moral relation to the kingdom of evil; for even in his tenderest childhood, thus even before he was able to distinguish between good and evil, the boy lay in these bonds.

Of greater importance to us in this connection is the announcement, that the spirit had often thrown the child into the water, even into the fire, to destroy it. A trace of the demoniac's desire not only to pain and torment, but really to injure body and life, we have already met with in former narratives; in the present case, this tendency comes forth openly and unconcealed; therefore the devil, when he was obliged to depart from the child, left behind at least the appearance as if he had killed him, as a mark of his real intention. If the 'unclean spirits' are the 'angels of Satan,' we know what name our Lord has given to the latter: He calls him 'a murderer from the beginning,' as to destroy men is his peculiar, his natural desire. And this expression (whether applied to the fratricide of Cain or to the fall) leaves not a doubt of the originator of the effect which took place, nor of the warmth of the interest which he has therein. Even to the *servants* of Satan *as such*, it is not less natural to strive after injury, as it pleased their lord and their head to kill, and as it was needful for his *children*, the priestly enemies of Jesus, to do after the lust of their father; while it is the tendency of the Son 'not to destroy men's lives, but to save them;' and as this should be the intention of all His servants and followers (Luke ix. 55, 56).

The disconsolate father has answered the question of our Lord; he has, besides, gained a touching representation of the depth and extent of the suffering before him; he does not doubt that Jesus will grieve over it. The σπλαγχνισθεὶς (Mark ix. 22) is not the object of his request, 'have compassion on us,' but is only the fact of his supposition, 'that thou wouldst certainly have sympathy with us.' However, he is in doubt whether there was any power here in a position to help him. He had seen the disciples fail. Will the Master be able to effect anything? That his hope is deeply dejected is seen in the expression, 'if thou canst,'—if thou art able to do anything against this trouble, let thy compassion have free course. But of all the cases where human misery appeared before the eyes of Jesus, the one before us is perhaps the one in which His compassion seems the least active. His eyes did not overflow with the grief of sympathy; and the fervour which the bowed-down father uses in his lamenting and weeping words, certainly made on Him as little, if not less, impression than did the urgent βοήθει μοι of the Canaanitish woman. Instead of this, we see Him show forth His majesty. Occasion for its display seemed called for by the words of the petitioner: 'if thou canst.' In answer to this, He explains that here other factors are needed besides *His* power and *His* compassion,—one factor which he, the person in need, had completely overlooked—his *own* correct, heartfelt faith.

For the purpose of understanding it, it is important to restore the correct reading. In the *textus receptus*, 'if thou canst believe,' the force of Jesus' answer is weakened. If we strike out, on the authority of the best critical authorities, the πιστεῦσαι (the Codex Sinaiticus omits it), the sense is this: 'You speak of *my* power; thou forgettest *the* power which *thou* hast, and the employment of which is the indispensable condition of success.' Our Lord had, in the scene before His eyes, observed on all sides want of faith, weakness of faith; and, descending from the hill of transfiguration, He must have felt this want with greater grief. He wished to save the world by means of its faith, to urge men to faith. And thus it was said to the petitioner not to inquire after the measure of the power, and after the depth of compassion in the Master, but to cast a searching glance on the degree of his own faith. 'To the believer alone does it happen according to his wish, but to Him all things are possible.' Let us draw an instructive comparison. Just as our Lord says here to the beseeching father, He says immediately after (Matt. xvii. 20) to His disciples also: 'If ye have faith, nothing shall be impossible to you.' But the sense in the two cases is not completely the same. To *him* he said, By faith canst thou *obtain* everything; nothing shall be unattainable by thee. To them, however, He gives the assurance, 'By faith can you *effect* everything; nothing shall be too difficult for you.' *There* He had said, With the hand of faith canst thou take possession of everything, even bring down from heaven the distant benefit; but *here*, Your hand of faith will be able to conquer all hostile powers, to overthrow all powers. *There* the beseeching, praying faith, and his victory; *here* the working, effective faith, and its results.

We pursue the subject still further. In both cases there is the *same* truth; to the believer *nothing* is impossible. But is there in both cases also an equal truth in the opposite view, 'to the believer *alone* is it possible'? And if *not*, in which of the two is it an absolute, and in which is it a relative one? The answer is this: even the *weaker* faith is sufficient to *take*, for that has to do only with the merciful Lord. A *stronger* one, however, belongs to the *working*, for there it stands opposed to the powers of darkness, which wish to assert themselves. Our Lord's reply brought powerfully into movement the feelings of the father. The result was laid quite specially into *his* hand; now was he himself answerable for it. And he feels very decidedly the burden. We will not lay too much stress on the εὐθέως, as it is known that this particle in Mark often signifies merely the simple progress, without meaning haste and speed. But the κράξας signifies more than simple repetition. Just as this expression in oratory is repeatedly used for the most impressive sermon, so here it testifies to the deep impression made, even if the accompanying tears, which exist only in the received text, must be given up on account of the weight of critical authorities. 'As far as I am able I will willingly fulfil all conditions; what thou desirest I will do. Thou requirest faith; now I believe, will believe; and if my faith is not sufficient, help Thou Thyself my unbelief.' The words 'help Thou my unbelief' have indeed been explained by modern exegetical writers as meaning that the request was for the healing of the child, and that the want of faith was a simple avowal,—'I believe; help, notwithstanding my unbelief.'

The proof that this explanation is possible, as the dative is used, is not brought out; and the assertion that the 'help' by its context can only point to the suffering before us, is arbitrary. At any rate, the usual view of the situation suits much better, and harmonizes thoroughly with the voice of the anxious, depressed, longing heart. From our standpoint we may experience a pleasure in this acknowledgment; but it is more than doubtful whether it would have appeared satisfactory to our Lord. This forcible raising of the feelings, this artistic excitement, explains and shows, by the conditions given, how much it lay below the 'great faith' of the Canaanitish woman, and the 'so great faith of the centurion.' But a germ of faith was really present, and He who breaks not the bruised reed does not despise it.

Perhaps under other circumstances He would still further have continued the discourse. However, there was no place for it here. The saying, 'Jesus saw that the people came running together,' allows that there were reasons for 'rebuking the foul spirit,' on the ground that our Lord immediately proceeded, without suffering any further delay, to cure, because it became necessary, from the people collecting about Him, to desist from any further pastoral exhortations.

The manner in which He completed the exorcism is peculiar and remarkable. We have not so much in view the circumstance that He addresses the spirit according to the manner in which it manifested itself: 'thou dumb and deaf spirit.' Though, even in this, our Lord's conduct differs in the case before us from the general one, and it was necessarily different. In fact, previously the spirit which had taken possession of a man, in coming out was accustomed to *speak;* but here our eyes meet with mere *appearances:* the boy gnasheth, foameth, walloweth, without uttering an accompanying word. The possessed one is silent, the one possessing is silent, the father of the former alone opens his mouth in words of complaint and request. If this is explained by the childish age of the person attacked, who has neither a clear consciousness of his condition, nor is even fitted for an immediate relation with Jesus, we can understand by it the direct address on the part of our Lord. To the spirit which is concealed behind the manifestations, and which seems not to observe our Lord approaching, and not to fear His threatening presence,—to him does Jesus direct His 'come out.' 'To you, this dumb and deaf spirit, is my command.' And, by means of the expressly prefaced ἐγώ, He makes Himself recognised. 'I am He, whom thou knowest, to whom thou must yield; to me thou wilt not refuse obedience, as thou didst before to my disciples.'

An increased attention is demanded for the express order addressed to the spirit by our Lord which occurs in no similar narrative: 'and enter no more into him.' In other cases He had always simply used the 'come out.' If the cures of Jesus are radical, just because they come from Him, why then was there a special preparation to prevent a return? It has been shown from Mark ix. 18 and Luke ix. 30, that the possession of the spirit in this case was no fixed one, but only a periodical one; it was therefore right when our Lord says, 'Not only go out, but remain for ever away.' But the rationalistic view of the demoniacal condition can alone be set at rest by this solution. The representation, that the spirit at times entered into the child, and then went out of him to return at will, cannot be justified by the 'wheresoever he taketh him' of Mark, and the 'hardly departeth' of Luke. These features show nothing else but that the demon, permanently dwelling in the child, makes at certain times his presence felt in an exciting, heartrending manner; but otherwise he rested in him. The correct exposition refers us to a passage already explained on a former occasion, Luke xi. 24–26. Here our Lord puts the case, that a devil really driven out, after he had wandered through dry places, and sought in vain for rest, returns into the house which he had formerly used. The question, why He did *not* take this care in the cases previously considered, while here He admits a danger of that kind, but which He at once prevents, is explained by the fact that this person possessed was a boy. In a child, who would not be on his guard, and who could not be warned, the return of the devil was certainly possible. It is certainly possible in even a person of riper years; but in their case it could only occur through their own fault. He who does not watch with fasting and prayer, may become afresh the prey of the devil, and then it will be worse with him than before. But to prevent the guilt of a man in another way than by warning, lay beyond the power of Jesus, because it was beyond ethical possibility. On the other hand, He *Himself* must protect and preserve the *child;* and His work was only then a work of pure love in this, when to the 'go out of him' He added the security of a lasting freedom.[1]

Lastly, even the end is of interest. The devil obeys; but while yielding, he excites a paroxysm more powerful than ever; the boy was 'as one

---

[1] It is certainly conceivable, that even such expositors, who otherwise believe firmly the reality of demoniacal possession, are here inclined to regard the present case as natural epilepsy. Olshausen does not conceal that this time he agrees with Dr. Paulus. And yet the narrative before us opposes such a view still more decidedly than any similar report in the New Testament. The address of our Lord to the deaf and dumb spirit, and His command to it never to enter again into the boy, gives us the unmistakeable alternative, either to acknowledge a real possession on the part of a devil, or to adopt views which mar the clearness of the face of Jesus.

dead,' and many standing around said, 'He is dead.' We have already spoken of this; the severity of this *last* attack is the consequence of our Lord's command, 'Do not enter into him again.' The 'as one dead' was no deceiving appearance, as in Matt. xxviii. 4, but really a condition resembling death, out of which the child would not have awoke without the uplifting hand of our Lord. 'He lifted him up' (Mark ix. 27). Certainly the ἐγείρειν cannot here signify a simple uplifting, as this expression does in the curing of the mother-in-law of Peter. But as the 'as one dead' goes first, He proceeds to a peculiar giving of life to him who was otherwise falling into death. Bengel's remark, 'Nova miraculi pars,' is therefore by no means to be completely rejected. There now began for the child a new life, which he had received from the Son of God. And the 'he arose' shows a rising to walk, not only in the world of appearance, but in the kingdom which had been glorified in him ἐν μεγαλειότητι. Let us keep this firmly in view, now, when we leave the consideration of the healing of demoniacs. We have sought to conceive their probability, and to prove them as real witnesses of the power of the kingdom of heaven which was at hand. The Spirit of God, by which Jesus effected this, overpowered the unclean spirits, and broke the bonds of the prisoners.

The gospel narrative tells us yet of another manner in which the same witness has come forward equally real, and as openly manifested. Our Lord says, 'The hour cometh, and now is, that all that are in their graves shall hear the voice of the Son of God, and those who hear shall live.' And to John the Baptist was the word sent, 'The dead are raised up.'

THE RAISING FROM THE DEAD.

We have already explained why we have added these works of our Lord to the third group, and not arranged them among the symbolical miracles. We will glance over the several cases. The fourth Gospel reports the raising of Lazarus, the third that of the young man at Nain; and lastly, the first three Gospels relate an occurrence which we will at present leave undecided, whether it is to be recognised as a real raising from the dead or not,—for it is generally known that views differ largely on this point,—namely, the history of the daughter of Jairus.

There are, therefore, at least three narratives belonging to this class. It will surprise no one that Jesus was so sparing and so reserved in these manifestations of His power. He must have experienced the strongest motives before He determined on such a work, as is witnessed by His prayer at the grave of Lazarus. If sickness was something contrary to nature, dying was a divine arrangement, which would remain until the Parousia. One ought not to be overawed by the objection, that sickness is the foreboding of death, a warning of death, and the usual gate through which it enters. For, as far as our experience goes, it does not need to be on that account the divine arrangement: 'Abraham our father is dead,' so said the Jews to Jesus. And he *is* dead; for Adam's curse rested on him, as on all who are from Adam. But that Abraham, the Patriarchs, and still earlier Noah and the antediluvian race, suffered illness, sacred history at least does not tell us. It is first in Exodus, at the promulgation of the Law, that sickness occurs; then we hear of leprosy and other troubles. There is, in fact, a dying without sickness; this results after the strength, the foundation of life is quite consumed, as in this sense it is said of the patriarchs, 'They died old and full of life, and were gathered to their fathers.' Even the Saviour Himself—He died; but He was never ill. The picture of the dead Jesus stands at all times before our eyes, and we should bear it in continual remembrance. But the thought of a very sick, or even of an ailing and physically-suffering Christ, we cannot entertain.[1] A *sickness* our Lord could therefore consider something abnormal, could feel it as a demand for Him to attack it with His restoring power. But when death occurs, it is right to bow down under God, who allows man to die, and says, 'Return again to dust,' and, 'It is ordained for man once to die.' Even a Paul, however deeply he often longed for death, did not like to be ill, and called on the Lord to deliver him from 'the body of this death.'

Hence the *rarity* of raisings from the dead by Jesus, but also hence the perfect right of the supposition that our Lord must have had the most powerfully determining motives in each single case to induce

---

[1] The passage in Matt. xxv. 36 may, in this view, present a difficulty. Everything else that our Lord says (I was hungry, thirsty, naked, a stranger, imprisoned) applied to Him, for He was really in these circumstances. But 'I have been ill, and ye have not visited me,' is wanting in historical support. It will be said that our Lord does not here mean Himself, but His 'brethren;' however, He has said it all first and immediately of His own person, and He could have introduced nothing which would have been impossible in Himself. But what is then the real meaning of ἠσθένησα? Must it be translated by 'I have been sick'? Why do we not stop at the next meaning, I was weak? The Vulgate translates it rightly, 'infirmus fui.' Of an ἀσθένεια of Jesus in the sense of 'weakness' there is mention in Scripture; apart from the appearance of our Lord in Matt. xxvi. 37, 38, see 2 Cor. xiii. 4, 'He was crucified through weakness,'—'we are weak in Him.' And passages such as 1 Cor. iv. 10, 2 Cor. xi. 29, 1 Thess. v. 14, on the one side, but on the other, admonitions, as in Jas. i. 27, 'visit the fatherless and widows in their affliction,' are well suited to recommend this more general acceptation of the expression.

Him to proceed to such an act; and hence, lastly, the demand on the expositor especially to show satisfactorily this motive.¹ If such a motive cannot be shown in the case of the daughter of Jairus, it would be a strong argument against the accepting it as a real resurrection from the dead.

While we so strongly emphasize and place in the foreground the question of the motives of Jesus in the awakenings from the dead, we wish, at the same time, to bring out clearly that point of view by which apologetics will be here best promoted. In merely combating opposing views, there is here little to be done,—and perhaps that little may be also easiest spared. The miracles now before us, like those which will be shown in the last group, have been and must be peculiarly inconvenient to Schleiermacher. Against the raising of the dead, the postulate which he demands for the recognition of a miracle, viz. the proof of an analogy with human dealings, could not possibly be given. And thus his perplexity appears very plain. He endeavours to free himself from his difficulty (*Leben Jesu*, p. 232) in a violent manner. He considers the daughter of Jairus as only apparently dead, and makes use of the fact (certainly a very irrelevant one here) that people apparently dead, when they returned to consciousness, have made the assertion, that in their

---

¹ The demand, that everywhere there should be shown the motive which determined Jesus to restore a dead man to life, is intended to be much more definite; and it goes much further than to say that the feeling or tone should be limited only to that region within which this activity of our Lord must have been kept. Feeling justly revolts against the thought that Jesus had been able to call back to life those that had lost it by a natural cause, or by such as the fall of the tower of Siloam (*The Evangelia Infantiæ* [in the Apocryphal Gospels] narrate a great number of such cases, and by it betray their character); just so, on the other hand, that He would have been willing to renew a life which had found its end at the limit set to man, by awakening the old man who had fallen asleep. There must have been reason for the wish, 'Take me not away in the half of my days;' it must, so to say, be worth while for the person to return again to the earthly life.

trance their hearing did not leave them. He makes the same supposition also of the young man at Nain; he calls to mind the Jewish custom of early burial; he is influenced, besides, by the fact that Luke alone narrates the history. By means of this makeshift he has fallen into the most ordinary rationalism, and in the case of Lazarus he is left in the lurch. How he, who stands up for the authenticity of the fourth Gospel, deals with *this* narrative, will be considered later.

Now, as regards Strauss; he also has a difficult position here. He cannot point out an Old Testament prophecy, applicable to the present narratives, which needed to be applied to the Messiah. To him it did not even seem sufficient that it was necessary for the Messiah to surpass Elijah and Elisha, who, according to 1st and 2d Kings, raised from the dead, and that, according to the idea held by the Jews, He ought at least not to be behind them. Hence he maintains that there is a second genetic factor, that a cause must be found existing in Christianity itself. 'The Christians were not like other men, who have no hope beyond the grave, . . . death appeared to them nothing but a sleep. . . . The faith in the resurrection of Christ involved, indeed, the principal guarantee for the future resurrection; but, together with this passive resurrection, men desired to see also active proofs of the exercise of His power on the part of Him who was to raise the dead; He must not merely have been raised from the dead Himself, but have also Himself raised the dead;' this he says was the genesis of our histories.

It is easy to discover the deceptiveness of this manner of considering it. If any one says that Christianity is the religion of immortality and of the resurrection (Strauss' *Leben*, 464; Eng. transl. ii. 205), he is bound to answer the question, On what is this faith grounded? from what source did the Christians draw it? Out of the Old Testament? But it needed the sharpness of the eye of Jesus, and of the enlightened view of the apostles, to discover the ground of such a hope there (Matt. xxii. 29; Heb. xi. 16). Or out of the opinions of the Judaism of the time? But Strauss himself has shown what there was in the theory of immortality as held by the Pharisees. Which of the two views is obvious to impartial thinkers, —the one, that Christians once got hold of the fancy of immortality, of awakening from death, and then invented it to suit and to support the myth of the resurrection of Jesus, and of the raisings of the dead which He has accomplished; or not rather the other, that they, just *because* Jesus had risen, and proved Himself as the Prince of Life, comforted themselves with an eternal life? Thus at least the Apostle Paul inferred in 1 Cor. xv. But we pursue the subject for an interest embracing much more than merely to show this arbitrariness. It is our object to render the probability of these miracles of our Lord conceivable, and to do so by exhibiting the motives which moved Him thereto.

THE RAISING OF THE DAUGHTER OF JAIRUS.—MATT. IX. 18; MARK V. 22; LUKE VIII. 41.

Strauss, from the point of view which he generally entertains of the narratives of the raisings from the dead by Jesus, makes the assertion, with regard to the one before us, that its theme is the saying, 'The maid is not dead, but sleepeth,' and that this theme is incorporated as a miraculous story. We refrain from passing a judgment on this view, relying with confidence on a thorough examination of the evangelical representations. It is otherwise with a point which we ourselves consider a doubtful one, and which requires a closer discussion. The correct view of it, though in the end it cannot be doubtful, is not to be easily gained.

Expositors are reproached, that they have neglected to answer a question on which the whole turns—the question *why* our Lord performed this work. If the *fact* is merely stated, without elucidating the *deed* by this, the door through which a satisfactory view of the subject might be obtained remains closed. It does not seem good to return at once and immediately to the oft-considered question as to whether we have before us a real awakening from the dead, or if we have only the cure of a child sick to death, and already dying. We will certainly *endeavour* to walk in this path, but only so far as to point out that it does not lead us to any sure result; for, in order to decide the question, a totally different manner of proceeding is required.

All three evangelists narrate the incident, as already mentioned, in close connection with the account of the woman with the issue of blood. If we had Matthew's account alone, there could be no dispute on the point; for in chap. ix. ver. 18 he narrates, in unequivocal words, that the father of the child, falling at His feet, said to Jesus, My daughter ἄρτι ἐτελεύτησεν. Away, then, with this vain attempt to explain away these words: they are, 'my daughter is even now dead,' and nothing else. Strauss, although he cannot help calling the beseeching father 'naïve,' because he makes the supposition that the awakening again of the dead child is easy work for Jesus, still sees in Matthew the beginning of the fabrication with a special tendency, and in the reports of Mark and Luke the further development of the myth. He does not even spare the *name* of the suppliant mentioned by two of the evangelists, saying that Jairus comes from Jair, 'he will enlighten,' and is intended to show the vivifying enlightenment of Jehovah which He manifested to the maid.

Our view of the relations of the synoptic Gospels to one another is different in this case. The account in Matthew is only a summary one. Thoughts would arise in us as to its insufficiency, even if the representations of Mark and Luke were *not* before us. We hold specially that what Strauss calls only 'naïve' was quite impossible, namely, that Jairus, after the child was really dead, had been able to say to Jesus, Come, lay thy hand on her, and she shall be again alive.[1] We will compare it with the words of the nobleman in John iv. 49. When he thus besought him, 'Sir, come down ere my child die,' the meaning is evidently, that the presence even of this physician would be of no more avail to the dead person. Let us therefore hear the accounts of the two other evangelists, especially that of Mark, who depicts the scene in great detail; who tells, besides the name of the man, also his rank (one of the rulers of the synagogue). Luke says, ruler of the synagogue, and even shows the spot where Jairus fell at His feet (Jesus stood still 'nigh unto the sea;' He had only just crossed to the other side). He gives the words of the request as follows: 'My little daughter lieth at the point of death; come and lay thy hand on her, that she may be healed, and she shall live.' (In reality, this agrees with Luke, chap. viii. 42, 'she lay a-dying;' while in the 49th verse it is, 'she is dead.') Thus, at

---

[1] Even the text of Matthew himself seems to be opposed to this view. We read ζήσεται (ver. 18); but we have no right, without any further notice, to make it the same as ἀνὰ ζήσεται. In the New Testament, at least, ζῆν is never used in this sense.

the moment when Jairus had come to our Lord, the child was still in life, even although she was evidently approaching her death. But how further? Was there still life in her when our Lord appeared in the house of mourning? Is she really not dead? Here views differ.

The majority of expositors consider that the death of the child had really taken place in the meantime. They recall the circumstance, that the people from the house send the message, 'Trouble not the Master; His help comes too late, the sick one is already dead;' besides this, they remark that the conduct of Jesus to the maid, the 'Talitha kumi,' 'the taking by the hand,' the 'I say unto thee,' all give the impression of a real resuscitation from the dead; besides, the clause 'and her spirit returned again' of Luke (chap. viii. ver. 55) hardly allows another view. However, others have recommended the opposite opinion, with very plausible arguments. Schleiermacher says, that if, notwithstanding the express words of Jesus, that 'the child is not dead, but sleepeth,' the history is understood as if she had died, and been awakened by Him from the dead, it is as if one knew better than Christ Himself; that in this case one betrays a suspicious relation to those who laughed at our Lord on account of His declaration, that the child was only sleeping.[1] His exposition has received the most decided approval from Olshausen, who, in his *Bibl. Comment.* i. p. 327, declares

---

[1] Compare Schleiermacher on Mark's Gospel, i. p. 266: 'There is something quite different in this speech of the Redeemer to what He says to His disciples with regard to Lazarus. There He says to them, Our friend Lazarus sleeps, I will go to awaken him; He by no means says, He is not dead, but only he sleeps; and when His disciples understand His words literally, He announces it to them openly: When I said he sleeps, I meant that he is dead. On the other hand, here He puts them expressly together, and says, "The child is *not* dead; make not such a noise and such complaints as you are accustomed to do for a dead person: she is only sleeping." We will not declare this exegesis "extremely miserable," as Strauss is pleased to judge it.'

it quite unquestionable that we have before us a deep trance, a so-called asphyxia (to distinguish it from syncope). However, this view at first sight, though very captivating, still leaves some doubt. Yea, if our Lord had simply said, 'the maid is not dead,' we should probably yield to it; however, as He makes the addition 'she sleeps,' there is again room for the supposition that this sleep signifies death, and just because of His intention to awake her did our Lord use the symbolical expression. Hence from the words themselves we cannot gain a *certain* decision; and if the arguments for and against are balanced, the result must be an undecided 'non liquet.' Even Bleek (*Synops.* i. p. 404) remains contented with such a result.

In order to arrive at a sure result, we must, as we have before remarked, take with it the question, On what ground did our Lord perform this work in the house of Jairus? If we suppose in advance that we have before us a raising from the dead, our dilemma is in fact great,—to be able to give information as to the causes which moved our Lord to *such* a miracle. For no one will consider it a sufficient motive to consider that, as Luke narrates, this child was the only daughter of Jairus, and that thus the compassion of Jesus was evoked. The state of affairs at Nain was something very different. If, on the other hand, we treat it simply as the healing of the sick, the *readiness* of Jesus to come and help gives us not the least difficulty; for we know that, as often as in such a case He was approached by a suppliant, He was always prepared to do so. Let us put it in this secure position. When Jairus came to the Saviour, his child was still alive. He did, indeed, complain that she was near to death, but his solicitude only went so far, that Jesus should come (he besought Him that He would come into his house, Luke viii. 41) in order to make his child well, to preserve her life, which was in danger of departing. And for that our Lord declares Himself ready, and He 'went with him' (Mark v. 24). The real intention was thus to cure a sick person, to *preserve* her from the death which threatened her. Now, when they were on the way, there came, on the part of the people of the house, the news, Thy daughter is dead (ἀπέθανεν, Mark v. 35; τέθνηκεν, Luke viii. 49). And the news was actually correct. None will hold it probable that the inhabitants of the house were under a deception. News which were doubtful in any manner they would not offer to the grieved father, at least at a moment when he had communicated with the infallible physician.

A trance may occur,—certainly most rarely in a child,—but any one can easily recognise the death of such a one. Physicians speak of undeniable death-symptoms; and since theology has been busy with the rationalistic hypothesis of the trance of the crucified Christ, the circumstance has been discussed on all sides. It may be allowed, that in a grown person who knows what dying is, and who fights with death, the threatened life may retire into the innermost part of his being, and notwithstanding all appearance that it has departed, may be latently present; but in a child, who yields without opposition to the unknown enemy, the possibility is purely speculative, and the idea of a deception on the part of the household is void of all probability. No; the death of the maiden had really taken place.

And how now? Should our Lord have again turned back? Should He, after having raised the hopes of the father by His rising and going with him, have acknowledged that now He could help him no more (especially as His arrival at the house of Jairus had been delayed; that He had spent a long time with the woman who had the issue of blood, a delay which had certainly put the anxious father to a hard trial of his patience, as he would feel acutely the danger of delay)? We feel at once that He could *not* act thus; but this feeling must be correctly shown. We cannot point to it as a mere instance of a natural human feeling. Such a view would be incorrect, as to suppose our Lord could not have had the heart to deceive the awakened hope of Jairus; that He could not have been a witness to the grief of the father who had received courage from His so readily offering to go with him,— a witness to the breaking out of his grief at the news of the death, and to his experiencing the bitterest deception. *This* is not the proper key. But therein lies the question: Jesus had arisen to give help—and was He not to do so now? Impossible! If He had once resolved on and promised help, He must have done so without fail; whatever intervened, no hindrance could stop Him—*not even death.*

The state of the case is here also different from that of the raising of Lazarus. In the latter case our Lord deliberately put off His arrival at Bethany. Lazarus *was* to die, in order that He might awaken him from the dead; this was His aim and end. On the other hand, *here* He did *not* intentionally delay, but at the moment that He had received the petition He hastened with the father to his house; and if He stayed on the way, it was only because a work was there to be done which could not be put off. It was now shown that this delay had hindered the cure of the *sick* child; she had in the meantime died. And in this our Lord saw an indication on the part of His Father for Him so to help, as *only* now He could help, that is, by raising her from the dead. This, then, was the motive which constrained Him. Thus there has been answered for us a twofold question: first, What did our Lord do? He called back to life a dead person! and secondly, Why did He perform this work? It was the consequence of His previously declared readiness to come and help.[1]

In order to throw here and there a confirming ray of light on our representation, we still devote some attention to a few particular points in the Gospel narrative. At the moment in which Jesus *at the same time* as Jairus (this would lie in the reading παρακούσας, if it is the correct one) receives the message from his house, He recognises what He has to do, He knows what He will do; but immediately He turns His care to the father, that his disposition should be favourable to the divine thoughts and intentions. His hope was awakened by the readiness of our Lord; it was strengthened into confidence by what he saw done to the woman with an issue of blood. By the tidings announced connected with the remembrance of the τί ἔτι σκύλλεις τὸν διδάσκαλον, it might sink, yea, might be extinguished. The words, 'Be not afraid, only believe,' were intended to obviate this danger. 'Let not this message overcome you; keep your faith firm; direct the whole force of your will on your faith,—this is the only (μόνον) thing that is necessary to you now.' Similar to this is the expression to Martha, even though it was shaded by a reprimand: 'Did I not tell

[1] We have readily allowed that Matthew has reported the event in question only briefly and summarily, and that his representation of it is not clear. But far from allowing thereby any disparaging conclusion on the first Gospel, we make this circumstance available rather as a witness to its high value, and to its authenticity. Matthew does draw the true, the correct summary. Shortly and decisively he expresses himself, that here we have a resurrection from the dead, and as such a deed of Jesus, it has its necessary position in the rich gallery of His miracles which are described in the 8th and 9th chapters of the first Gospel. If we had only Mark and Luke, the opinion that our Lord had only cured an apparently dead and very sick child, would gain the highest appearance of right; and Schleiermacher's view would then, indeed, become the dominant one in Protestant exegesis.

thee, if thou wouldst believe, thou shouldst see the glory of God?' (John xi. 40.)

It was not only when they came into the house or to its immediate vicinity (as Luke represents it) that Jesus turned back the accompanying multitude, but immediately after the message of the death had been delivered,—thus in the very moment when He knew what He was to do. (Thus Mark reports in words, chap. v. 37, 38, which bear in themselves the guarantee of literal correctness; in verse 37 it says, 'He suffered no man to follow Him,' and then in the 38th verse, 'and He cometh to the house.') Hitherto He had suffered the thronging multitude; and it was even thereby that the work of faith in the woman with the issue of blood had been possible. Now, when His eye rests on the work shown Him to do,—a work which from its nature must be done in stillness,—He begins to ward off unbidden witnesses. He makes a selection even among His disciples. Only Peter, James, and John were allowed to continue the journey with Him,—the same three whom He took with Him to the Mount of Transfiguration, while the nine remained in the valley; the same three whom later He called into His immediate neighbourhood at Gethsemane, and who also formed a closer circle about Him (sometimes with Andrew, as in Mark xiii. 3; John xii. 22). When He had entered into the house of mourning, He at once sent away the people there collected. Only the father and mother of the lifeless child, and the three trusted disciples, were allowed to be present. And even to them (Mark v. 43) was the express injunction given, that they should ponder in their own hearts on the work they had seen, without intentionally spreading it abroad. We agree here as little with Meyer's stereotyped resource, that Jesus this time, as much as He could, wished to prevent the enkindling of fanatical hopes of the

Messiah, as in any other case. The retirement which our Lord desired for this work, and the silence which He recommended at it, were necessitated by the peculiar manner in which it arose. Only those should see it who had the most immediate interest in the child, and those who had in equal measure a part in our Lord. Those who stood nearest to the passive object, and those nearest the active subject, were the truly called witnesses, and were also to remain the only ones; as in a similar way the vision on the Mount of Transfiguration remained the secret of the same three disciples, Matt. xvii. 9.

When our Lord had come near to the house of Jairus, He saw there the tumult which customarily took place after a case of death, that is, He remarked the weepers and the loud mourners,—Luke, ἐκόπτοντο, those who smote on their breast; 'plangentes' (Matt. ix. 23, τοὺς αὐλητάς), those who raised a wailing cry (חָיִל, Jer. iv. 8), with which was mingled the funeral music (appointed by the αὐλή, חָלִיל). The Jewish obsequies were in full operation. The traditions of it in this particular form are not very old. We meet with the first traces of them at the time of Jeremiah. In 2 Chron. xxxv. 25, after mention is made of the death of King Josiah, it is stated, 'And Jeremiah lamented for Josiah, and all the singing men and singing women spake of Josiah in their lamentations to this day, and made them an ordinance in Israel.' See also Jer. ix. 17: 'Thus saith the Lord of Hosts, Consider ye, and call for the mourning women, that they may come; and send for cunning women, that they come: and let them make haste, and take up a wailing for us, that our eyes may run down with tears, and our eyelids gush out with water.' The custom had indeed a double meaning,—at once to show plainly the pain, in order then to fight against it. If our

Lord comes forward to stop it, and assures them that the maid sleeps, it is, as we have seen, to be understood with regard to the intended raising from the dead; He wishes that the appearance of the house should agree with His intention. They laugh at Him, not in derision, but with a painfully incredulous smile,— she is only too certainly dead.

Our Lord obliges them to leave the place; and, with the persons interested, He enters into the chamber where the dead child is laid out. Talitha kumi! We know that Mark is accustomed to introduce in Hebrew the important and effective words of the wonder-working Jesus,—not as if they were magic formulæ, but because they remain incapable of being forgotten by the witnesses; and because just in this form, as the commands of power of the Son of God, are they so comforting to the consciousness of the Christian, just as the 'Abba' comes from his mouth with the experience of peace. And the maid stood up and walked; 'for she was of the age of twelve,' adds Mark. She was no small child, who could not walk, but she already counted twelve years. Bengel says, 'Rediit ad statum ætati congruenter.' Our Lord orders that they should give her something to eat. He wishes not only to prove the reality of the life restored to full health, but also that, after this mighty attack on the course of nature, it is again allowed to take its usual order. The apprehensions of the parents also wanted time to calm, for 'they were astonished with a great astonishment.' In another sense, also, their nature would be altered for ever, for, as in a similar case, it is said, 'and he believed with his whole house.' Such was here our Lord's intention, and perhaps the real result. If faith had been deficient in the father after such an event, it would certainly never have been attainable by miracles.

THE RAISING OF THE YOUNG MAN AT NAIN.—
LUKE VII. 11-17.

The manner in which Strauss passes to the consideration of this narrative, gives to apologetics a warning well worthy of being taken to heart. He begins with the remark, that even the remembrance of the Old Testament types of Elijah and Elisha, both of whom raised from the dead the only son of a mother (the former, indeed, that of a widow), render it conceivable how Christian myth-making has made a considerable progress since the history of Jairus; and, in fact, orthodox theology does speak of a progress of that kind in the raising from the dead. On one side there is some weight in it, as Jesus raised from the dead, first one on the bed of death, then upon the bier, and lastly even from the grave. On the other hand, it is also advanced that our Lord called back to mortal life, first a child, later a young man, and lastly a man.

This is not only a useless and aimless speculation, but it supposes a real danger. Perhaps it may be objected that there is danger of encouragement being given to the mode of mythical consideration; but so much is certain, that by such suppositions exegesis is limited in its extent, and that in single cases the door is opened for arbitrary suppositions.

It is certainly correct that, among all the evangelists, the one whom we have to thank for the narrative before us, notwithstanding the clause in chap. i. 3, 'to write unto thee in order,' has at any rate in the first part of his writing observed the chronological order the least. So in the seventh chapter, when he says, 'And it came to pass the day after,' it is impossible to exempt the following narrative from its connection in point of time with the immediately preceding one of the captain at Capernaum. For the ἐν τῇ ἑξῆς cannot signify anything 'later,' but only 'on the day following.' (Luke has also introduced the history of the lunatic, chap. ix. 37, with this formula; but all the evangelists testify to the fact that it followed immediately after the transfiguration of Jesus.) This determination of the time would, however, be found now inconvenient; and on that account, the reading approved by the best critics, ἐν τῇ ἑξῆς, must give place to the weakly attested ἐν τῷ ἑξῆς, in order that one may be able to place the raising of the young man at any later time approved of. The motives for this arbitrary act were not only those expressed by Stier (*Reden Jesu*, iii. p. 73); for the opinion, that the plural in the message of our Lord to the Baptist, 'The dead are raised,' supposes several raisings of the dead on the part of Jesus, is just as erroneous as is the assertion, that otherwise Jairus would not have dared to have any more hope for his child after she was dead, and which rests on the latter narrative being misunderstood. The true motive for this arbitrary altering of the text was rather this, that it had been found more convenient to commence the resurrections from the dead by Jesus in a child that had only just died, than in a young man already on the road to the grave. But even here Gottfried Arnold's true saying is suitable: 'Reason and good opinion state that the spirit never depends on human laws.'[1]

We leave aside the questions principally connected with archæology, which have partly been satisfactorily

---

[1] Meyer himself has also decided for the reading ἐν τῷ ἑξῆς, and that on verbal grounds. That Luke, in fact, always writes τῇ ἑξῆς, never ἐν τῇ ἑξῆς. There are certainly to be found in his writings a few passages where he leaves out the preposition. But it is a hazardous conclusion, that the evangelist could never have made use of the formula, in itself quite indisputable, ἐν τῇ ἑξῆς, and that thus in this case the authority of the codices should not be considered forcible.

settled, and partly left unanswered by exegetical writers. We look for this otherwise quite unknown town of Nain in Galilee, not on the authority of Jerome, but on account of the 'on the day after;' although we do not undervalue the difficulty which arises to this view from the 17th verse. Our Lord touches the bier, and by that signifies to the bearers that they are to pursue the way to the grave no further; He will give again life to the youth, the son to the weeping mother. Her tears were not to yield to the voice of a comforter, but they are stopped by the possession again of her only child.

Now there arises the question, By what motive was Jesus moved to perform this deed? Our narrative belongs to the small number of those where He performed a miracle without previously receiving a request. That such was wanting in this case, we see at once is quite natural. The demand to raise a dead person *could* not be directed to Him. Let us think of the highest grade of a strong faith, or of the most extreme point of a narrow-minded pietism in the Christianity of the present day; in neither of these cases would the request to Jesus come from a human mouth, 'Awake again the dead.' One could urge on Him, 'Cure the sufferer, keep back the expiring life; see, he whom Thou lovest lies sick;' but if death has occurred, no one would pray, 'Give me back my dead.' And thus it is that it never happened in the whole extent of the gospel history. Jairus indeed hastens to Jesus when his daughter lay sick unto death and in the last throes; but when the news came that she was dead, it was said, 'Trouble not the Master any further, for the maiden is dead.' The sisters in Bethany did send to our Lord that he should come quickly, in order that He might cure their sick brother; but when he was dead, they gave up hope, and said only, 'Lord, if Thou hadst been here, our brother had not died.' Certainly there broke out once from Martha, 'I know even yet, what Thou askest from God, that will He give Thee.' But the words make the same impression as those of Peter on the mountain of transfiguration, on which Mark's judgment (chap. ix. 6) is, for 'he wist not what to say, for they were sore afraid.' Martha spoke in the tumult of her feelings, and was not herself clear as to what she said. The thought of an earnest request for the raising of the dead could have no place in her heart. Mary was certainly far from thinking of it. We can quite *conceive* it. It is appointed to every one to die. Though it may be wished that this hour be put off for a long time, or that the threatened danger should yield to a palliative, still, *when* death has occurred, all wishes are given up, and grief, pure, and in this point hopeless, or no more restrained by hope, enters into its rights and asserts itself.

If, therefore, the request for the awakening of a dead person could not be directed to Jesus, such a factor could not have caused his action; therefore he must have experienced *peculiar*, deep, inward motives for the unexpected deed. What were they? It will *not* do to draw an answer from the general explanation of our Lord, that 'as the Father raiseth up the dead, and quickeneth them, even so the Son quickeneth whom He will' (John v. 21), because we have not now to deal with the *general* question, why He called back into life dead persons in general, but with the more *special* one, as to the ground of his θέλειν in the present case. Why did He manifest His life-giving power specially upon this youth? The reproof of arbitrariness is applicable to every answer which is not taken from the gospel narrative itself, and proved from it. But from the narrative, we are only able to say that the motive of Jesus was His deep, inward compassion for the widowed and orphaned mother. Strauss has proved the special acuteness of his observation, in judging that the peculiarity of this representation of St. Luke consists in the numerous impulses affecting the feelings and the interest considered, which is here much stronger than in the case of Jairus. To Strauss these only show the motive for the composition of this narrative, while to *us* the same opinion occurs from the course of the real events and from the representation of the act. But that this opinion really results from them, we have first exegetically to prove, in order afterwards to consider the question, How it is to be understood that this compassion could have been in Jesus the motive for such an act? Let us now follow the narrative itself, and we see that the very way in which the evangelist depicts the scene, as also the saying of Jesus which he reports, is calculated and put in such a manner as to show that our Lord is governed by compassion, and was disposed to show it. For that purpose he introduces the state of matters as depicted in the 12th verse.

It was an 'only son of his mother' who was about to be snatched away from the already widowed woman; she was thus now completely forsaken; the great multitude of people accompanying, 'much people of the city was with her,' testifies to the high degree of sympathy which this case of death had awakened in Nain. Then the remark of the 13th verse, 'the Lord had compassion on her,' which is to show immediately the subsequent conduct of Jesus, is in harmony with this. And to this also agrees the 'weep not.' This is a very different message from the apparently similar, though really different command, 'weep not,' to the household of Jairus. In the latter case we have a command of Jesus for the purpose of restoring quiet; here, however, the cheering is from sympathy. We must not overlook the concluding words, 'and He delivered him to his mother.' We certainly find it the same in the narrative of the lunatic (but that only in Luke's account, chap. ix. 42); but here they are of especial importance, when we compare them with the representation of the raising of Lazarus. There our Lord spake, 'Loose him, and let him go;' it is *not* said, He gave him to his sisters. But the motive of His deed was there quite different. It was far from His intention to still the tears of the sisters. Hence we can draw from the announcement, that He delivered the young man into the hands of his mother, confirmatory views for the supposition, that He accomplished His work out of pity to the bereaved woman. That, according to the 16th verse, the whole multitude broke out in praises to God, and in acknowledging Jesus as a great prophet, does not invalidate our judgment; for this result was by no means the special intention of our Lord.

But if now, on the strength of the evangelist's representation, no other answer is to be given to our question, the further problem arises, as to why our Lord so completely yielded in this case to His compassion, Why He suffered Himself so thoroughly to be led by it? Why here also was there not that groaning,[1] in order to suppress the psychical emotion? The question is difficult to answer. It could be proved by the explanation, that in this case the πνεῦμα was in perfect understanding with the ψυχή. But where a sure view is denied to us, probability has a certain right to be heard, in so far as it does not rest merely

---

[1] We understand the 'groaning,' which in John xi. is repeatedly mentioned of Jesus, as a spiritual working of our Lord, directed against the movement of His own soul. We think also that the correctness of this view is convincingly proved. We consider incorrect the explanation lately made, and especially by Gumlich (*Theol. Studien und Kritiken*, 1862, p. 260 and fol.).

on fancy. Our view is, that our Lord has here shown a type of what was to be accomplished in Himself at no very distant time. The raising of Lazarus by Jesus has often been judged as a prelude to His own resurrection. Strauss himself has expressly acknowledged the right of considering it in this light (certainly in the interest of his own tendencies). But still more indisputably is it allowable to bring the event before us in a relation of that kind to an occurrence in the termination of the career of Jesus Himself. When in fact our Lord drank the cup of death, there stood the *mater dolorosa* at the foot of the cross, with similar though deeper grief than the woman at Nain. Jesus Himself was also, in a certain sense, 'the only son of His mother, and she was a widow.' We know how He looked down with compassion upon her, and spoke to her His 'weep not,'—not in words alone, but by means of a testamentary disposition. Among all His ties of kindred, that to His mother was the only one to which He felt bound. For even the so-called 'brothers,' even though it should be convincingly proved that they were the real sons of Mary,[1] were not in a complete sense His brothers. Hence He experienced towards the woman who bare Him a peculiar compassion, different and deeper than if the blind and the lepers, or the needy in general, had depicted all their necessities to Him,—a compassion not by means of His suffering pity, but in sympathy with His own experience of pain. And if it now happened that a woman came before His eyes in trouble, in a position in which He would soon have to see His mother, there is thus shown a degree of the expressly reported ἐσπλαγχ-

---

[1] The newest treatise by Laurent (*Neutestamentl. Studien*, pp. 152-193) on this question, decides it in this way. We certainly plead just as little for all the details of this treatise, as for the collected fruits of these studies in general.

υἱσθη, which makes the probability of this *act* of compassion conceivable.

THE RAISING OF LAZARUS.—JOHN XI.

For the extraordinary exertions which Strauss has made against this narrative, exegesis as well as apologetics are deeply indebted to him. He has cleared the air; he has strikingly and victoriously shown, that all the half measures of accommodating theology, however numerous and manifold they may be, are in this case to be condemned as pure impossibilities. With a well-deserved irony he turns against those who seek, 'with the pens of modern poets,' to conceal the unexplained difficulty and their own restlessness. Clearly and sharply he shows others that, notwithstanding all their evasions, they only reach the most common rationalism. As gently as he judges Renan (whose exposition, however much it may provoke the reader, is really, in its principle at least, *more reasonable* than what many others have said in a manner less hurtful to the feelings), he also declares to him that, with such an endeavour to make the raising of Lazarus a mere intrigue of the family, the matter becomes 'not essentially better.' Lastly, he has proved that even Schleiermacher's view is an impossible one. This theologian asserts that we have before us here no deed of Jesus, as our Lord ascribes the work not to Himself, but to His Father.[1] Strauss shows what this really means in plain language; for by this mode of explaining them, *all* the miracles of Jesus would either vanish before

[1] See Schleiermacher's *Leben Jesu*, p. 233: 'The miracle as a deed of Christ possesses quite a different character. For while He prays to God to hear Him, He takes the effect as a *divine* one resulting from His prayer. He Himself thus steps outside the region of miracle, excepting the firmness of His conviction that what He asked would also happen on the part of God.'

our eyes (as without a glance upwards to His Father, or without a prayer to Him, did our Lord certainly accomplish no single one), or they would be placed altogether under one new point of view only. Also in this way a real difference between the Lazarus miracle and the other miracles of Jesus would in no wise occur. The critic has thus so far rendered quite thankworthy services.

We now turn to Strauss' own view. He proceeds negatively and positively at the same time. After he has attempted to show that the history could not have happened as it is told, he tries to prove the genesis of the 'myth.' The incredibility of the occurrence appears sure to him, on external as well as internal ground. In regard to the former, the reality of it is destroyed by the circumstance that the synoptics know nothing of it. On the other hand, the internal improbability is evident, partly from the conduct of Jesus before His arrival at Bethany, which, as here stated, would be 'revolting;' partly from the feigned prayer at the grave of Lazarus, which would be the 'affair of an unskilful actor.'

If this negative explanation, even in its outlines, appears a very weak one, Strauss has, on the other hand, in the positive half of the exposition, unfolded the whole glory of his power of showing probabilities and drawing conclusions from them. At the head he places the assertion, that the root of the Johannine narrative is the interest that existed to support the Christian doctrine of the future resurrection of the dead through Christ's coming again, by means of a miracle, which should witness to its having happened in the past. As a proof that at a future time all that were buried should rise at the voice of the Son of God, it was necessary to show that He had called forth from the grave with a mighty voice during His mortal pilgrimage, one who had already fallen into corruption. But for this end, the history of Jairus was applicable just as little as the narrative at Nain. It was necessary to invent an incident which would relate to the latter, just as the superlative does to the comparative and positive. The justification of this view is shown by the disclosure of the theme of the myth, then furthered by the designation of its base, and lastly completed by proving how the author of the fourth Gospel arrived at the persons acting, and how he was led to the form of his composition. The *theme* consists of the sentence, 'I am the resurrection and the life;' for all the details rest on the carrying out of this. On the other hand, the *base* may be the history of the raising of the daughter of Jairus. This latter must evidently have served the poet as a pattern; the close relation of the several features prove it,—here as there the commencing of the announcement of the mere sickness, and then of death resulting from it; here as there the designation of death as a sleep,—'the maid sleepeth,' 'our friend Lazarus sleepeth;' here as there the going to Jesus with 'Trouble not the Master, the child is dead,' 'Lord, if Thou hadst been here, my brother had not died;' lastly, in both cases the same conduct of Jesus to the mourners,—in the one the forbidding of demonstrations of grief, in the other the trial of the weeping sisters. 'Is it not therefore plain that the fourth evangelist, taking his plan in general from the groundwork of the history of Jairus, has followed out the raising of this subject into the superlative degree?' But for such actors as were needed for the material of the dramatic composition, the author has obtained them by a circumspect use of the synoptic Gospels. We have in Matthew and Mark at Bethany an anointing woman, in Luke an anointing sinner; and the sisters Mary and Martha in an uncertain place. These threads are now found drawn together in the narrative before us, in such a form that at the same time the peculiarities of the persons, faintly pointed out in the synoptic Gospels, have become of use. Of a real Lazarus the older sources knew indeed nothing, but only of one in a parable. And that this latter had been borrowed from Luke, and changed into a real one, is based not only on the striking resemblance between John xi. 1 and Luke xvi. 20: 'There was a certain sick man, Lazarus of Bethany,' 'There was a certain poor man, Lazarus by name,' but also on this, that both died and are buried; that one of them, as the rich man wished, rose from the grave; and that the Jews, notwithstanding this, did not believe, as Abraham had predicted, this result in the parable. And from this is drawn the conclusion, that as we have so plainly seen whence the fourth evangelist obtained his Lazarus with his surroundings, and as it is inconceivable that the others, *if* he had really existed, and had been raised from the dead by Jesus, should have omitted it, it is evident that a mythical poem lies before us, the object of which is not to be mistaken.

Before we turn to the examination of this critical attempt, we again must attest the full justice of the view, that the fourth evangelist was conscious of giving the report of a real raising from the dead, which Christ had accomplished, and that all endeavours to question it are in vain. In order not to repeat what has been said at length, we again call attention to the often-overlooked, or at least not sufficiently-estimated passage (chap. xi. 39),—a passage that, by means of two or three witnesses, cuts off any possible excuses. We read: 'Martha, the sister of him that was dead, saith unto him, Lord, by this time he stinketh, for he hath been dead four days.'

The 'by this time he stinketh' is Martha's opinion; thus she at any rate considered Lazarus already in a state of corruption. The evangelist calls this witness 'the sister of him that was dead.' Why this designation? Certainly not to inform the reader that Martha was the sister; that was known long before. But still less to show, as Meyer says, 'the natural shuddering of the sister's heart;' but in order to pledge by this phrase (it is not of Lazarus, but of him that was dead) his *own* word in testimony that the buried one was really dead. And lastly, he adds: 'for he hath been dead four days,' thus establishing the fact, which was known to every one interested in the circumstance, that it was so long since he had given up the ghost, since he had been buried. We are still informed that the Jews entertain the fancy, that for three days the soul floats about the dead body; that on the fourth it departs, and gives it up to corruption. And the judgment will be immoveably fixed, that unreasonable obstinacy alone can doubt that the evangelist wishes to narrate a real awakening from the dead, and that he has narrated one. Even Strauss himself asserts this. But how does this agree with his peculiar view?

The fact that the synoptic Gospels are silent on this event, he points out as the rock on which its historical credibility is irremediably wrecked. Whether this circumstance really resembles a rock, which causes unavoidable shipwreck, may remain at present undecided; but the *difficulty* really is present. The manner in which it was formerly attempted to be solved satisfies no one now. Schleiermacher's resource, that the history has less a didactic value than a pragmatical significance, which has been damaged in the transmission, could easily be proved by Strauss to have miscarried. Another remark of this theologian has indeed gained attention, but nowhere any real acknowledgment. For even granting the possible case, that the family saw themselves compelled, by the plots on the part of the Jews (mentioned John xii. 10), to leave Bethany, the remembrance of the event is by no means necessarily connected with their personal presence still in the κώμη; it must, under all circumstances, have still been retained there. Hence the apologists of the present day have endeavoured to throw light on this dark point by new exertions. It has been said that the synoptic Gospels confine themselves to the Galilean miracles. But this is not in accordance with fact; for as far as St. Luke is concerned, this manner of explanation does not at all agree with the care with which he depicts the latter part of the life of Jesus.

Other writers [1] have taken a higher standpoint, and decided that this history belongs to the class of those reserved to John; that this disciple had a special mission for the communication of things deep and full of mystery. The mysterious character of the history does not consist in the representation of it, but in the act itself; and the disciple whom Jesus loved, who lay on his breast, was alone able to narrate it. The justice of such a manner of considering it can be acknowledged, without our being on that account *obliged* to admit, or even *able* to admit, that the question has thereby been satisfactorily solved. The plain confession, that we must leave it as it is, deserves certainly the preference over a new hypothesis, in case the latter cannot be made quite clear. Hence we do not show great self-denial in being silent on our own indi-

---

[1] Meyer is of opinion, that from this point of view the problem appears as solved (*Comm. to the Gospel of John*, 4th ed. p. 379). We acknowledge that the representation of such an intentionally mechanical, and almost capricious and objectless carrying out of the 'restriction of the older evangelical historical writings to a limited region' is certainly not possible.

vidual conjecture, because we are not able to fulfil the required condition, and in substituting for it the following consideration as a tolerably satisfactory solution. When the biblical critic comes upon any difficulty, the first law is, that he should not exaggerate it; and in case this should have happened, that he should bring it back to its right proportions. In the case before us it has been exaggerated, and it is right to guard against such unjustifiable over-estimation. So much is indisputable fact, that all four evangelists, although they (John not excepted) each report certain miracles of Jesus in common, also each give single narratives peculiar to themselves. It may therefore be asked, Why this special narrative is *only* found in the first, and that one *only* in one of the others? But nobody concludes, that because only *one* evangelist has it, that it must be untrustworthy. Because Mark *alone* has the history of the deaf and dumb, no one is therefore inclined to suspect it. Why then, because John *alone* narrates the raising of Lazarus, is it on that account *not* trustworthy? We might perhaps conclude that it is just this miracle that should stand out prominently, that such a manifestation of the power of Jesus would have been passed over by no evangelist, 'that it should have been wanting in no complete Gospel, even if only by a mere collector of traditions' (Strauss, 477; Eng. trans. ii. 223).

But these are only modern views, which we may not impute to the authors of our Gospels. We have already entered our protest against the comparison of the miracles of our Lord one with another, from the point of view as to the greater or lesser difficulty of their being performed, and have rejected the question, ' Which is easier to do, this or that?' If such a question is allowed in this matter, who knows whether the contemporaries of Jesus, the disciples included, would not have judged quite differently from us. So much is fact, that the healing of a demoniac formerly left a deeper impression than the awakening of a dead person. No such estimates of degree were present to the eye which performed them. We read in John ix. of the cure of a man that was born blind. No other Gospel tells us that Jesus cured a man that was *born* blind. But yet it has never been asserted that this history *could* not be true, since the synoptics tell us only of simple healings of the blind. Although one may not agree with this inference, it is still an unjustifiable conclusion, that the history of the raising of Lazarus is not trustworthy, because the synoptics on their part relate fewer raisings of the dead occurring before their eyes. If we acknowledge in general the difficulty which is caused by the silence of the first three evangelists on this event, we desire that it should not be exaggerated. Its real value is much too small to be of any decided weight in the balance. At any rate, there must be brought forward other circumstances to make the difficulty greater. As already said, Strauss has made available as such additional witnesses the peculiar inner improbability of the event, and the probability of the narrative when viewed as a myth. To begin with this latter statement, we must repeat our opinion, that Strauss has here unfolded in full force his wonderful power of bringing forward probabilities and drawing conclusions from them. His arguments will tempt many an *ignorant* reader to put the question, 'Could it not have really happened like this?' At the same time, there would occur immediately to every *unprejudiced* one the opposite question, 'Why cannot what is here explained as a poetical working-up and weaving of threads, which are separate and scattered about in the synoptics,—why can it not be the whole historical truth?' A more untenable ground than that the persons coming on the scene are nothing else than forms of fancy and phantoms, has not been advanced; and the confidence with which this is assumed is solely explainable by the view, that this result is attained by other grounds, and that criticism has only to solve the problem of justifying it at any price. It is an experience to which common life as well as scientific life bears witness, that a prejudice once entertained forms a fixed crystallizing point, to which all further motives occurring are added by degrees, so that they tend to confirm the supposition already cherished. The eye is sharp in finding out all suspicious circumstances; it *sees* them in the light, it *places* them in the light which prejudice has already prepared for them, while it is dim and blind to every other possibility, even though close at hand. Combinations, which to an unprejudiced observer appear extremely important, are reckoned as insignificant; and difficulties, over which another cannot pass, are put aside in an easy, genial manner.[1] And thus can a picture be conjured up, which most opportunely

[1] It is only in this way that we can explain the newest work of Volkmar, one relating solely to history, *The Origin of our Gospels*, Zurich 1866, unless in judging it we take into account the thorough animosity against Tischendorf's treatise (in defence of which we ourselves are not inclined to enter the lists). The Gospels may certainly be indifferent to an acknowledgment which is thus formulated in page 18: 'Jesus the teacher from God the Father, of redeeming *love*, of full love, even of love to His enemy,' even though it is embellished with a few pompous phrases. The acknowledgment of Jesus from heathen mouths would satisfy him (as pointed out in other places), while the Biblical sources are unsatisfactory and burdensome to him. The whole penetration of the author hence took instinctively the direction of finding out and combining together all that seemed to call in question the genuineness of the Gospels; while, on the other hand, all that opposed his suspicions be considered as unimportant, unenlightened, and uncertain. But how he can expect, that men who have read the sources just as well and just as carefully as himself should on his authority and guidance concede that the witnesses for the fourth Gospel are first met with in the second half of the second century, is difficult indeed for us to conceive.

recommends itself by its pleasing, and indeed artistic forms, but which breaks down in the main thing, that is, in truth. While Strauss resolves the narrative of Lazarus in St. John into a myth, he has himself given us a specimen of fancy, which will draw from *all* readers an acknowledgment of his splendid power of arrangement and of drawing conclusions, but from *none* of anything further. He has certainly shown two points of the evangelical account which, taken historically, may seem purely impossible. But, in fact, one must first either share the prejudices of Strauss, or realize his views, at least, clearly and precisely, before we can conceive how these features of the narrative can really be a stumbling-block to any one. For, *on the one hand*, there must be 'such a mode of proceeding on the part of any one,—that is, of preferring to allow a friend to die when he might have saved him, in order afterwards to have the power of reviving him,' which 'in the case of a real man, even the most divinely endowed and most closely united with God, would be inhuman and revolting.' Certainly a man, as Strauss represents Jesus Christ, a Jewish rabbi, who surpassed his companions in office without specifically differing from them,—such a man could not thus have acted, but would, on the receipt of the message, have immediately started, as a sympathizing friend, to Bethany. But even with an 'embodied conception' we gain nothing; a conception that acts (we do not say this in jest, but in deepest earnest, see *Leben Jesu*, 475) lies beyond our understanding. But the Son of God, who was guided by what was the design and the will of His Father, in this delaying and remaining, and in this finally rising and going, could and must yield the obedience to which He felt Himself bound, according to John v. 19, 20. *On the other hand*, according to Strauss, the thanksgiving prayer of Jesus at the grave of Lazarus must appear as the conduct of an actor, and that a very unskilful one. How? Is, then, a thanksgiving to God so destitute of every degree of inner truth, that it can be conceived only in the mouth of an actor? or, if *that* is not exactly to be asserted, does the loudly outspoken thanksgiving justify the degrading comparison? Our Lord has elsewhere addressed to God a thanksgiving aloud: 'I thank Thee, O Father, Lord of heaven and earth, that Thou hast hid these things from the wise and prudent, and hast revealed them unto babes: even so, Father; for thus it seemed good in Thy sight' (Luke x. 21). Does *this* come under the same judgment? or is it only the express declaration of the petitioner, that He intended to bring His offering before the ears of the assembled people, which is not otherwise justifiable and conceivable than on the stage? As if the most satisfactory light is not spread on this circumstance by the tendency of the whole work as shown in the 4th verse, that it was in fact a manifestation of the Father through the Son, and of the Son through the Father! And is this really all that Strauss has to bring forward against the historical credibility of the narrative? In fact this is all, really all! And can he really be of opinion that *this* will afford more than a mere counterpoise to the impression of truth, which history has brought forward in accordance with experience in the course of nearly a thousand years? A particular avowal he himself could not suppress. He has not given it in his interpretation of the narrative before us, but in a later connection: 'The profundity of the fourth evangelist excites our admiration . . . it is impossible not to see his eagerness for the inward and the spiritual; but this goes hand in hand with a propensity for what is most objective, most material in form' (*Leben Jesu*, 595; Eng. transl. ii. 393). We take action on this assertion, and think we may affirm that the critic has here spoken his own judgment. In fact, this mixture so distasteful to him of the most admirable 'profundity,' with its hold on the most outward and most sensible, whence does it arise? What key gives the explanation? No other will be found than this, that the external and sensible, or, more justly expressed, the historical reality of the events depicted by the apostle, is itself the source of this so-called 'profundity.' What John saw with his eyes, heard with his ears, felt with his hands, and afterwards understood and conceived, that is it which fitted him to be the exponent of the 'spiritual gospel.' Any other way of explanation is contrary to all experience. There have always been reflective minds, and speculating overprecise people; but this profundity of St. John is no mere reflectiveness, and has nothing in common with theosophic speculation. Perhaps one has no right to hazard the conjecture, whether Strauss, after he had completed the section on the resurrection of Lazarus, was really filled with thorough confidence in the correctness of his view, or whether there did not remain in him that sting of doubt of which, as is well known, Spinoza used to make no concealment. But there is a fact which justifies us in deciding on the second alternative. He has published a polemic entitled, *Die Halben und die Ganzen* (The half and the whole). For the *second* part of it he had *not* the motive which stimulated him in the *first*. Now, as it is impossible that he can be of opinion that he can agree with his chosen opponent at so little cost as he has done here,[1]

---

[1] The second half of this polemic is one of the most unimportant that Strauss has ever published; and only perhaps on the part of the well-known writer in the *Liter. Centralblatt.* (1865, No. 47) could it have obtained the praise, that it was comparable to an eyesalve for the blinded. One does not hereby disagree with this theologian, that a few exegetical meanings can be drawn from it,—meanings which by no means characterize

the suspicion arises that he considers it a convenient opportunity to come back again to the history of Lazarus, and as much as possible to weaken the opinion against the justice of his view of it (strange, but not also peculiar). But what does he do? He attacks the view which his opponent has given of the family relations in Bethany. He rejects it with scorn. He calls it a 'giddiness' ('Schwindel'). That may be. He will be of opinion that he can justify this harsh expression. But how does he conclude? He concludes: '*Consequently* the history of Lazarus in St. John is not to be held without " giddiness."' *This* conclusion he can never justify. In the whole literature of theological polemics, we have hardly met with a case which is open in a similar manner to the reproach of an unwarrantable feint. That is *not* called νομίμως ἀθλεῖν.

his standpoint, and of which it is known all the same that they are disputed by exegetists of all views. With regard to the first point taken into consideration by Strauss, we also are convinced that apologetics have gained nothing by the Tiburtinian Inscription, and that, by acknowledging a possible double governing of Quirinus over Syria, the difficulty of the history of the taxing is not taken away. Apologetic recognises its true interest when it ignores the assured results of historical investigation, when it ignores in the case before us the irrevocable conclusion, that at the time of the birth of Jesus, under the still existing government of Herod the Great, a Roman census over Judea was an impossibility. How far we are inclined, and how little we are necessitated, to give up the real substance of St. Luke's narrative,—that is, the birth of Jesus in Bethlehem, and the forced journey of Joseph and Mary to the town of David,—we hope at a future time satisfactorily to show. However, we expect from Strauss the avowal, that views of the relations of the family at Bethany can be entertained quite different from those expressed by the theologian attacked, without our being thereby necessitated to doubt the historical credibility of the narrative in the 11th chapter of the fourth Gospel. Are these combinations mere makeshifts to support the latter? Does it fall as untenable without them? With what right does any one dare to assert this? The whole conduct of the critic in the second part of his polemic gives the impression, that he is either not inclined really to agree with those whom he calls 'the whole,' or that he was conscious that he was unable to do so with such means as he had at his disposal.

V.

FOURTH GROUP.

THE MIRACLES OF JESUS AS PROPHECIES OF THE FUTURE SOVEREIGNTY OF THE KINGDOM OF HEAVEN ON EARTH.

THE form of expression which we have chosen as a title for this group, embodies the opinion that the miracles belonging to it bear a twofold character. The exposition of them must therefore also be made from a double point of view; but only one of the two views need be a convincing one. In fact, if they are intended to prophesy the future sovereignty of the kingdom of God on earth, their character must be predominantly a prophetic one. But as this prophecy is expressed by means of an action, and thus is a language of signs, the symbolical element is often (*certainly not always*) indispensable. Only it does not take its place here in the sense of our second group, where the earthly gift signifies the *present* heavenly treasure which has become attainable, but it is rather a *future* condition that is symbolized by the sign. A future condition. It is not the everlasting order, the *regnum gloriæ* as the Parousia of Jesus will restore it, which is prophetically depicted in these miracles, but more thoroughly the victorious *development* which the kingdom of heaven will take on *earth*. Still more, as these deeds of our Lord happened especially, or rather exclusively, before the eyes of the disciples, they were intended to give them, in their position as elect organs of the kingdom of heaven, the certainty of victory, which they would need for the cheerful and courageous execution of their office.

There is hardly a single miracle of Jesus which can be considered in its character as quite simple,—certainly not those which we have specially designated as symbolical; but all of these might be placed in another group; for though our Lord intended, by the healing of the sick of the palsy, chiefly to show symbolically the reality of the power manifested in Him to forgive sins, still the cure was at the same time an act of mercy to the man in bodily distress. The miracles, however, of our *fourth* group have in no respect this object in themselves; for only in one single case, which we shall consider later, can we allow it to be so, even in a most limited sense. In *them*, the twofold nature of their character is rather this, that the symbolical element forms the substratum on which the prophetic is raised; the one is more the form, the other the real substance. We divide these miracles of Jesus into two classes: The one was performed by our Lord on the Sea of Galilee (Strauss calls them anecdotes of the sea, legends of fishermen and sailors); the others have been accomplished over the powers of nature so far as it produces,—so far as it offers meat, fruit, and wine.

PETER'S DRAUGHT OF FISHES.—LUKE V. 1-11.

The evangelist Luke alone gives us information of an event which was repeated in like manner in the days of the resurrection of Jesus, but with many modifications. An account relating to this narrative is found in Matthew and Mark, but they have made no mention of the miracle. Without discussing more fully the harmonistic questions, we must at any rate enter our protest against the assertions of those who think they find here that the third evangelist is in contradiction to himself. They say that (in chap. iv. ver. 38) he has reported an event which supposes an acquaintance between Jesus and Peter, while here it is narrated as if a connection between them had been made first by means of this event.

Strauss is of opinion, supported not merely by this circumstance, nor by a pretended difference between Luke's reports on the one hand and the representation of the first two evangelists on the other, but principally by his own known prepossessions (as he this time does not scorn to use the analogy of the call of Quinctius Cincinnatus), that we have before us a myth which has become a narrative of a miracle, and which brings to view the later prosperous activity of the apostles (in accordance with the words of Jesus, 'I will make you fishers of men') under the form of a rich draught of fishes. However, the apparent contradiction between the assertions of Luke in the 4th chapter and the present narrative, has sufficed for others to consider that the third evangelist had derived the latter from later traditions, and that he has confused the historical sequence. This false view rests partly on the false supposition, that only *one* act is conceivable by which our Lord required His disciples to follow Him (the calling of the *first* disciples, especially that of Peter, *must* have proceeded through several stages), and partly on a superficial view of the miraculous deed itself which is now before us.

We turn to it in laying stress on the fact, that our Lord, before He addressed Himself to Simon in the 4th verse, had taught the people out of the ship. By this we shall be shown, if not the source from which the blessing symbolized in the miracle flows, at least the medium through which it passes. The real doctrinal tendency is, however, to be found chiefly in the command of Jesus, 'Launch out into the deep, and let down your nets *for a draught*,' that is, for the purpose of catching something. There is no dispute about the *general* meaning. When our Lord had said earlier, 'Follow me, and I will make you fishers of men,' we at once recognised the symbol of the fishing net, which will be applicable until the συντέλεια τοῦ αἰῶνος. So here also nothing else can be meant than the reception of men into the borders of the kingdom of heaven, in order that it may be peopled with souls. Peter, and those who were with him, had *received* this call already for a more or less length of time; they had already had their duty confided to them.

Now, however, further instruction is communicated to them *on* this object of their life;—not instruction as to how they should begin—how *they* should behave, but information of quite a different kind. Peter advances the doubt as to whether the attempt might not be fruitless, for they had laboured the whole night in vain; but 'at Thy word I will let down the net.' It is important that we should emphasize the right point. All that has been said of the faith already possessed by the disciples,—of a faith which is shown in this obedience, even as Bengel observes, 'senserat Petrus virtutem verborum Jesu,'—is borne out by the text. It appears exclusively in the assertion of the future apostle, 'I will do it at Thy bidding.' This is the point on which the effect of the incident hangs. If Peter is really made to acknowledge that he, if left to himself and his own will, would not cast out the net, that his own reflection would keep him back from doing so, he thus places himself in the position, that in case any result should occur, Jesus must be honoured as the wonderful dispenser. 'If I do catch anything, this happens not in the natural order of things, or of chance, but it comes from *Thee.*' But it is just this which is the intention of our Lord. It is to be manifested in the light, that He and He alone is the cause of the result,—He draws the souls, His ministers are only the organs. As Paul explained it later, 'I have laboured more than they all; however, not I, but the grace of God which is in me; he who planteth is nothing, and he who watereth is nothing, but God who giveth the increase.' Does this activity of the fishers of men thus bear fruit? The real source of it is the blessing of the Lord.

The result becomes at once manifest: 'Then they enclosed a great multitude of fishes, so that their net brake; they beckoned to their partners who were in the other ship that they should come and help them; and both ships, under the pressure of their burden, threatened to sink.' It seemed as if the sea gave up all the fish which moved in its sphere. It is our right and our duty to deal with this detailed description in such a way as to *give*, or more correctly to *leave*, to each feature its prophetic or symbolical significance. There is certainly the danger of an arbitrary interpretation; but it was only meant in the sense of *application* when Augustine referred the tearing of the net to heresies. Again, only those who in advance take the whole narrative as a myth, can consider this incident as referring to a schism of the Church occasioned by the activity of Paul, and the two vessels to the rising of Gentile Christian Churches by the side of the Jewish Christian ones.

We must not allow ourselves to be driven by such aberrations to the insipid conclusion, that the rich blessing is only a general one, which all these details are symbolically to signify. We ought and must, however, emphasize a threefold one: *First*, There are masses which the disciples of Jesus will gain, not here and there single people; they are fishers, no mere anglers; they throw out the net for large draughts. *Secondly,* The ministers of Christ need mutual support; not one alone can do it, but their united strength is needed. *Lastly,* The gain is greater than they can compass; the measure of the blessing is an overflowing one.

The understanding of the symbolico-prophetical miracles is often simplified *to us* by our being in a position to follow them to the point of their fulfilment, —the view of this fulfilment often opening up to us the sense of the prophetic sign. In the case before us this key does not seem to fit. Indeed, Peter's fishing of men achieved very considerable success; but as to its results, these were still far from what had been promised by the symbol in our narrative. The thousands which entered into his net cast out on the first Feast of Pentecost are still in a disproportion to the symbolism of this draught of fish. But the question is, whether we should apply it to the *person* of the apostle. The various promises which our Lord made to Peter, either by word or by sign, all prepare, if we confine ourselves to this point, important difficulties. These doubts are not removed by making the *faith* of the disciple the ground of explanation. They are, however, solved by adopting the opinion that the office is the καλὴ παραθήκη of the promises. Here in the symbolical event it is quite indisputable; here, where the united labour of all the workmen called was needed to gather in the fulness of the blessing, under the weight of which the net brake and the ships threatened to sink, the persons disappear behind the work and the call.

Special attention is demanded to the way in which the disciple acted at the sight of the over-abundant blessing. Of himself, as well as of his companions John and James, it is said that the feeling of astonishment overwhelmed them—that, in fact, Peter sank at the feet of our Lord, beseeching Him, 'Depart from me, for I am a sinful man, O Lord.' 'Lord' he calls Him, not as before, 'Master' (ἐπιστάτα). This latter address (peculiar to Luke, and equivalent to διδάσκαλε in John; see John xiii. 13, 14, Lord and Master) was in relation to the teaching which Jesus had given; the former had its motive in the power now unfolded. The deep emotion of the disciple is explained by the 5th verse. While he said, 'At Thy word I will let down the net,' he had given up all right, in case of success, to speak of a lucky chance; he was obliged at all events to acknowledge it as a mighty working of Jesus. And the more extensive the blessing, so much the more majestic did the power appear to him, and so much the more was he immediately conscious that it was divine. Hence, then, his adoration. It is not, however, a joyful bowing down before the recognised Son of God, but an anxious homage inspired by fear and trembling. He speaks, in fact, just like that demoniac who also fell down before him, 'Depart from me, torment me not.' Psychologically, this is easy to be conceived. If the feeling of one's own sinfulness is vividly awakened, the appearance of the divine must *then* call forth fear, even when it is employed in blessing and bestowing. The person confessing his sin cannot greet with joy such a power in its neighbourhood; he does not feel at ease; it must depart from him if he is again to breathe freely. Even though this powerful hand had now showered down rich gifts on him, what surety was there that, unlimited as it was, it would not show itself as an avenger and destroyer; at least an experience of this kind, on account of previous sin, would have been the ordinary one felt. The 'depart' is, however, in the mouth of the disciple, no expression of confusion or surprise, but a request meant in real earnest. Peter could not flee, for he was in his own place, just as that demon was in his οἰκία; he could only beseech, 'Depart from me.' 'Fear not' is our Lord's reply to him.

As the following words are not connected with a γάρ, they cannot be understood as the foundation of a consoling encouragement. The apparent consolation is rather in itself an absolute command, which was fulfilled immediately it was uttered. We compare the 'Fear not' with the similar expression, 'Peace be to you.' Just as the latter, in the form of a wish, effects a real communication, so the former, in the shape of a command, causes a real liberation. As Christ speaks, so it takes place; as He determines, so it comes to pass. To this immediate effect of power is added the promise relating to the future. Our Lord promises the disciple, that He, notwithstanding his sins, will show Himself to him only as a blessing; and that did he experience in the course of his earthly communion with the Master. Hence we understand, that at that last draught of fishes (John xxi.), notwithstanding the rich blessing, he entertained no anxious thoughts; he is accustomed to it; he finds it in accordance with the usual order; he even recognises in it the proximity of his Lord. The concluding words, 'From henceforth thou shalt catch men,' establish Peter peculiarly in his office. The same thing relates to the 'putting me into the ministry' of Paul (1 Tim. i. 12); but these words give at the same time the authentic explanation of this symbolical prophetical act. The word ζωγρῶν, in connection with ἀνθρώπους, apparently forms a tautology, or at least a superfluity of words; for the ζωγρῶν *is* in itself a fisher of men. But this is the very intention, that there should be brought to light the call to help men to a real life.

The 'henceforth thou shalt catch' gives, lastly, not only the signification of the constancy with which *the apostle* would effect this work,—from henceforth for ever, until he can no more gird himself, but 'another shall gird thee, and carry thee whither thou wouldst not' (John xxi. 18),—but also the notification that the office should continue until the consummation of ages, and that the blessing which is here symbolized should never be taken away from this office. How does the attempt to do away with the spiritual office appear in the light of our Lord's word (Strauss, *Leben Jesu*, xix.; Eng. ed. 1, xvi.)? Chiefly as a vain one? Or does it not rather appear as a vain one, just because it is blasphemous, and despises the counsel of Gamaliel?

By the side of the narrative we have just considered is ranged an event which Matthew alone has reported, in so far as it also brings to view the calling of Peter to fish, only that we do not see in the hands of the disciple the net, but the fishing-rod.

THE MONEY IN THE MOUTH OF THE FISH.—
MATT. XVII. 24–27.

The conviction that we have before us here a symbolical miracle of Jesus, that is, one performed with a prophetical object, is held by us, in this case at least, by the mere proof of the untenableness of all results to justify and to recommend it taken from any other standpoint. Hence we state the view of Strauss only in its chief feature, without subjecting it to a thorough criticism.[1] The critic seeks the *genesis* of the 'myth' in the history of the tribute money; the *motive*

---

[1] We find ourselves completely at variance with other erroneous attempts at explanation. Thus Weisse, in his *Evangelien Frage*, Leipzig 1856, p. 265, proposes the following view: 'In the mouth of the first fish Peter would catch he was to find the piece of money which he owed as tribute to the temple; that is, the first best disciple which he, as a fisher of men,

to its 'fabrication,' however, in the question ventilated later among the Christians (of which, by the way, we know nothing from Church history), whether they, as the royal priesthood, were bound to contribute to the Jewish temple worship; in reality they would have denied it, but fictitiously, for the sake of peace, answered in the affirmative. Instead of combating this groundless assertion, we will rather see if we cannot arrive at a satisfactory insight into this enigmatical event by means of unprejudiced exegesis. For enigmatical it does in fact appear, if it is not so, as Schleiermacher judges, that the act is inconceivable in its ethical motives, and only explicable in a magical way. It bears—this is undeniable—at first sight a monstrous character in itself; it does so in a far higher degree than the history of the barren fig-tree.

In the neighbourhood of Capernaum the receivers of the tax (δίδραχμον) ask Peter if his Master is accustomed to pay this tax? There can be no doubt of the tax itself; the expression used is, in fact, the designation fixed by the Greek translator of the sum which Moses (in Exod. xxx. 13) had demanded from each Israelite who had passed his twentieth year, as a heave-offering for the building of the sanctuary, once for all, but which was collected after the captivity yearly for the temple service. As all the members of the covenant people, those living out of Palestine not excepted, had to perform this religious duty, delegates from the temple travelled between the 15th and 25th of the month Adar, for the purpose of collecting it in the provinces. They appear here in Galilee, and turn to Peter. Certainly they first reminded the disciple of his obligation, and then would catch for the kingdom of heaven, will be reckoned to him, instead of the obligations to which he was bound as an enslaved servant of the law, but with which he now, having become free by faith, can satisfy in that way.' Strauss' view deserves the preference over this.

demanded how Jesus stood in regard to this tax. There might be a doubt in the matter. Priests and Levites were tax-free. Our Lord was indeed neither the one nor the other, but He was certainly a recognised teacher, who carried on no earthly calling. The precedent of the past year would give an explanation of it. Had He paid it? or had the tax been remitted to Him? The 'Yes' of Peter decides the question in the affirmative. This is neither a hasty, nor even an unjustifiable reply. The disciple does not prejudge the conduct of his Lord, but he only affirms a fact of the past. It is with this fact that the dialogue which commenced between both in the 25th verse is connected. The representation of the evangelist allows no other supposition, than that Christ by His own inner intuition had gained knowledge of this incident. Whoever raises the otherwise unjustifiable objection, that then omniscience must appear on the part of Jesus, is not on that account bound to the view in opposition to the text, that our Lord had with His ears listened to the conversation held probably in his neighbourhood. This is irremediably shattered by the explicit words: 'And when Peter was come into the house.' There is the house Jesus had been staying in while the scene took place outside. The evangelist John writes (chap. ii. 25), 'Jesus needed not that any should testify of man, for He knew what was in man.' This saying is applicable here. When in fact Peter, under the fresh impression of the want he had just experienced, comes before the eyes of his Master, our Lord saw in him not merely unrest and excitement, but at the same time recognises their grounds; he read them in the face of the disciple. 'And He prevented him,'—without letting him first narrate what had happened, He began the conversation with him. In the first place, it was intended thereby to give Peter a view of what was right in this case. The uncertainty of the Jewish receivers as to whether Jesus had to pay the tax for the temple had the very conceivable result, that the disciple himself pondered this question in his thoughts. And it is with the quiet deliberation which he had had with himself that the 'preventing' of our Lord is certainly connected. The parabolic nature of the speech includes the subject of taxation in general. Taxes are indispensable in every organized community; but it is manifest that there must be everywhere some exemptions.

An earthly kingdom is chosen as an example. The conduct of the 'kings of the earth' (the added genitive is to be carefully observed) is a type of the analogous action of the heavenly King, while in a kindred sphere (Matt. xx. 25) the practice of the 'princes of the Gentiles' is the exact reverse of the laws of the kingdom of heaven. They demand taxes from the inhabitants of their territory, partly in order to possess means to defray the expenses of the state, and partly to keep awake the feeling of subjection. But they distinguished between the 'children' and 'strangers.' From the former, the members of their household, the princes (see 1 Tim. v. 8, ἴδιοι, οἰκεῖοι), they demand neither custom nor taxes, but only from the subjects; in strict sense, from those to whom they are merely rulers, and not fathers. Our Lord intentionally makes Peter affirm this fact, which is in accordance with experience. He does this while giving instruction in the form of parables also at other times (see Luke vii. 42). The application (as in this passage in St. Luke) He keeps to Himself. But, in fact, the application is in the words, 'Then are the children free.'[1] Formally, in-

---

[1] As our Lord restricts Himself to the point of view of the 'freedom of the children,' an otherwise approximate consideration is excluded. The

deed, the plural belongs to the 'children' spoken of in the preceding verse; but in reality our Lord meant no one else than Himself. He alone stood to His heavenly King in the relation of ἴδιος καὶ οἰκεῖος (John viii. 35, 'The Son abideth in the house for ever'). He alone had thus a claim to freedom from a tax which was demanded and instituted in the interest of the 'house of God.'[1] This claim, both in deed and in truth, applied to Him. But He will not now make it available; to avoid offence He prefers to renounce His right. The express refusal to pay the tax, especially if it was founded on the reason as stated between Him and His disciple, would inevitably have caused a scandal. But it is important to gain the right point of view, which by no means rests on the fact that our Lord was not acknowledged by the Pharisees as the Son of God. *This* view was not at other times taken by Him. Not only did He cure on the Sabbath day, but He also founded His right to such a Sabbath working upon the claim of a Lord over the Festival Day, and of being greater than the temple, not caring for and unaffected by the offence which He would thus cause. The statement, that in these latter cases it was His declared adversaries, while in the present one only unprejudiced minds, who were opposed to

making Jesus liable to this tax was inadmissible also in this account, because, according to the explanation of Moses (Ex. xxx. 12-15), it was a sin-offering: 'Give an offering unto the Lord, to make an atonement for your souls.' A slight reference to this is, indeed, found in our narrative (in the ἀντί of the 27th verse), but, in connection with the whole incident, it cannot with propriety be dwelt upon.

[1] In this we must agree with Dorner ('über Jesu sündlose Vollkommenheit,' Gotha 1862, p. 37), that our Lord showed beforehand this free position towards holiness as one also appropriate to His followers. The plural σκανδαλίσωμεν (ver. 27) makes this view almost unavoidable. Besides, the 'free' (ver. 26) reminds us of the saying (in John viii. 36), that 'the Son will make those who believe on Him *free*.' But still we are able neither to comprise the disciples among the children, nor even limit the prophetical tendency of the event to the 'free' position, to holiness.

Him, is unsatisfactory, because the fear of 'giving offence' can never be made to depend on the persons who take the offence, but solely on the ground which causes the offence. Bengel was much more acute in seeing it. He who has of all exegetists, especially in our narrative, taken the deepest views, makes upon the feature before us the suitable remark, 'Facillime ubi de pecunia agitur, scandalum capiunt a sanctis homines negotia mundana curantes.'[1] At any rate, Jesus could never *give* 'offence'; even if 'the ignorance of foolish men' took such from Him, he remained pure; and the saying suits Him, 'Blessed is he who is not offended in me.' Hence also in general He was not in a position to avoid an offence, for every renunciation of His claims would have been a disavowal of the truth.

There was, however, one relation in which 'that they should not be offended in me' could be His motive of action, and that was the *money* point. We call to remembrance the admonition which the Apostle Paul gives to the Church at Corinth (1 Cor. vi. and foll.), 'Instead of striving over temporal possessions, why do ye not rather take wrong? why do ye not rather suffer yourselves to be defrauded?' In a similar way our Lord says, 'We will pay the tribute, so that *from this* no offence may arise.' But why was it not paid at once? Why the miracle? 'Non erat in crumena pecunia,' answers Bengel. This generally sufficiently correct view requires now a more thorough definition. We know that there was a fund out of which the general needs of the whole circle were borne, and that Judas (often faithless) was the

---

[1] Bengel with justice speaks of the *negotiis mundanis*, although it relates to a tax for the service of Jehovah. For money, for whatever objects used, is always and everywhere an ἀλλότριον, and belongs to the things of this world.

administrator of it. Conjectures as to whence the contributions came are inadmissible; however, it is allowable from single assertions to draw the conclusion that the amount was a moderate one. When Philip (John vi. 7) broke out in the well-known exclamation, it is thereby seen that two hundred denarii far exceeded the amount in their possession. At the present moment there was certainly no money in hand; Peter is not at all in a position to fulfil his obligation. It is hardly probable that the fund should by chance have been exhausted; the monetary want was indeed caused by this, that our Lord was alone with the one disciple, while the others, including the bearers of the γλωσσόκομον, were far away. At any rate, we have to make the double supposition, that on one side Jesus had resolved to pay the tax, and that on the other the necessary sum was not at His disposal; it was therefore necessary to procure it in an extraordinary way. The fact that Jesus does not ask the question (like to the one He made in a similar case to another disciple), 'Whence are we to take the money?' should also be excluded from the uncalled for advice which many exegetists have given our Lord in the present situation, as the plain command, together with the not less explicit promise, warns us from the error of doing away with the miracle by strange meanings, and raising difficulties which border closely on the ludicrous. The event was not otherwise than as it is precisely stated, and is to be understood literally. Certainly it is not expressly stated that the disciple executed the directions of the Master, and that everything was fulfilled as He predicted; but Matthew's method of representation is not the same as that of the writer of Genesis; and even Strauss has acknowledged that in a gospel the observance of the behest and the fulfilling of the prophecy of Jesus stand to reason.

But how then? It has been said 'that even the exegetist most believing in miracles does not know how to answer the question, Why was such a strange miracle necessary? yea, even why was it allowed?'

As long as the motive for the deed is sought in the *mere* interest to prevent a monetary want, and to avoid a possible offence, embarrassment will certainly arise. But the wonder will disappear in the same proportion as we learn to conceive the miracle as a symbolical prophetical one. While Peter is receiving and carrying out the command of our Lord, the picture of the future 'fisher of men' stands before our eyes. But we see not Him who throws out the net in order to win souls for the kingdom of God, but Him who places the demand before single people who are won, and who offer to Him earthly coins. As it is especially the Christian manner of considering money as an ἄδικον, ἐλάχιστον, or ἀλλότριον, the apostles have naturally judged it especially from this point of view; and how far was it from their thoughts to have their activity paid for with *this* hire! But, as pilgrims in this world, they also stand towards money in a not repellent attitude,—they would have appeared as strangers,—they would have given offence if they had debarred themselves thoroughly from it. And they themselves have expressed their opinion, that the churches collected together by their labours ought to bestow on them this earthly possession. 'If we have sown unto you spiritual things, is it a great thing if we shall reap your carnal things' (1 Cor. ix. 11 and foll.)? St. Paul calls it his glory that he was a burden to no one; he would rather die than that this witness should be kept back from him; yet still he considered it to be right when the church at Philippi had sent the sum of money to the prisoners at Rome. But still more complete definitions are needed. If the apostles agreed to this proceeding, it was not in the interest of their own position, in order to have it for their own support, or in order to be able to bestow alms. In *this* point of view, Paul asserts that he has desired neither silver nor gold nor raiment, but that his hands served him for his necessity, and that he had eaten his own bread; and Peter replies to the beseeching beggar, 'Silver and gold have I none.' The interest does not appear to us to be in the forcible words : 'We will give ourselves continually to prayer and to the ministry of the word' (Acts vi. 4), for the apostles have always considered Christian taxes as a divine service, as an offering in the interest of the kingdom of heaven.

Let us see what is the state of matters in our narrative? Was the fish to furnish a sum of money for any use that might be chosen? No; but a fixed coin for a definite purpose was demanded,—a coin, not with the emperor's image and superscription, but the tax for the service of Jehovah, for the maintenance of the temple. After our Lord had shown to His disciples the temple already in ruins (Mark xiii. 2), they could no more experience any peculiar piety towards this sanctuary even *before* the extreme catastrophe. Jerusalem itself lay still in their hearts for the sake of the saints there; but they themselves were to build among men a better tabernacle of God. For the purpose of this new habitation, they were shown another material than the gold of Ophir and the cedars of Lebanon; so far and so much, however, they needed for their work money as a means. They should demand it from Christians possessing it, and they would receive it from them in a sufficient measure. This is the authority with which they are clothed by means of the symbolical deed; and this is the promised prophecy of Him who can say, Mine is both the silver and the gold. 'In medio actu submissionis emicat majestas.' Thus Bengel judged of the narrative we have just considered. In the one now to be brought before us, the majesty of the Lord breaks forth not in a single ray, but in the fulness of its splendour.

THE STILLING OF THE TEMPEST.—MATT. VIII. 23, ETC.; MARK IV. 35, ETC.; LUKE VIII. 22, ETC.

We find ourselves again in the place where the miraculous activity of our Lord was the most manifested. However, the narrative places us not on the *shore* of the Sea of Galilee, but upon its *waves*, which here must flow for the glory of the Son of God. It is certainly in a double form that the majesty of their Master shines down on the disciples in the open sea. However, when they see Him walking on the waters as on the dry land, they do not look upon a peculiar miracle, but are only witnesses of an event similar to that when He was manifested to the eyes of the three chosen ones on the mount of transfiguration. Mindful of the task before us, we therefore limit ourselves to the first of the two narratives. We follow Mark's account. The supposition that it is the most complete will be justified of itself. Schleiermacher holds that none of the evangelists have reported the event in strict accordance with truth. Hypotheses are here permissible; what is wanting must be supplemented, and what is founded on fact must be settled by analogy. Let this be the task to be undertaken, though the solution of it cannot be demanded. He himself has not attempted it, and stands perplexed in regard to the narrative. Strauss knows how to answer it. He says Jesus *might* after a hard working day have departed with the disciples from Capernaum, have gone to sleep in the ship, have on the storm arising been awakened by the dispirited disciples, and have opposed their faintheartedness; but He could *not*, as the evangelists have reported, have rebuked the winds and the sea. *This*, he thinks, is a myth, the origin of which is to be sought for in the 106th and 107th Psalm ('He rebuked the Red Sea, He commanded the stormy wind, which lifted up its waves; they cry unto the Lord in their trouble, He saved them out of their distresses; He maketh the storm a calm, and its waves are still; then are they glad because they are at rest, and He bringeth them to the haven where they would be'),—a myth, the fabrication of which had its cause in the desire of Christianity to possess a guarantee of protection, of which the Church might be assured in all its combats on the side of our Lord. Let us consider whether there is a necessity for this doubtful view, or whether we cannot with confidence assert that the event is an historical fact, that the passage in the Psalms is more than an Old Testament type, and that the early Christian views are more than merely an application that may be admissible.

The evangelist Mark places the beginning of this narrative on the evening of the day on which our Lord has spoken His parable sermon: 'And the same day, when the even was come;' and 'they took Him even as He was in the ship.' These last words refer to the 1st verse of the 4th chapter, where it is said, that on account of the multitude of the people thronging Him, Jesus had entered into a ship, and thence had taught those assembled on the shore. When He had ended, He requested the disciples to go to the other side; and they took Him 'as He was still in the ship,' that is, without His first leaving it; and immediately they commenced the voyage, 'and they launched forth' (Luke viii. 22). The continuation of the representation of the third evangelist makes it probable that our Lord, soon after the breaking up of the assembly, was sunk in sleep, while Mark shows Him to us later, when the stormy wind was raging, sleeping in the hinder part of the vessel on a pillow. (The προσκεφάλειον, probably a soft cushion inviting to rest, not the wooden back of the πρύμνη itself; at least the Septuagint has in Ezek. xiii. 18 thus translated the כְּסָתוֹת—'Woe to you that make cushions for the heads for great and small, in order to catch souls.') The fact that Jesus fell asleep after the trouble of a day of hard work, has neither been found by the evangelists as incompatible with the truth, 'that the Keeper of Israel neither slumbers nor sleeps' (at least this 'want' in the narrative did not give them cause for the fabrication of a supplementary miraculous history; see Strauss, *Leben Jesu*, 492); nor can it cause us the least surprise. As long as our Lord walked in the flesh, He was also subject in waking and sleeping to the order of nature. He was worn out by the fatigue of the day, and needed refreshing in sleep. It has certainly been asserted, that while sleeping He merged into His Father, and received in dreams His revelations; thus it was overlooked, that the Scripture mentions prayer alone as the medium of Jesus merging in His Father, and that only subordinate tools have received in dreams the direction of God; see Num. xii. 6. While He Himself enjoyed refreshing rest, His companions were the prey of restlessness and anxiety. A stormy wind had arisen, and the ship was driven and tossed. The mariners were accustomed to the glassy smoothness of the Sea of Galilee being suddenly changed into lofty waves, and they knew how to take the proper precautions. But this time the storm must have taken place with peculiar suddenness, and with unwonted violence, for they had exhausted all their means. The water pressed into the vessel, and filled it, until there was the extreme danger of sinking. 'And He was asleep.'

That our Lord remained in undisturbed slumber, though the waves might wet Him and the storm roar round His head, has, indeed, much deeper grounds than merely in the *securitas potentiæ*. The sleep lasted as long as nature's need demanded. When the organism after the lowering exertion has received back its elasticity by rest, the freshened feeling of life drives away slumber of itself, and man awakes. In the present case, Jesus had rested too short a time for such a spontaneous awakening to have occurred. At any rate, there is certainly a mystical effect, which threatening danger exercises on the sleeper, so that he is awakened suddenly out of the deepest slumber; but sinful man alone, just because he alone knows of such danger, can perceive this effect when close at hand. The child, even, who is still innocent, does not experience it; his sleep, therefore, remains undisturbed, because even waking he is free from care, where grown-up persons tremble. And thus force from without could alone break the power of the sleep of Jesus. We see how it is here applied.

In the first place, however, a question of harmonizing presents itself to us. For according to Matthew, the disciples break out in the words, 'Lord, save us: we perish.' Similarly Luke says, 'Master, Master, we perish.' On the other hand, according to Mark, they said, 'Master, carest thou not that we perish?' Those expositors who judge of the second evangelist, that he is accustomed to colour the reports of the rest, have in this case no easy position; for that would be a very curious embellishment to change the beseeching request into a formula including a reproach. Others have indeed sought to unite both together, so that first the reproach, and afterwards the request, was spoken aloud; but this conclusion is quite impossible. In a moment of inward confusion and outward distress, one might indeed assert something contradictory; but this certainly would not be the expression of heterogeneous feelings. A 'Lord, save us,' in the mouth of the disciples, does, certainly, hardly excite the feeling of a judgment in favour of probability. For supposing that they had even, in this the commencement of their communion with our Lord, been inclined to believe Him capable of such a power, it would be difficult to reconcile it with their unmeasured astonishment *after* the miracle.[1] But if from this we decide in favour of Mark's account, it will be asked, How are the words to be understood? We would compare it with the expression of Mary at Cana, They have no wine! This last in no way excludes the demand that our Lord should perform a miracle; she simply wished to let Him know the dilemma which had arisen. The intention of the disciples was here similar. It appears unnatural that Jesus should sleep in such danger; at least, they think He ought to share their anxious solicitude.

How natural it is to man to require all persons threatened with him to be attentive in a general calamity, is seen by a striking example in Old Testament history. Jonah the son of Amittai slept in the lower part of the ship when the storm had arisen: 'So the shipmaster came to him, and said unto him, What meanest thou, sleeper? Arise, call upon thy God, if so be that God will think upon us, that we

[1] From the text of Matthew, one can hardly justify the arbitrary assertion, that the expression of astonishment at the deed of our Lord proceeded from the mouth of 'people' who were in the ship as well as the disciples; while the accounts in Mark and Luke decidedly exclude such a supposition. Even Matthew means by the 'people' (chap. viii. 27) no one else than the disciples. This description, in view of the manifestation of divine power, was the appropriate one; at the same time, it makes the astonishment of the witnesses conceivable in itself.

perish not' (Jonah i. 6). Quite in the same sense is our 'Carest Thou not?'—Thou actest as if the storm is over, as if this danger deserves no attention. Now we must not emphasize too closely the plural, as if the disciples separated themselves from Jesus, and considered themselves only in danger, and that He Himself was safe. They say in the form of communication, without intending a direct question, 'Carest Thou not that we all together perish?' Our Lord arises. But a new difference among the synoptical Gospels meets us to arrest our attention.

According to Matthew, Jesus at first turned toward the disciples with a reproach, and then directed His attention to the storm and the sea. On the other hand, Mark and Luke testify to the reversed order of His conduct; and both are certainly in this also the more faithful reporters. The midst of the storm was hardly the right moment for a reproof to the disciples; at least, it could only be effective when it had been first effectually proved that they were wrong in their care, that they had acted as faithless fools. This miracle is not to be judged from the same point of view as the cures. If often a moral influence preceded the latter, that order was in its right place; for it was important to produce the right state of feeling for the reception of the benefit. On the other hand, here the work of Jesus itself was its own preparation for the reproof which followed; the witnesses of the miracle that had been accomplished were only by witnessing it in a position to value its spiritual interpretation. Thus our Lord turns first to the storm and to the sea. The brief report of Matthew, 'He rebuked the wind and the waves' (Luke has 'the raging of the water'), is supplemented by that of Mark, that He said, 'Peace, be still.' We speak with justice of a supplementing (no dilation) by the second evangelist. For the word 'rebuked,' on all sides attested, must plainly have been accomplished in some way intelligible to the witnesses. But we are now arriving at the right understanding. The words in themselves are plain; and whether the 'Peace' relates to the storm, or, on the other hand, the 'Be still' refers to the roaring waves, or whether we prefer not to see any such distinction, is a matter of no importance. According to physics, the one as well as the other ought to be applied to the storm, which indeed raises the sea, and which alone can be considered as a power of nature. The evangelist himself appears to have understood our Lord as if He had directed His command exclusively to the raging sea. Let us pass this by.

Much more important is the question, How does Jesus here appear to us, and how is His conduct conceivable? They have a light task who poetically speak of hostile powers which He sent back bound, within their limits, and necessitated to quietness. They have an easy task; and yet they make the understanding of the passage the more difficult. For to perceive demoniacal sounds in the howling tempest, in the roaring storm, is purely an affair of modern feeling. Scripture knows nothing thereof. It sees absolutely in the storm and in the tempest, the lightning and flames of fire, manifestations of the almighty power and greatness of God, without ever representing them as powers seeking to assert an evil, corruptible, blasphemous will. If it is then the Lord of heaven and earth who makes the winds His angels, and for His ministers the flaming fire, it is certainly easily said that the Son who can rule His Father's household, and at whose command, according to His own declaration, legions of angels stand,—that even here He was in a position to command the powers of nature.

But this is not the marrow of the question. Why did He not accomplish what it pleased Him to do by the simple direction of His will? Why these words? That the spoken sounds were not the indispensable condition to the result we know; but they were no less requisite than the laying on of hands on the sick. The end must positively have been for the sake of His own people.

We are urged to the same idea, also, from another point of view. To speak to things or to the powers of nature is not a possibility. One can only *speak* to those who possess the faculty of speech as well, that is, to *men*. Everything that our Lord said on earth is the property of men; for them was it intended, and to them it is delivered. What follows? The 'Peace, be still' is spoken for the sake of the disciples. Let us keep this result, in the first place, steadily before us. We now continue. There immediately arose a complete calm; the tempest was silent, the sea became as a smooth mirror, and without being tossed about, the ship lay on the quiet surface.

Jesus now turns to the disciples on the strength of His deed. We discover even here differences among the reports; but they are of no importance. Matthew, 'Why are ye fearful, O ye of little faith?' Luke, 'Where is your faith?' Mark, 'Why are ye so fearful? how is it that ye have no faith?' The general reproach relates to their fear, their want of courage, of manliness, which, notwithstanding the threatened danger, should have raised its head, and been sure of a good issue, viz. the 'going out of power from Him.' Such a confidence *is* possible. It flows principally from thoughts on Providence, and on its preserving power. The 91st Psalm exalts the happiness of the man who 'dwelleth in the secret place of the Most High,' and 'abideth under the shadow of the

Almighty,' and who says to the Lord, 'My refuge and my fortress,'—'my God, in Him will I trust.' But how easily does this confidence depart at the immediate view of danger, even from the pious; how soon does his courage fail him! If it is to *remain* with him, there is need of a power which would keep it erect; and as such Jesus indicates faith.

What have we to understand by this? It cannot possibly indicate *again* the faith in Providence, and in the protection which it promises. For that is just the confidence which is apt to fade in the moment of danger; and it is not *our* exertion, but only a *new* strength which can preserve it and can heighten it. The faith which is in a position to unfold such a quickening power on the glimmering light of confidence, can be nothing else than the 'faith in Jesus!' Faith in God and faith in Jesus certainly hang sufficiently together; but they are also as distinct in experience as in apprehension. Scripture also places them *beside* one another, and in no way does it mingle them as entirely united. See John xiv. 1, 'Ye believe in God; believe also in me.' On the other hand (Mark xi. 22), 'Have faith in God.' 'Where is your faith?' Thus, then, does the Lord ask, Have you forgotten who I am? Do you not think *whom* you have with you in the ship? He accuses them not simply of this little faith (Matt. vi. 30), their want of confidence in the protecting hand of Providence; but His reproach is this, that they had here denied their faith in Him, the Messiah. Otherwise they would not have been able to show themselves so timid, but in the midst of danger must have preserved the full feeling of security, without waking from His slumber Him who was with them, and whom they knew belonged to them.[1]

[1] Much in this sense, while narrating a later case, the second evangelist in his reflection raises a similar accusation against the Twelve (Mark vi.

We now take the result gained previously, that the words 'Peace, be still' had been spoken for the sake of the disciples. Let us then place it together with the shown import of the rebuke. What is then the sum? No other than this: That they are safe for His sake; and if they had maintained faith in Him, they would have also felt safe for His sake, so that they, not even in imminent dangers, could ever become the prey of cowardice.

The question as to the *motive* to this miracle can now be no more doubtful. From a certain point of view the wonder would arise why our Lord did not make use of a mere exhortation,—'Fear not: all the hairs of your head are numbered; the waves raise their noise; but God is greater in the height.' Thus in fact a mere teacher would have acted; and after the danger was past, the disciples would have been somewhat ashamed of their timidity. But the Son of God wishes to procure a firmer confidence in the future organs of His kingdom, than that which rests on the foundation of a general trust in God. They needed such a one. The Apostle Paul in 2 Cor. xi. sketches a picture of the dangers with which he had been surrounded in his assiduousness in his calling. 'Thrice I have suffered shipwreck, a night and a day I have been in the deep' of the sea, 'in journeyings often, in perils of waters, in perils of robbers,' of Jews and of Gentiles, 'in the city, in the wilderness, and among false brethren.' But on what ground said he, 'in all of them do we overcome'? Because he knew that he was in Christ; in the name of Jesus the apostles felt themselves safe, inviolable among all

52). After describing the later stormy sea voyage, after delineating the 'trouble, the amazement, the wonderment on the part of the disciples,' he writes with regard to the preceding unfolding of the power of Jesus in the miraculous feeding: 'For they considered not the miracle of the loaves; for their heart was hardened.'

dangers;—they have learnt this by the prophetic act of their Lord.

At this view of the narrative we stop, without overstepping the boundary we have drawn. The history has been made to show, that the Jesus who here commands the storm and the sea is also in a position to soothe the waves of an excited mind, and conduct it to peace. It may be an admissible application, but it is quite an erroneous view, that our Lord really intended to bring to light His power over the heart's disquietude by this miracle. This is not the place to bring to remembrance, that Scripture has used the wave tossed by the tempest as the symbol of a tottering, disquieted mind. The stormy sea was the *cause* of the anxious care of the disciples; but the *cause* of an anxiety cannot possibly be its *symbol*. By commanding the storm, our Lord takes away the ground for this disquietude; His deed, therefore, cannot signify what He is able to do in *another* sphere; it can only prophesy of what the disciples have to provide against in *the same* sphere during the whole course of their activity. The exposition has thus attained its object.

THE MIRACULOUS FEEDING.—MATT. XIV. 13, ETC. (MARK VI. 32, ETC.; LUKE IX. 10, ETC.; JOHN VI. 1, ETC.); MATT. XV. 32, ETC. (MARK VIII. 1, ETC.).

The history of the miraculous satisfying of thousands with a few loaves, is the only one which all the evangelists (even the fourth) have reported in common. It is true that John and Luke only relate one of these feedings, while Matthew and Mark give the details of two (separated from one another by no considerable interval of time). The duplicate occurrence of the event has, in fact, been doubted, on the ground that the disciples, with all their experience of the first case, showed again the same restlessness in the second. But the argument loses its significance in face of the fact, that they a third time, after they had been witnesses of both miracles, appeared no less dismayed, and experienced the rebuke of our Lord for their foolish thoughts (see Mark viii. 17–21).[1]

On these narratives Schleiermacher has expressed the opinion, that circumstances meet together in them which make every view of the case impossible, and justify an hypothesis. In this case Strauss also raises a claim for his view, that he should not be confined to one conjecture only. He seeks the root of the 'myth' in the 107th Psalm ('They wandered in the wilderness, hungry and thirsty, that their soul fainted in them; they cried unto the Lord in their trouble,— and He satisfied the longing soul, and filled the hungry one with goodness'), and in the historical facts of the feeding of Israel in the desert, as well as the mitigation of famine by the miraculous hands of Elijah and

[1] The recognition of the instructive connection in which these feedings are related by Matthew, leads us to a firm conviction that the cases are different. The first, related immediately after the account of the death of the Baptist, pursues the same interest, full of instruction, which lies unrecognisable in the Johannine narrative. A new epoch in the activity of Jesus commences,—an epoch which John marks by placing us suddenly in a time far distant from the preceeding fifth chapter; Matthew, however, makes the epoch special, separating as he does the life of Jesus in its several divisions (compare chap. iv. 12 with chap. xiv. 13). On the other hand, the thread of the narrative in the second case is quite a different one. Matthew had narrated the history of the Canaanitish woman. Our Lord says there, 'First let the children be filled.' And now follows immediately (chap. xv. 29–31) the account of how Jesus had showered on these children His benefits with full hands and $μὴ ὀνειδίζων$; then (ver. 32) the incident, that He without being asked sets a table for them, so that they eat and were all filled, and there still remained over quantities of fragments,—of crumbs, one of which the Canaanitish woman had first received at her urgent request. In fact, we have indeed in the first Gospel something more than a mere chaotic aggregation of single narratives.

Elisha. 'Hence they also expected from the Messiah a miraculous increasing of the means of nourishment at hand.' But that the 'myth' should receive the very form selected, that it should appear as a distribution of bread, rests on the rite of breaking of bread in the ancient Church. 'The history of the feeding of the multitude contains no feature which could not be derived on the one side from the Mosaic prophetical type, and on the other from the antitype of the Christian Lord's Supper.' Thus the desert in which Jesus accomplished the feedings answers to the Mosaic type, while the late even-time points to the festival of the Lord's Supper. Further, the embarrassment of the disciples at the thought of making provision for so numerous a multitude, calls to mind the reflection of Moses (Num. xi. 21), and the helplessness of the prophet's servant (2 Kings iv. 43); while the way and manner in which the conduct of Jesus is depicted (Matt. xiv. 19), appears perfectly conformable partly to the institution of the Lord's Supper, partly to the ancient Christian rite as Justin has depicted it. The wine was certainly wanting; but the early Christian festival of the Lord's Supper was often designated only as the breaking of bread (the bread being the substance of the matter. The collecting of the crumbs that remained over was, lastly, on one hand, a reminiscence of the history of the manna; on the other, a reference to the abhorrence of the early Church to destroy anything of the elements of the Lord's Supper).

We must in this critical attempt acknowledge some skill in the arrangement of facts and drawing inferences from them, although it is far behind the clever mastery with which Strauss has brought his arguments to bear on the account of the resurrection of Lazarus. There we expressed the fear that ignorant people might allow themselves to be befooled by the blinding representation; in the present case we have not the least ground for a similar fear. The fact that the critic makes a double course flow together to the genesis of the 'myth,' is in itself a considerable stumbling-block to the reader's consent. The circumspect estimate in the conception which would have been presupposed, contrasts very strangely with the natural dress in which the narrative appears, and the simplicity with which the occurrence is reported. To this may be added, that many single features in the mythical construction will not suit, and that the violence with which this construction is sought places the gravity of the reader in a very trying position. The manner in which the critic endeavours at one time to put out of sight the fish which were used with the bread in feeding the multitude, and at another time to bring them into notice, can only produce either indignation or a mocking laugh.

The proof of the historical reality of the narratives also, in this case, hangs on the question as to the motive *out* of which, and as to the end *for* which, our Lord did these works. A double answer has been given, each of which is founded on very probable grounds. Some adopt the *one*, that Jesus resolved out of compassion to the hungering people to make the miraculous feeding. The express words of the text point to this. For although in the passage, Matt. xiv. 14, 'He had compassion towards them,' the healing of the weak was the principal motive, this compassion still manifestly appears in the immediate satisfying of the famishing ones. At any rate, the view aimed at in Mark (viii. 2) is not at all to be mistaken: 'The multitude being very great, . . . He saith, I have compassion on the multitude, because they have nothing to eat.' But, granted that our

Lord performed this miracle from compassion, there is still the question, whether in doing it He had no further object. If we acknowledge the answer simply as mentioned above, we should have to assign it to the narratives of the first group, where the *pure* manifestations of the helping love lay before us. But we can *not* satisfy ourselves with this. The *motive* for a sign does not thoroughly exhaust its object, and least of all in *this* case. Here, in fact, in no wise was it the want *in itself* that awakened the compassion of Jesus, but rather the manner in which the need had arisen.

When we read, 'They have now been with me three days,' our Lord does not thus emphasize the fact that bread was wanting, but that He had compassion on the people, because they, having for His sake neglected their calling and their work the whole day, have been brought thereby into this dilemma. And this is certainly no immediate simple compassion, but a feeling resulting from a reflection which contains the point of difficulty. Others have therefore made the attempt to find out the motives of Jesus from the Johannine account of the miracle. The tendency of the fourth Gospel, as is well known, is to seek and centre the interest in our Lord as the living bread: 'Moses gave you not the bread from heaven, but my Father gives it to you: I am the bread of life.' With regard to the close connection between this doctrinal speech and the feeding preceding it, the opinion has been accepted, that Christ by the latter had desired to point out symbolically the highest end of His appearance—to communicate to man *life*. If this view were the correct one, we should not have arranged this narrative in the present fourth group; it should rather have found its appropriate place in the second. But we must beware of doing this. Even according to St.

John's report, the feeding of the multitude appears by no means as the foundation for a later instructive lesson, but simply as the occasion resulting from events to which it has been annexed. Yea, this occasion of teaching was not *taken* by our Lord of His own movement from the miracle, but it was the conduct of the satisfied people which first *gave* Him cause for it. The most cursory comparison of the passage, John vi. 26, carries at once this conviction; hence it is purely impossible to see in the miracle performed the symbolical reflection of the lesson following after it, which has a *special* motive, and to draw from this latter any conclusion as to the intention of Him who performed the miracle. But is there not a *third* view?

We hope to recommend the view which we have thus attained, at least to place it safe above the reproach of arbitrariness, by the fact that we have taken our proof solely from the text itself. That our Lord wished by the miraculous feeding of thousands to bring to light an important truth, is shown not less by the repetition of the deed (this is the only case where such a miracle has been performed a second time[1]), than by His indignation against the disciples because they neither understood nor perceived it: 'Do ye not remember, perceive ye not yet, neither understand (Mark viii. 17, 18) what is this truth?' We find it in the answer which Jesus gave to the

[1] We guard ourselves expressly against the view that our Lord had TWICE guaranteed the disciples, while sailing, a safety in their distress. For in the second case of a stormy passage there is certainly no question of a danger to which they had been exposed. Here the difficulty is in quite a different direction. Of a miraculous draught of fishes, Gospel history certainly tells us not merely of one case, but the second happens in the days of the resurrection, and does not belong to those miracles with which we have to do; besides, it should be judged by a different standard.

Twelve when they pointed out to Him the threatened dilemma, and besought Him to send away the multitude: 'It is not necessary,' He replies to them, 'that they should depart.' However, He does not continue, '*I* will feed them,' but says (and the three evangelists report His words in the strictest uniformity—Matt. xiv. 16, Mark vi. 37, Luke ix. 13), 'Give ye them to eat.' This *ye* demands earnest attention; and that so much the more imperatively, as it was, in fact, according to the following narrative, the hands of the disciples from which the hungry ones received the satisfying bread.[1] Certainly it stands to reason that the increase of bread proceeded from Jesus alone, that the disciples had no part in that; but just on that account is it so much the more important that He commands, Give *ye* them to eat. What He tells them to do, *that* will He put them in a position to do. By means of this command, which receives its accomplishment here through them, He gives the promise that *at all times they would be able in His name to procure food for the people.*

If this view is assured by the words of the text, there arises the further question, In what sense are the apostles who are called to be able to communicate in the future course of their evangelical mission the satisfying bread to the people in need? As we steadily oppose the opinion that the *whole* event is to be symbolically understood, still more decidedly do we reject the typical comprehension of a *single* feature. The fact that Scripture now and again represents the apostolic annunciation under the picture of food offered (see 1 Pet. i. 25, ii. 2, 'the gospel which is

---

[1] The complaint of many expositors, that the manner of increasing the bread is not made more evident,—that, in fact, it cannot be said whether it is done already in the hands of Jesus or in those of the apostles distributing it, or even if only in those of the people receiving it,—is explained solely by the want of insight into the signification of the incident.

preached unto you . . . the sincere milk of the word;' also Heb. v. 13), by no means justifies the view of the forcible 'Give ye them to eat,' which, though before shown as the conception of duty, would now decide it to be a beneficent promise. Also, if we look on the miracle of feeding as a prophecy given to the disciples, the 'bread' then retains rather its natural significance; it is to be understood thoroughly in the sense of the 'daily bread' in the Lord's prayer.[1] Thus the disciples are placed in a position to help the starving ones to their daily bread. Which starving ones? All, without distinction? We call to mind how our Lord had had a motive for His miraculous bounty in this, that the people had continued with Him three days. The desire to hear His preaching ($\epsilon\pi\iota\pi o\theta\epsilon\hat{\iota}\nu$, 1 Pet. ii. 2) had repressed the earthly necessity, the higher care had driven away the lower—the assembly was a multitude of Marys. Those who for His sake had forgotten themselves, them has the miraculous hand of Jesus cared for. His ministers also should in like manner only remove a want that has thus arisen; but *that* they should really be able to accomplish this,—that is the promise which is given to them, and inculcated by the miracle that was performed.

There is the question as to whether the prophecy comprised in this miracle has been really accomplished. An affirmative answer cannot certainly be given in any particular case. It even appears as if the apostles

---

[1] We firmly believe that in the fourth petition of the Lord's prayer the earthly bread is exclusively meant; yea, that the $\epsilon\pi\iota o\acute{\nu}\sigma\iota os$ even characterizes the bread asked for as earthly,—'Give us this day our *earthly* bread.' The explanation warranted by the text, that it signifies the bread 'for the future' or 'for the morrow,' however it might be applied, irremediably fails from the passage in Matt. vi. 34. We are hence positively referred to the root $o\dot{\upsilon}\sigma\acute{\iota}\alpha$, as now the usual acceptation of the thus derived $\ddot{\alpha}\pi\alpha\xi$ $\lambda\epsilon\gamma\acute{o}\mu\epsilon\nu o\nu$, necessary bread, *panis quotidianus*, $\tau\rho o\phi\grave{\eta}$

had expressly declined the solution of this problem: 'It is not reason that we should leave the word of God and serve tables' (Acts vi. 2). But let us look closer. Our Lord has, as is known, announced a similar prophecy, not by the symbolical language of a miracle, but one plainly spoken: 'Seek ye first the kingdom of God and His righteousness, and all these things shall be added unto you' (Matt. vi. 33). No one doubts that this prophetic expression has been fulfilled. The difference between it and the result of the narratives under consideration is only this, that in the latter case the circle of the recipients, on the one hand, is more closely defined than the crowd of those who eagerly press after the word of God; and that, on the other hand, the consequent blessing appears effected by the service of the apostles. But have they not, in fact, really proved by their preaching and activity that it is effective?—'Godliness with contentment is great gain' (1 Tim. vi. 6); 'Godliness has promise of the life that now is' (chap. iv. 8). It behoved the apostle, in appealing to facts of experience, to make assertions to the Corinthians which, in a variety of respects, prove how the Lord gave to His own the glory manifested by Him in the wilderness, and caused it to be seen conspicuously in their favour. See 2 Cor. viii. and ix. (especially chap. ix. 8, 10, and 15). To himself could Paul well apply the words full of triumph: 'God will both minister bread for your food, and multiply your seed, and increase the fruits of your righteousness, that you should be enriched in every-

---

ἐφήμερος, would form a tautology with the σήμερον; as, besides, the οὐσία in the only passage in which it meets us in the New Testament is to be understood of temporal goods (Luke xv. 12, 13), we can consider the true value of the ἐπιούσιος only as the designation of the earthly bread that is needful for the sustenance of the body. In the clause of the present narrative (Mark viii. 3), 'If I send them away fasting, they will faint by the way,' lies the true import of the fourth petition of the Lord's prayer.

thing ... *through us,* causing thanksgiving to God.' If our view is correct, we ought then to consider these miracles of Jesus as prophecies of the future dominion of the kingdom of heaven on earth; for there it really did rule, where those who sought it had all the wants that arose in connection with their holy work miraculously supplied.

But we cannot leave these narratives without touching on a circumstance to which our Lord Himself (certainly on a later occasion) has directed the attention of His disciples. When they, in fact, not long after the second feeding, had misunderstood the warning they had received of the leaven of the Pharisees, 'It is because we have no bread,' Jesus held a conversation with them on the unfolding of His power, of which they had been witnesses (see Mark viii. 19): 'When I brake the five loaves among five thousand, how many baskets full of fragments took ye up?' They answer, 'Twelve.' 'And when the seven among four thousand, how many took ye up?' They answer, 'Seven.' When He afterwards reproaches them, 'How is it that ye do not understand?' He wishes to teach them, that even now, when they (Mark viii. 14) had only one loaf, they should be convinced that it would be quite sufficient for their need. But we must not pass over the relation of the numbers in this conversation. We do not, however, mean the numbers of the baskets (twelve and seven), of which Volkmar on the one hand, and Luthardt on the other, have made an unjustifiable use. In the first case, there were twelve, in the second, seven baskets full, just because there was so much bread over. Enough of that! Another point is strange, that is, the quantity of fragments in the two cases stand in a very remarkable disproportion to each other. In the first feeding, five loaves, five thousand eaters, and twelve baskets full of fragments. On the other hand, at the second feeding, seven loaves, four thousand eaters, and yet a remnant over of merely seven baskets. That is not in accordance with arithmetic; according to its laws, the second time the remainder should have been much more abundant. But what is to be shown here, what will be learnt here, is this, that the divine rule and blessing are not to be reckoned by any law; that it does not fit into human categories; that the wisdom from above mocks at earthly rules, and has everywhere its own standard.

Analogous to the miraculous feedings is an event which is recorded in the fourth Gospel alone. The impossibility, however, of considering one part of this Gospel apart from the whole, necessitates us to limit our contemplation of the miracle of Jesus at Cana to its principal points.

THE TURNING OF WATER INTO WINE.—JOHN II. 1–11.

The considerations which Strauss has made upon the narrative before us, form the section of his entire work which has the most completely failed; and this result was certainly an infallible one, if he did not wish to be unfaithful to his principles. Here he was certainly not in a position to be able to bring forward an Old Testament type which could have suggested a fabrication to show its fulfilment in the Messiah. He does make a weak attempt to render available for this end the bestowal of water on the people perishing from thirst in the wilderness (Ex. xvii.; Num. xx.); but of water, as is well known, there was no want at Cana. A clever fabricator, as Strauss endeavours to prove the fourth evangelist to be, would have placed Jesus, the supposition of the origin of the myth being granted, not in a house where there was a wedding, but in a desert where thirsty crowds surrounded Him, in order that He might refresh them from springs miraculously opened, especially as in this Gospel there is such frequent mention of the living water. Hence the critic found himself driven to view the turning of water into wine as merely a completion of the miracle of feeding, *i.e.* that just as the latter corresponds with the bread in the Lord's Supper, so the former is identified with the second element in the Eucharist. But for this hypothesis, he has in advance forfeited the good sympathy of his readers, in that he has already pointed out, while discussing the subject of the miraculous feeding, the want of drink, from the one-sided emphasis placed on the κλάσις τοῦ ἄρτου by the early Church. It has indeed been asserted, that the fourth evangelist has had especial grounds, in regard to the festival of the Lord's Supper, for placing by the bestowal of bread the furnishing of wine, although we do not receive any convincing proof of it. The manner, then, in which Strauss treats of the details of the narrative, is only so far worthy of him as it gives above measure the unreasonable demands which he believes himself entitled to require of his readers. Only an unusual conviction of the superiority of his own judgment could make him require any one to agree to his assertion, that the saying of Jesus to Mary is meant to 'outdo the question of Jesus as a child to His parents,' in Luke ii. 49, or that the remark of the master of the feast was intended to explain a passage in one of the synoptic Gospels (Luke v. 39). Lastly, we take objection to the fact, that he has declined to admit (p. 512; Eng. transl. ii. 274) that the evangelist himself has not by any single word referred to such a view of the narrative. In truth, he has *not* done so; but he has not omitted to do *something else;* he has most particularly shown his own comprehension of this act of Jesus Christ: 'This beginning of miracles did Jesus in Cana of Galilee, and manifested forth His glory; and His disciples believed on Him' (John ii. 11).

'He manifested forth His glory.' But what is this 'glory' of Jesus into which John looked through the symbol? That it was no other than that of the Only-begotten of the Father (chap. i. 14) it is hardly necessary for us to say. But by this self-evident answer is not settled the real question, as to how far a beam of glory, shining from the act performed, had enlightened the disciples. That they recognised therein the supernatural power of their Master, expositors have hardly once acknowledged; but so much the more confidently have most exegetists acquiesced in the view advanced by Lampe, that the *benignitas, philanthropia, beneficentia* of Jesus here first come out in their glorious light. Meyer especially calls attention to the 6th verse, for the purpose of proving that the point of difficulty rests on his philanthropy. In the main, the conjecture of Olshausen, that our Lord by this miracle wished to show His antithetical position to the strict asceticism of the Baptist, is only an attempt to give a surer support and a greater definiteness to the vague view of Lampe. But by the former view, the uncommon stress which the evangelist lays on this event becomes as little evident, as by the latter the conception of the 'glory' comes to us shorn of all its brightness. What appears proper as a practical application cannot be given as a real exposition.

We would much rather decide in favour of Hofmann's view, that our Lord here has given to His own disciples 'an earthly representation beforehand of that heavenly marriage feast, when He will drink the fruit of the vine with them in the kingdom of His Father' (*Schriftbeweis*, iii. 407), did not the representation of the evangelist point in quite another direction, and one in which we arrive at a more satisfactory view. I refer to the manner in which Jesus procured the wine. He did not increase the little store gradually, as was the oil in the widow's cruse, which was not to be consumed. Still less did He produce the wine required by a mighty word of command. But His action is developed on the principle of a change. It is impossible to mistake that the description is intended to concentrate the attention upon that presumption. The servants received the command to fill the jugs with water (ver. 7); they knew (ver. 9) that they had drawn water. They were to bring (ver. 8) what they had drawn to the master of the feast, and he bears witness (ver. 10) that it is good wine. The entire attention is concentrated on the miraculous change effected by the power of Jesus. Let us, in the first place, consider its *symbolical* meaning. Do we not see the glory of Him who neither destroys nor creates, and who yet makes the old new: 'Old things are passed away; behold, all things are become new' (2 Cor. v. 17). It is the 'glory' of the Restorer—the Redeemer. But besides this symbolical, there is also the *prophetical* meaning. The kingdom of God will succeed in completing the transformation of the old into the new on earth. 'Behold, I make all things new;' thus says (Rev. xxi. 5) He that sat upon the throne; and the seer writes, 'I saw a new heaven . . . and a new Jerusalem.' The miracle at Cana, in the fourth Gospel, reveals the whole efficacy of Christ on earth. This strong position, taken at its commencement, confirms us at once in the conviction, that it shows both symbolically and prophetically the dominion which the kingdom of God will gain upon the earth in its victorious course. 'This beginning of miracles did Jesus;' but what a contrast between this 'beginning' and the end! There the work of renewing, here that of judgment. And yet, even in the latter is manifested the glory of Him who guarantees the victory of His kingdom on earth. The former had its correct position at the beginning, the latter the equally necessary one at the end.

THE CURSING OF THE FIG-TREE.—MATT. XXI. 18-22; MARK XI. 12-14, 20-23.

The fact that our Lord performed this miracle exclusively before the eyes of His disciples, and that He joined to it a discourse on their future zeal and activity, enables us to characterize it in advance as symbolical and prophetical. Here the saying applies: 'What I tell you in darkness, that speak in the light; and what ye hear in the ear, that announce on the house-tops.' If this standpoint is taken, the difficulties dissolve of themselves,—difficulties which in all other ways of considering it appear inexplicable. However, before we proceed, it is necessary for us to understand the relation in which the representations of the event by the first and second evangelist stand to one another. Not that they are in mutual contradiction; only that the preference of greater detail is to be credited to the one over the other.

It is, indeed, a matter of indifference, that in Matthew, immediately after the condemning words of the Lord, there follows the account, 'and presently the fig-tree withered away,' while, according to Mark, it is only on the day following that the tree was found 'dried up from the roots.' But this difference in the reports does not affect the matter itself, only the observation on the part of the disciples. The judgment of Jesus was certainly followed immediately by the results, but just as indisputably was this result observed by the Twelve on the following morning. However, it is of some importance that, instead of the

'Let no fruit grow on thee henceforth' in Matthew, we see substituted in Mark a 'No man eat fruit of thee hereafter.' But it is chiefly the reflection which the second evangelist has added that deserves attention. It seems at first sight confusing, and yet it really helps to understand the narrative. It is not, as Strauss asserts, that Mark had by this clause 'made a slip of the tongue,' but by the remark, 'for the time of figs was not yet,' He has made the anger of Jesus comprehensible; but the words must certainly be rightly understood.

Instead of the view generally accepted, 'it was not now the time of figs,' many able expositors have preferred the phrase which is *also* textually possible, 'it had been no good year for figs.' But apart from the fact, that, indeed, at the time of year in which the event occurs (not long before the time of the Passover) the fig harvest was still far off, in this new method of explanation the very marked words (Mark xi. 3) 'having leaves' would appear not less indifferent, as it would take away from the eye every ground for the sorrow of Jesus on the tree being merely covered with leaves. Hence, if we keep to the ordinary and manifestly natural reading, the important question seems to us to be: To what have we to refer the argument at the end of the 13th verse, that our Lord found *only* leaves? This certainly gives the motive for His sorrow; but the fact that it was not yet the time for figs cannot possibly explain the circumstance that the tree was solely covered with leaves and without fruit.

A satisfactory light is shed on the verse immediately we refer to what went before the concluding remark, 'It was in fact not the time for figs.' Our Lord experienced hunger whilst He was on the way. In His need of food He looks around, and His eye sees *a* fig-tree in the distance (we desire the ἀπὸ μακρόθεν to be compared with μακράν, which resembles it in Matt. viii. 30), 'in the way' (Matt. xxi. 19),—a fig-tree which, differing from all the others, had leaves already. There stood many on the road from Bethany to Jerusalem; in fact, Bethphage must have received from them its name. This circumstance was quite unusual at that time of year; but as the fruit of the figs is developed earlier than the leaves, the leaves only coming out as the fruit ripens, Jesus would expect to find figs also on the tree that was covered with leaves. This expectation is shown by the particle ἄρα. He approached the fig-tree 'having leaves' with the well-grounded opinion that He would also find fruit on it as well. *So much* was unusual, that the tree should already appear covered with leaves; but under these circumstances it would justly be expected that it would also have had premature fruit. Hence Jesus *seeks* for it; but the tree has deceived the expectation which it had awakened; and because it had nothing else than leaves,—'Nothing but leaves!'—our Lord breaks out (hence the 'answered' in the 14th verse) in the condemning words.

But if the outward state of matters is hereby satisfactorily explained, our wonder arises as to how Jesus could have let His anger act in such a way against a tree which can have neither a will nor a responsibility of its own, against a tree which His heavenly Father had planted and clothed with this premature fulness of leaves (like the lilies of the field), because it did not answer His need of food, but deceived His expectation. This is just the point on which it is important to take our stand for its consideration. In the first place, we will cast a glance on the connection of the whole passage which belongs to this event. Our Lord had entered into the town of Jerusalem, He had visited the temple,—'and having looked round about upon all things' (Mark xi. 1), He returned at eventide to Bethany. On the following morning, when He again wished to visit the town and the temple, He performed the present sign. It thus stands in the midst between the searching glance which surveyed everything and the purification of the temple which was about to take place; and it is by this circumstance that we see the great probability of its referring to the last combat with the leaders of the Jewish theocracy. To this we add a second view: That a fig-tree should be made the symbol of Israel is probable, not only in accordance with the symbolism of the Old Testament, but in virtue also of a former parable of our Lord's, the signification of which He was now in a position to explain.

Our narrative contains, in fact, nothing else than a continuation, or rather the completion, of the parable in Luke xiii. 6-9. This latter had in reality remained incomplete; it had ended with a request which pointed to the future: 'Lord,' thus spake the gardener, 'let it alone this year also, till I shall dig about it, and dung it: and if it bear fruit, well; and if not, after that thou shalt cut it down.' Now, when Jesus was at the end of His work, this *one* year asked for had passed. But what was the result of his digging and dunging? It brought forth, investigation proved ('he looked round about on all things'), even now no fruit! And now had arrived the hour when the 'cut it down' which was formerly considered was to take place. And this is what our Lord shows symbolically, not by the *word* of a parable, but by a symbolical *deed*. It thus shows symbolically and prophetically the judgment passed on Israel,—a judgment which was to be fulfilled by those before whose eyes the miracle took place, and who saw with astonishment the result. We ought to say that

Jesus Himself testifies to the correctness of this view; for the discourses following it in Matt. xxi. 28-44 are nothing else than an explanatory commentary on the withered fig-tree.

In the head of this narrative, expression is given to the thought, that our Lord *sought* fruit, and that He *expected* it, on account of the leaves which were there. Israel was set up in order that it might bring forth fruit; and this was to consist not in works of righteousness, but in faith in the Messiah who had appeared. The leaves being visible, naturally cause *this* fruit to be expected. For the undeniable piety towards the law and the prophets, the punctuality and anxiety with which the sacrifices and ceremonies were performed, seemed to place in security the joyful reception of Him to whom they all pointed. Nevertheless, it failed to appear. The nation rejected the Angel of the covenant who came to His temple. The tree *full* of leaves proved itself to the searching eye to be *void* of fruit. Our Lord is angry; and as there was no motive present for 'tolerance,' 'anger' proceeds to the act of judgment. The 'children of the household' have not accepted their Lord; they must therefore give up being the people of the possession and of promise. They have not employed their talent in faithfulness; it was therefore taken away from them. The tree was indeed to remain by the way, but withered with the token of dejection that had taken place, unmoved by the stream of new life which henceforth will go through the world,—a monument of the divine earnestness against the despisers of His grace. Hence the thought will no more occur to any one to seek fruit on the tree manifestly dead: 'No man eat fruit of thee hereafter for ever.' If any one requires truth, consolation, peace, strength, or whatever it may be, he will pass over from Israel as a tree withered and laid aside.

But the narrative also explains *by whom* this symbolico-prophetical deed should be performed in its thorough execution. In fact, after the disciples on the following day had remarked the withering of the tree that had taken place, and had expressed their perception of it to Jesus, they received the answer, that if they had faith they would 'do as it was done to the fig-tree.' These words require the strictest attention. It is erroneous to consider as parallel to them the passage, John xiv. 12: 'He that believeth on me, the works that I do shall he do *also*.' The meaning is not, 'You shall *also* do as I have done to a fig-tree,' but rather, 'It is you who will really perform what I have done symbolically; it is you will bring to pass on Israel the judgment which I have performed allegorically on the fig-tree.' Our Lord adds, that they would also say effectually to the mountain, 'Be thou removed, and be thou cast into the sea.' If we understand the fig-tree parabolically, it follows that we have also to consider the mountain in a similar manner. And what does it signify? Nothing else than Paganism; for Paganism, as such, is to sink into the sea, just as the demons went down into its depths. It is to vanish off the face of the earth, while the dried-up fig-tree—dead Judaism—is to remain as a sign. The Gentiles themselves, however, are to enter into the kingdom of God, as a tree full of the fruit of righteousness by Christ to the honour of God. The execution of the judgment of Jesus on the Jews is the negative, the introduction of the Gentiles into the kingdom the positive side of the apostolic mission. And in faith ('If ye have faith') the apostles have performed their task; the result was made manifest. They always offered salvation to the Jews, but generally in vain. When they then shook the dust from off their feet, when a Paul said, 'I go henceforth only to the Gentiles,' they performed the negative as well as the positive side of their mission. Let us understand our narrative in this sense, and then it will not appear as a clumsy fabrication, as Strauss affirms. But we shall indeed be considered justified in having shown the miracle to be an actual prophecy of the dominion which the kingdom of God will gain by the ministration of the disciples on earth.

PASSAGES OF SCRIPTURE ELUCIDATED OR REFERRED TO.[1]

OLD TESTAMENT.	PAGE
Exodus iv. 6, 7,	90
viii. 15,	15
xvii.,	259
xxx. 12-15,	*234*
xxx. 13,	231
Leviticus xiii. 1-7,	92
xiii. 7,	94
xiv.,	94
xiv. 2,	90
Numbers xi. 21,	251
xii. 6,	241
xx.,	259
Deuteronomy xiii. 1,	23
xxvii. 18,	109
xxviii. 22,	53
xxviii. 28,	130
1 Kings xiii. 14,	74
2 Kings iv. 3,	251
iv. 8,	174
v. 11,	*92, 95*
xx. 8-11,	48
2 Chronicles xxxv. 25,	200
Psalms xviii. 14,	113
lxxiv. 9,	*43*
xci.,	246
ciii. 12,	*107*
cvi., cvii.,	240
cvii.,	250

	PAGE
Proverbs xii. 14,	69
Isaiah xix. 9,	113
xxxiv. 14,	138
xxxv. 5,	109, 119
xlix. 23, etc.,	168
Jeremiah iv. 8,	200
ix. 17,	200
Ezekiel xiii. 18,	241
Jonah i. 6,	244
APOCRYPHA.	
1 Maccabees iii. 18,	84
Tobit v. 12,	109
vi. 8,	138
Baruch iv. 35,	138
NEW TESTAMENT.	
Matthew i. 27, 32, 34, 39,	132
iv. 8,	132
iv. 9,	128
iv. 12-25,	*55*
v. 18,	98
vi. 11,	147
vi. 23,	110
vi. 26,	68
vi. 30,	247
vi. 33,	257
vi. 34,	*256*

[1] Those printed in black type are commented on; the others merely referred to. If the figure is in italics, the text is in a note.

272 PASSAGES OF SCRIPTURE ELUCIDATED OR REFERRED TO.

Reference	PAGE	Reference	PAGE
Matthew viii., ix.,	55	Matthew xxv. 36,	188
viii. 2-4,	88	xxv. 41,	139
viii. 5-13,	102	xxvi. 37, 38,	188
viii. 6,	139	xxviii. 4,	186
viii. 14, etc.,	51		
viii. 16,	47	Mark i. 23,	171
viii. 23, etc.,	239	i. 29,	51
viii. 28-34,	150	i. 32,	95
viii. 30,	265	i. 34,	172
ix. 1-8,	78	i. 39,	139
ix. 6,	205	i. 40-44,	88
ix. 13,	64, 69	i. 45,	96
ix. 18, etc.,	191	ii. 1-12,	78
ix. 20, etc.,	54	ii. 27,	74
ix. 22,	20	iii. 1-6,	73
ix. 27-31,	110	iii. 5.	61
ix. 30,	97	iii. 22-27,	165
ix. 31,	96	iv. 23,	126
ix. 32-34,	164	iv. 35,	239
x. 7, 8,	40	v. 1-20,	150
x. 8,	91, 92	v. 22, etc.,	191
x. 25,	166	v. 25,	54
x. 31,	68	v. 28,	57
x. 46,	110	v. 34,	57
xii. 7, 8,	64	vi. 32,	249
xii. 9-14,	73	vi. 52,	247
xii. 16-21,	125	vii. 24-30,	140
xii. 17,	97	vii. 31-37,	120
xii. 22-29,	165	vii. 33,	111
xii. 27,	134	vii. 36,	96
xii. 28,	47	viii. 1, etc.,	249
xiii. 16,	119	viii. 12,	123
xiv. 13, etc.,	249	viii. 17-21,	250, 254
xv. 21-23,	140	viii. 18,	119
xv. 32, etc.,	249	viii. 22-26,	110
xvi. 3,	67	ix. 14,	173
xvi. 19,	86	ix. 18,	134
xvi. 20,	118	ix. 21,	94
xvii. 9,	97, 200	ix. 31,	96
xvii. 14,	173	ix. 38,	135
xvii. 24-27,	230	x. 23,	61
xviii. 18,	86	x. 46,	110, 118
xix. 16,	55	x. 52,	101
xx. 25,	233	xi. 1,	61
xx. 29-34,	110	xi. 12-14,	263
xx. 34,	112	xi. 20-23,	263
xxi. 12,	96	xi. 22,	247
xxi. 18-22,	263	xiii. 2,	238
xxi. 28-44,	267	xiii. 3,	199
xxii. 29,	191	xiv. 4,	67
xxii. 41,	117		
xxiii. 15,	133	Luke i. 77,	88

PASSAGES OF SCRIPTURE ELUCIDATED OR REFERRED TO. 273

Reference	PAGE	Reference	PAGE
Luke ii. 49,	260	Luke xiv. 1-6,	70
iv. 18,	169	xiv. 3,	64
iv. 24,	145, 173	xiv. 5,	15
iv. 26,	145	xv. 12, 13,	257
iv. 27,	89, 92	xvi. 17,	85
vi. 33,	171	xvi. 20,	212
vi. 38,	224	xvii. 11-19,	88
iv. 41,	139	xviii. 25,	85
v. 1-11,	223	xviii. 35,	110
v. 8-10,	163	xix. 9,	69
v. 12-14,	88	xxii. 51,	51
v. 17-26,	78	xxiv. 32,	60
v. 31, 32,	91		
v. 39,	260	John i. 14,	261
vi. 6-11,	73	ii. 1-11,	259
vii.,	101	ii. 11,	50
vii. 1-10,	102	ii. 25,	232
vii. 11-17,	202	iv. 40,	163
vii. 39,	57	iv. 46,	102
vii. 42,	233	iv. 47,	81
vii. 50,	63	iv. 49,	193
viii. 2,	139, 164	v. 6,	66
viii. 22,	239	v. 14,	81
viii. 26-39,	150	v. 16,	73
viii. 41, etc.,	191	v. 17,	37
viii. 43,	54	v. 19,	37, 218
viii. 48,	63	v. 20,	48, 218
viii. 49,	103	v. 21,	38, 48, 205
ix. 1,	47	vi. 1,	249
ix. 2,	40	vi. 6,	105
ix. 10, etc.,	249	vi. 7,	236
ix. 37,	173, 203	vi. 26,	254
ix. 38,	51	vii. 20,	135
ix. 42,	207	viii. 36,	234
x. 9,	40	viii. 37,	137
x. 17, 18,	129	viii. 48-52,	135
x. 18,	170	ix. 3,	83
x. 21,	219	ix. 4,	69
x. 55,	44	ix. 13-38,	108
xi. 11,	121	ix. 34,	93
xi. 14-22,	165	ix. 39,	126
xi. 20,	15	x. 20,	135
xi. 21,	161	xi.,	209
xi. 24-26,	185	xi. 25, 26,	48
xi. 27, 28,	170	xi. 33-38,	59
xii. 24,	23	xi. 35,	123
xiii. 6,	15	xi. 40,	199
xiii. 6-9,	266	xi. 42,	48
xiii. 10-17,	65	xi. 52,	145
xiii. 15,	71	xii. 10,	214
xiii. 29,	107	xii. 21, 22,	107, 190
xiii. 32,	47	xii. 31,	129

S

274 PASSAGES OF SCRIPTURE ELUCIDATED OR REFERRED TO.

	PAGE
John xiii. 6,	96
xiii. 10,	89, 93
xiii. 13, 14,	228
xiv. 1,	247
xiv. 12,	268
xiv. 30,	129
xv. 3,	89
xx. 17,	97
xxi.,	229
Acts ii. 22,	42
iii. 6, 7,	44
iii. 12–26,	40
iv. 8, etc.,	40
iv. 29,	174
v. 15,	58
vi. 2,	257
vi. 4,	238
vii. 57,	124
x. 36–39,	40
x. 38,	164
xix. 12,	58
xix. 13,	134, 171
xxvi. 18,	115
Romans i. 19, 20,	41
i. 21,	100
ii. 28, 29,	45
iv. 11,	45
iv. 19–21,	39
v. 13, 14,	97
viii. 26,	123
x. 7,	158
xi. 25,	114
xiii. 12,	100
1 Corinthians iv. 10,	188
vi.,	235
viii. and ix.,	257
ix. 1,	237
ix. 5,	53
ix. 9,	68
xiii. 12,	115
xv. 29,	191
2 Corinthians iii. 14,	114
iv. 6,	115
v. 17,	262

	PAGE
2 Corinthians vii. 1,	93
ix. 9,	160
xi.,	248
xi. 29,	188
xii. 12,	46
xiii. 4,	188
Ephesians iv. 18,	114
iv. 29–32,	100
v. 14,	124
vi. 12,	167
1 Thessalonians v. 14,	188
2 Thessalonians iii. 17,	43
1 Timothy i. 12,	229
iv. 8,	257
v. 8,	233
vi. 6,	257
2 Timothy i. 10,	129
iv. 11,	104
Titus iii. 4,	44
Hebrews ii. 14,	129
v. 13,	256
viii. 13,	146
x. 35,	106
xi. 13,	106
xi. 16,	191
xiii. 17,	123
James i. 21,	93
i. 27,	188
iv. 8,	93
v. 9,	123
1 Peter i. 25,	255
ii. 1,	93
ii. 2,	255, 256
iv. 7,	177
v. 8,	162, 177
1 John iii. 3,	89
iii. 8,	47, 69
Revelation ix. 1,	158
xii. 10,	170
xx. 2,	170
xx. 5,	262

THE END.